GALÁPAGOS

GALÁPAGOS
A Natural History

by
Michael H. Jackson

UNIVERSITY OF CALGARY PRESS

1994 Second printing
1995 Third printing
1997 Fourth printing
1999 Fifth printing
2001 Sixth printing
2002 Seventh printing
2004 Eighth printing
2005 Ninth printing
2006 Tenth printing
2007 Eleventh printing
University of Calgary Press
2500 University Drive N.W.
Calgary, Alberta, Canada T2N 1N4

Canadian Cataloguing in Publication Data
Jackson, M. H. (Michael Hume), 1959-
　Galápagos, a natural history

　First ed. published as: Galápagos, a natural history guide.
　Includes bibliographical references and index.
　ISBN 978-1-895176-07-0 (bound). —ISBN 978-1-895176-40-7 (pbk.)

　1. Natural history—Galápagos Islands
—Guidebooks. 2. Galápagos Islands—Guidebooks. I. Title.
QH198.G3J32 1993　　　　508.866'5　　　　C93-091246-2

Canadä　We acknowledge the financial support of the Government of Canada through the Book
Publishing Industry Development Program (BPIDP) for our publishing activities.

We acknowledge the support of the Alberta Foundation for the Arts for this published work.

Cartography authorized by the Instituto Geografico Militar of Ecuador.
Permit number 8400194-IGM-DT-600964, May 15, 1984.

Figures and line drawings prepared by Monica J. Jackson.
Uncredited photographs by Michael H. Jackson.

Front cover: Male great Frigatebird displaying on Genovesa Island.
Back cover: Domed giant tortoise from Alcedo Volcano, Isabela Island.

Printed and bound in Canada by Houghton Boston Printers & Lithographers Ltd.

∞ This book is printed on acid-free paper.

Table of Contents

To Anne, Frederick and Monica

Preface

The natural history of these islands is eminently curious, and well deserves attention. Most of the organic productions are aboriginal creations, found nowhere else; there is even a difference between the inhabitants of the different islands; yet all show a marked relationship with those of America, though separated from that continent by an open space of ocean, between 500 and 600 miles in width. The archipelago is a little world within itself, or rather a satellite attached to America, whence it has derived a few stray colonists, and has received the general character of its indigenous productions. Considering the small size of these islands, we feel the more astonished at the number of their aboriginal beings, and at their confined range. Seeing every height crowned with its crater, and the boundaries of most of the lava-streams still distinct, we are led to believe that within a period, geologically recent, the unbroken ocean was here spread out. Hence, both in space and time, we seem to be brought somewhat near to that great fact—that mystery of mysteries—the first appearance of new beings on this earth. (Charles Darwin 1845)

This succinct, classic, paragraph from Darwin's *The Voyage of the Beagle* summarises Darwin's feelings about the Galápagos Archipelago, and can hardly be bettered today. Darwin visited these islands 150 years ago aboard HMS *Beagle* while on a five year surveying voyage around the world. He was able to spend only five weeks in the archipelago during September and October 1835, but his astute observations during this short period were to set the stage for the development of the theory of evolution by natural selection, as well as a century and a half of scientific exploration in the Galápagos. No other single person has done so much to put these islands on the map.

In 1959, a century after the publication of Darwin's momentous book *The Origin of Species*, the government of Ecuador, to whom the islands belong, declared all areas of the Galápagos as a National Park, except those areas already colonised by that date. By 1982, a century after Darwin's death, visitors have been coming to these islands in the thousands, and a wealth of

xi

information has been discovered about diverse aspects of the natural history of these "curious" islands. It has been my intent in this book to provide a digest of the observations and results obtained by the hard-working scientists, who have put up with the discomforts of working on tropical desert islands to further our knowledge of one of the world's most wonderful wild places.

The Galápagos Islands were declared a World Heritage Site in 1979 by the member states of UNESCO. This designation recognises the Galápagos Islands as one of the world's most significant natural areas, and highlights the need to conserve the Galápagos as a unique part of mankind's natural heritage. The World Heritage Convention has been adopted by more than 70 member states and, as of January 1983, 136 natural and cultural sites around the world have been approved. These include such special areas as: Dinosaur Provincial Park, Canada; the historical centre of Rome, Italy; Serengeti National Park, Tanzania, and Yellowstone National Park, U.S.A.

In 1987, the coasts of the Galápagos Islands, together with a 15 nautical mile band, were declared a Marine Resources Reserve by President Febres-Cordero. The details of the management of this reserve have not yet been clearly laid out, but it is a step in the right direction.

As I prepared this second edition, I noted that 1992 marked the 500th anniversary of Columbus' discovery of the Americas. Though Columbus never visited the Islands, they are officially named "Columbus' Archipelago" (Archipiélago de Colón), and many islands have official names which derive from Columbus' voyage (Pinta, Santa Maria, etc.). I can only hope that when the 600th anniversary comes around, that the Islands are still a magnificent refuge for wildlife. The next few decades will be critical for the survival of the Galápagos ecosystem as we know it—there are many pressures on the resources and many conflicts to be resolved (see Chapter 12).

In this second edition, I have included new information gleaned from several visits to the Islands over the past few years as well as from new books and scientific papers. To give you an idea of the amount of ongoing research, when I carried out a computerized literature search for the years 1984 through 1991 in *Biological Abstracts*, I came across nearly 500 papers that related to the Galápagos. Much of the information found in these articles has been integrated into this edition. As well, I have tried to update population estimates and other numbers as well as trying to include changes in the classification of species.

I write with the sincere wish that people who read this book may understand and appreciate these special islands a little better as a result. I hope that the information contained in this guide will help you enjoy your trip to the islands, but also that it will encourage you to take good care of the islands and their wildlife. The Galápagos ecosystem is fragile, and can easily be destroyed by thoughtless behaviour. With good care the Galápagos Islands will remain a magnificent place for future generations to visit and experience. Please remember that the Galápagos Islands are a National Park, and that all native life is protected by law. Do not pick any flowers or collect any souvenirs. I also urge you to consider supporting conservation in the Galápagos by a donation through one of the organisations mentioned in Appendix 4.

The fire which, during March of 1985, burnt over 200 square kilometres of southern Isabela is another example of the Galápagos Islands' vulnerability to man's presence. If man and nature are to coexist in the Galápagos, we must be more careful than ever to prevent man-caused impacts from destroying any more of this magnificent natural heritage.

I have tried throughout this book to avoid the use of scientific jargon, but there are some words that I have used for the sake of conciseness or clarity. As some of these may not be familiar to the reader, these are defined in the glossary (Appendix 2).

Unfortunately, in a book of this size and scope, many groups of plants and animals, especially the invertebrates, have been given a brief treatment. I have tried to equate the depth of treatment of various groups with their level of interest to visitors.

This book is organised as follows: Chapters 1 to 3 provide historical, environmental and scientific background to the Galápagos Islands' natural history; Chapters 4 through 11 provide detailed natural history information about the plants and animals found in the Galápagos; Chapter 12 discusses the management and conservation of the Galápagos National Park; and Chapter 13 provides visitor information and notes about the various visitor sites. An index and checklist of plants and animals with page references is provided in Appendix 1. For those readers who are not familiar with the metric system, a list of conversions is provided in Appendix 3.

If you encounter errors in this book, or have additional information which you think should be included in a future edition, please write to me at the University of Calgary Press. I plan to keep this book up to date by revising it every five years or so. Any suggestions will be gratefully accepted.

M.H.J.
Victoria, 1993

Galápagos National Park Rules

The Galápagos Islands remain well preserved as a natural environment in large part due to the National Park Rules. These rules are established by the Galápagos National Park Service, and enforced by park wardens and trained guides. The following rules are excerpted from a National Park Service brochure:

1. **NO PLANTS, ANIMALS, OR REMAINS OF THEM SUCH AS BONES, PIECES OF WOOD OR OTHER NATURAL OBJECTS SHOULD BE REMOVED OR DISTURBED**. Such actions are illegal and may cause serious harm to the island's ecological conditions.

2. **BE CAREFUL NOT TO TRANSPORT ANY LIVE MATERIAL TO THE ISLANDS, OR FROM ISLAND TO ISLAND**. Before landing on any of the islands, check your clothing for seeds or insects and destroy them or keep them on your vessel for disposal later on. Check your boots or shoe soles for dried mud before leaving the boat. This material will frequently contain seeds and spores of plants and animals. Inadvertent transport of these materials represents a special danger to Galápagos.

   Each island has its own unique fauna and flora, and other plants and animals can quickly destroy this uniqueness. These rules apply to pets as well as other animals and plants. **DO NOT BRING THEM TO THE ISLANDS**. One of the most destructive forces in Galápagos are feral organisms (domesticated species gone wild) which have been brought to the Galápagos by man.

3. For the same reasons expressed in rule No.2 **DO NOT TAKE ANY FOOD TO THE UNINHABITED ISLANDS**. It is easy to introduce, together with food, insects or other organisms which might be dangerous to the fragile island ecosystems. Fresh fruits and vegetables are especially dangerous. The orange seed you drop may become a tree.

4. **ANIMALS MAY NOT BE TOUCHED OR HANDLED**. All wild animals dislike this and will quickly lose their remarkable tameness if thus treated by human beings.

5. **Animals may not be fed**. Not only can it be dangerous to your own person, but in the long run it can destroy the animal's social structure and affect its reproduction. You came here to see a completely natural situation. Do not interfere with it.

6. **Do not disturb or chase any animal from its resting or nesting spot**. Be very careful with breeding colonies of seabirds. Don't drive boobies, cormorants, gulls or frigatebirds from their nests. These birds will fly from their nests if startled, often knocking the egg or chick to the ground, leaving it exposed to the sun. (A newly hatched booby chick will die in 20 to 30 minutes if exposed to the sun; frigatebirds will also eat any unguarded chick).

7. **Litter of all types must be kept off the islands. Disposal at sea must be limited to certain types of garbage, only to be thrown overboard in selected areas**. Keep all rubbish (film wrappers, cigarette butts, chewing gum, tin cans, bottles, etc.) in a bag, to be disposed of on your boat. The crew of the vessel is responsible to the National Park for proper trash disposal. You should never throw anything overboard. A few examples of the damage that can be caused:

   • sea lions will pick a tin can off the bottom and play with it, cutting their highly sensitive muzzles;
   • sea turtles will eat plastic thrown overboard and die, for it blocks their digestive tract;
   • rubbish thrown overboard near an island will usually be carried to shore where, as it accumulates, it will convert a once beautiful area into a rubbish pile, in addition to causing problems for the plants and animals.

8. **Do not buy souvenirs or objects made from plants or animals of the islands**, with the exception of articles made from wood. The best way to discourage this trade is simply not buying any of these articles. If anyone offers you any of these souvenirs, please advise the National Park.

9. **Do not paint names or graffiti on rocks**. It is against the law and is extremely ugly to look at. Immortality can't be more important than the Islands' natural beauty.

10. **All groups which visit the national park must be accompanied by a qualified guide approved by the national park**. The visitor must follow the instructions of the guide.

11. **The national park is divided into different zones to facilitate its management and administration**. There are certain sites where tourist activities are permitted, and others where the public is restricted or prohibited.

The boat captains and guides know which are the visitor sites and will be responsible for obtaining the proper permits. Nevertheless, the personnel in the office of the National Park is available to answer any questions you might have.

12. **DO NOT HESITATE TO SHOW YOUR CONSERVATIONIST ATTITUDE**. Explain these rules to others, and help to enforce them. Notify the National Park if you see any serious damage being done.

Acknowledgements

This book would not have been possible without the help and advice of many persons and organisations. I wish to take the opportunity here to thank them.

This book was originally written as part of a Master's thesis with the Faculty of Environmental Design, University of Calgary. Stephen Herrero supervised this project and gave me much advice and encouragement, as did Richard Revel and William Taylor, who were on my supervisory committee. The Faculty of Environmental Design also gave me financial aid in the form of research assistantships.

Several people helped me at various stages of development of the manuscript, giving me constructive criticism, editorial advice and proofreading help. Thanks are due to the following for their invaluable help: Juan Black, Robert Bowman, Linda Cayot, James Cragg, David Gammon, Sylvia Harcourt, Michael Harris, Alan Hayes, Friedmann Köster, Peter Kramer, Yael Lubin, Godfrey Merlen, Tui and Alan Moore, Tim Myres, Bryan Nelson, Tony O'Regan, Duncan Porter, Günter Recht, Bob Reynolds, Jo Anne Reynolds, Gary Robinson, Tom Simkin, Linda Sutterlin, Luon Tan Tuoc, and Tim Toth.

I wish to thank the staff of the Charles Darwin Research Station and the Galápagos National Park Service who were my mentors during my stays in the Galápagos Islands. I owe a special debt to Ian Thornton, whose book was my guide and teacher throughout my time in the Galápagos. Virtually all the information in this book has been gained from the work of other scientists. I am profoundly grateful to those authors referred to in the bibliography, as all of them have contributed in some way to this book. Errors in the interpretation of their work, however, remain my own.

Several employees of Metropolitan Touring and Galápagos Cruises companies were very kind and helpful during my various stays in the Galápagos. I wish to thank David Balfour, David Fox, Lucho Maldonado, Vigdis and Peter Stapely, in particular. My fellow guides were a constant source of companionship and discussion, for which I thank them. Julian Fitter also deserves my thanks for sending me to the Galápagos as a guide in the first place.

I would like to thank my wife Monica, Barrie Baptie David Day, Aileen Harmon, Stephen Herrero, Paul Humann, Dwight Knapik, Dianne Pachal, Gordon Pritchard, Tui de Roy, Barry Taylor and Tim Toth for permission to use their photographs in this book.

Mary Bereziuk, Janet Harper and Martha McCallum typed various parts of the manuscript for me, saving me a great deal of time.

I wish to give special thanks to Monica, who, incidentally, I met in the Galápagos, for preparing maps, drawings and figures for this book and for her support and encouragement throughout the project. My parents too, gave me much help, support and encouragement right from the start of the project.

I also wish to thank the staff of the University of Calgary Press for bringing this book into print.

In addition to all those who helped me prepare the first edition, I wish to thank the following for their help with this second edition: Gayle Davis-Merlen for her help with finding recent scientific papers, Sylvia Harcourt-Carrasco and Alfredo Carrasco for their help with the chapter on conservation, John King for his detailed editing of the manuscript, Cliff Kadatz for typography and design, Felipe Cruz for his helpful discussions and companionship, Fiddi and Jane Angermeyer for their hospitality aboard the yacht *Andando*, Tammy Fowler for her help in retyping the manuscript, Gary McCracken for his information on Galápagos bats, Sue Baptie for her information on George Vancouver, John Woram for his help with the history chapter, Peter Grant for his help with the land birds, Stewart Peck for his help with the terrestrial invertebrates, Jerry Wellington for his help with the marine life chapter, Eileen Schofield and Duncan Porter for their help with the botany sections, Haraldur Sigurdsson for his help with the geology, Kathy Nelson of the University of Victoria for her help with computer bibliographic searching, Robby Robson for the use of his laser printer, Craig MacFarland for his comments and to countless others who have helped me in my travels to and around these wonderful islands.

This book has been published with the help of a grant from the Alberta Foundation for the Arts.

Historical Background

1

During the four and a half centuries since their discovery, the Galápagos Islands have had a rich and varied history. Buccaneers, whalers, fur seal hunters, scientists, the military, convicts, fishermen, farmers and homesteaders have all left their mark on the islands and their biota. This chapter provides a brief outline of human involvement with the Galápagos Islands up to their declaration as a national park in 1959. For further information on the history of the Galápagos, I highly recommend John Hickman's *The Enchanted Islands: The Galápagos Discovered.*

Discovery

The Galápagos Islands were officially discovered in 1535 when the then Bishop of Panama, Fray Tomás de Berlanga, and his ship were becalmed and carried out to the islands by the ocean currents while on a journey from Panama to what is now Peru. His account of the islands, written to his emperor, Carlos V of Spain, included the first descriptions of the giant tortoises and iguanas. He also commented on the extraordinary tameness of the birds. The Bishop and his crew were without water when they arrived in the islands and had trouble finding it. Two men and ten horses died and the crew were reduced to chewing cactus pads. There is a legend that the islands were visited earlier by pre-Columbian voyagers (Heyerdahl 1963), but the evidence for this is tenuous.

It was in about 1570 that the islands first appeared on a map. Two maps appeared at this time, one was drawn by Abraham Ortelius and one was by Mercator. The islands were called "Insulae de los Galopegos" (Islands of the Tortoises). They were also called the "Encantadas" (Bewitched Islands) because of the way in which the strong and variable currents made navigation difficult.

Pirates, Whalers and Other Early Visitors

The first use of the islands was by pirates. From the late 1500s to the early 1700s, these pirates used the Galápagos as a refuge and base for their raids on the Spanish colonial ports. They stocked up with water and tortoise meat in the islands. The most unusual loot brought to the islands was a cargo of eight tons of quince marmalade in pottery jars. It is possible that hidden caches of gold and silver remain to be discovered. Several large tapered clay jars have been found by divers in James Bay, Santiago Island and it is thought that these were discarded by visiting pirates.

The first crude navigation charts were made by the buccaneer Ambrose Cowley in 1684. Many islands were named after Cowley's fellow pirates or for the English noblemen who helped the pirates' cause. Buccaneer Cove, Santiago, was a favourite anchorage of these sailors. Here they could find water (in season), salt, firewood, tortoises, and could careen their ships. It is almost certain that the buccaneers were responsible for accidently introducing rats to the islands, while careening their ships.

Robinson Crusoe's prototype, Alexander Selkirk, visited the Galápagos Islands around 1708 with the privateer captain Woodes Rogers. Selkirk was picked up from the Juan Fernandez Islands in 1708 and came to the Galápagos when Woodes Rogers took his two ships to the islands for a refit after sacking Guayaquil.

The first scientific mission to the Galápagos came in 1790 under the leadership of Alessandro Malaspina, a Sicilian captain, sent by the King of Spain. Unfortunately, the records of this expedition were lost. In 1793 the English Captain James Colnett came to the islands to investigate the possibilities of whaling and made the first reasonably accurate navigational charts of the islands. His investigations began an era of whaling that lasted for much of the next century. The damage done to the whale populations must have been enormous. At the same time the exploitation of fur seals began; these were hunted almost to extinction. Whalers and sealers were also responsible for greatly diminishing and, in some cases, eliminating certain races of tortoise. Whalers' logs show that at least 15,000 tortoises were removed for food between 1811 and 1844 (Townsend 1925). Probably well over 100,000 were taken in all.

Around the time of Captain Colnett's visit, the first post office barrel was erected on Floreana. It was originally set up to facilitate the delivery of mail to England and the United States. Letters left in the barrel would be picked up by homebound ships and eventually delivered to their destination. The beach by which it was placed became known as Post Office Bay. The original box has disintegrated, but it has been replaced several times and is still used by visitors today.

The Post Office Barrel on Floreana Island.

Captain George Vancouver visited the Islands in 1795 with HMS *Discovery* and HMS *Chatham*. Vancouver's crew considered the Galápagos to be "the most dreary barren and desolate country I ever beheld" and "nothing but large Cinder without any sign of Verdure or vegetation," though they also noted the land populated "with Seals & Penguins in vast abundance, whilst the surface of the adjacent sea . . . swarmed with large Lizards swimming about in different directions & basking at their ease."

Early Colonists

The first resident of the Galápagos was an Irishman named Patrick Watkins. It is thought that he was marooned on Floreana in 1807. He spent two years growing vegetables which he exchanged with visiting whalers for rum. In 1809 he stole a whaling ship's long-boat and took five captured sailors with him as "slaves." Only Watkins reached Guayaquil alive.

In 1813, the U.S. warship *Essex* came to the islands, captained by David Porter. His mission was to destroy the British whaling fleet in the islands. He was successful in doing this with the help of intelligence gained by reading mail at the Post Office Barrel. He was also responsible for accidentally releasing goats on Santiago Island.

Table 1. Island Names and their Derivations

English Name	Origin	Spanish Name	Origin
Abingdon	Earl of Abingdon	**Pinta**	Caravel Pinta
Albemarle	Duke of Albermarle	**Isabela**	Isabella of Castille, Queen of Spain; 1451–1504
South Seymour	Lord Hugh Seymour	**Baltra**	acronym from USAF, WWII?
Barrington	Adm. Samuel Barrington, R.N.	**Santa Fé**	Spanish city
Beagle	HMS *Beagle*		
Bindloe	Captain John Bindloe	**Marchena**	Fray Antonio de Marchena
Brattle	Nicholas Brattle	**Tortuga**	Spanish for turtle
Bartholomew	Lt. David Bartholomew, R.N.	**Bartolomé**	
Caldwell	Adm. Caldwell, R.N.		
Champion	Andrew Champion, whaler		
Charles	King Charles II	1. **Santa Maria** 2. Floreana	1. Caravel Santa Maria; 2. Pres. Juan José Flores
Chatham	William Pitt, First Earl of Chatham	**San Cristóbal**	St. Christopher, patron saint of sailors
Cowley	Ambrose Cowley, buccaneer		
Crossman	Richard Crossman		
Culpepper	Lord Culpepper		
Daphne	HMS *Daphne*		
Duncan	Adm. Viscount Duncan, R.N.	**Pinzón**	Brothers Pinzón
Enderby	Samuel Enderby, whaler		
Guy Fawkes	The English conspirator		
Hood	Adm. Viscount Samuel Hood, R.N.	**Española**	España (Spain)
Indefatigable	HMS *Indefatigable*	**Santa Cruz**	Holy Cross
James	King James II	1. **San Salvador** 2. Santiago	1. First island discovered in America; 2. Spanish for James
Jervis	Adm. John Jervis	**Rábida**	Convent "de la Rábida"
Nameless		**Sin Nombre**	Spanish for nameless
Narborough	Adm. Sir John Narborough	**Fernandina**	Ferdinand II, King of Spain
Plaza		**Plaza**	Presidente L. Plaza
North Seymour	Lord Hugh Seymour	**Seymour Norte**	
Tower		**Genovesa**	Genoa, Italy, supposed birthplace of Columbus
Wenman	Lord Wainman	**Wolf**	Ecuadorean geologist

Official names are given in bold type. Underlining indicates name used in this book (if not official). *Sources*: Slevin (1959), Black (1973), and Woram (1989).

The Galápagos were officially annexed by Ecuador in 1832 and were named "Archipiélago del Ecuador." At this time, a small colony was established on Floreana; it soon turned into a penal settlement as many political and other prisoners were sent there as well as prostitutes. The ensuing history for the next century was one of repeated colonisation attempts by settlers, and with penal colonies, most of which were ill-fated. Efforts were made to exploit fisheries, tortoises, dyer's moss (a lichen), and salt mines. Only the fisheries continue and only on a small scale. Settlement at Villamil on Isabela dates from 1893 while Puerto Ayora (Academy Bay) on Santa Cruz, was started by a group of Norwegians in 1926.

Between 1850 and 1950, both Britain and the United States attempted to lease or purchase the islands on several occasions but their attempts were resisted. In 1892, the islands were officially renamed "Archipiélago de Colón" in honour of the 400th anniversary of the discovery of the Americas by Christopher Columbus (Cristóbal Colón), but to this day "the Galápagos" remains the most used name. At this time too, the various islands were officially renamed in Spanish. Up to this time a variety of names, both English and Spanish, had been used, but even now there is little consensus as to their use. Santa Cruz has had eight different names in its short history and Santiago six! Table 1 lists some of these names and their derivations.

Later Visitors and Modern Residents

The most famous visitor to the Galápagos was Charles Darwin, aboard HMS *Beagle*, captained by Robert Fitzroy. Captain Fitzroy made accurate navigational charts of the islands which were used until World War II. Darwin visited only four islands (San Cristóbal, Floreana, Isabela, and Santiago) but made extensive collections of plants and animals and observations of their natural history (Sulloway 1984). His chapter on the Galápagos in *The Voyage of the Beagle* (1845) remains a classic and is well worth reading. Observations made here and elsewhere on his voyage, especially regarding parts of South America, stimulated him to ponder the subject of evolution. Twenty-four years later, he published the classic *The Origin of Species*, which shook the foundations of biological thought and led to profound changes in man's philosophy of nature. Since Darwin's time, a number of scientific expeditions have been made to the islands, all of which have contributed to our knowledge of the islands' natural history.

During the 1930s, some strange deaths and disappearances occurred on Floreana (see Treherne 1983). These involved a somewhat crazed German philosopher, Dr. Friedrich Karl Ritter, his mistress (Dore Strauch Koerwin from Berlin), Heinz and Margaret Wittmer from Cologne, the self-styled "Empress of the Galápagos" (Baroness Eloisa von Wagner Bosquet), and her three lovers. They were the only inhabitants of Floreana at the time and there

HMS *Beagle* hove to in the Strait of Magellan. (From Slevin 1959.)

was little friendship between the groups (or within some of them). To cut a long story short, within a few years the Baroness and a lover disappeared without trace, the other lover died trying to get to San Cristóbal in an open boat, and Dr. Ritter died, supposedly of food poisoning from eating spoiled chicken, although he was a vegetarian! To this day, no one has a clear story of what really happened though three books and many articles have been written about the "Floreana story." Margaret Wittmer continues to live on Floreana with her son Rolf, daughter Floreanita, and grandchildren. She runs the post office and a cafe on the sparsely populated island.

During World War II, the United States was allowed to build an airbase on Baltra Island, which was used to patrol the approaches to the Panama Canal. One airstrip is still in use. There is now an airport on San Cristóbal Island also. At the end of the war, Baltra and its airstrip were returned to Ecuador.

Small settlements remain on the four larger islands, Isabela, Floreana, Santa Cruz, and San Cristóbal, with a resident population of over 12,000 in 1990. The residents make a living from a combination of tourism, cattle ranching, fishing and agriculture. Though Puerto Baquerizo Moreno on San Cristóbal is the capital of the Galápagos province, most visitor activity occurs at Academy Bay on Santa Cruz Island, where both the Charles Darwin Research Station and the Galápagos National Park Service have their head-quarters.

Sailor with a boat-hook for turning over tortoises. (Courtesy of BBC Hulton Picture Library.)

The first legislation to protect the islands was enacted in 1934, but it was not until 1959 that effective legislation was passed. The work of the conservation organisations connected with the Galápagos is discussed in Chapter 12.

Charles Darwin as a young man, circa 1840. Painted by George Richmond.
(Courtesy of Mr. George P. Darwin.)

Environmental Setting

The country was compared to what we might imagine the cultivated parts of the Infernal regions to be. (Darwin 1933)

I scarcely hesitate to affirm, that there must be in the whole archipelago at least two thousand craters. . . . Nothing could be less inviting than the first appearance. (Darwin 1845)

Born of volcanic fires deep beneath the Pacific Ocean, the Galápagos Islands are unique. This uniqueness is largely a result of the way the islands came in to being, and their isolated location.

All living things are intimately related to, and dependent on, each other and the physical environment in which they live. An appreciation of the physical environment in which plants and animals are living is essential to an understanding of their natural history. Much of the extraordinary nature of the plants and animals of the Galápagos results from their unique physical environment.

In this chapter we will look at some of the major features of the Galápagos environment and the ways in which they affect life in these islands. It includes discussions of the geographic position, the geology, the oceanography, and the climate of the islands.

Geography

The Galápagos Archipelago consists of thirteen large islands (greater than 10 km²), six smaller islands and over forty islets that have official names (see Table 2 and Fig. 1). Many small rocks and islets remain unnamed. These islands are well isolated from other land masses and straddle the equator at the 90th meridian west. The nearest land, mainland Ecuador, is some 960 km to the east. To the northeast lies Cocos Island (720 km) and Costa Rica (1,100 km). Sixteen hundred kilometres to the north is Guatemala, while to the south about 3,200 km lie Easter and San Felix Islands.

Table 2. Island Areas and Heights

Common	Area		Height	
Name	km²	mi²	m	ft
Isabela	4588	1771	1707	5600
Santa Cruz	986	380	864	2835
Fernandina	642	248	1494*	4900*
Santiago	585	226	907	2974
San Cristóbal	558	215	730*	2395*
Floreana	173	67	640	2100
Marchena	130	50	343	1125
Española	60	23	206*	675*
Pinta	60	23	777*	2550*
Baltra	27	10	100*	328*
Santa Fé	24	9.3	259*	850*
Pinzón	18	7.0	458	1502
Genovesa	14	5.4	76*	250*
Rábida	4.9	1.9	367	1203
Seymour	1.9	0.7	–	–
Wolf	1.3*	0.5*	253*	830*
Tortuga	1.2	0.5	186	610
Bartolomé	1.2	0.5	114	359
Darwin	1.1	0.4	168*	550*
Daphne Major	0.32	0.12	110	366*
Plaza Sur	0.13	0.05	23*	76*

* = measurement is uncertain. Total land area of the archipelago is 7882 km². The highest point is Volcano Wolf, Isabela, at 1707 m. The total length of coastline is 1336 km. *Source*: J. Black (1973).

The total land area of the islands is about 8,000 km² spread over about 45,000 km² of sea. Isabela, the largest island, has a land area of 4.588 km² and four other islands have an area greater than 500 km². The archipelago is 430 km long from Darwin Island, in the northwest, to Española Island in the southeast. From Point Cristóbal at the southwest of Isabela Island to Genovesa Island in the northeast is 220 km.

Geology

If we were to drain away the ocean from the eastern Pacific around the Galápagos, we would find that the sea floor has a dramatic underwater topography. These mountains, ridges, plateaux and valleys tell us a great deal about the origins and development of the archipelago. The bathymetric diagram (Fig. 2) shows the islands as the tips of huge submarine volcanoes, many of which have coalesced to form a submarine platform called the Galápagos Platform. Thus, though the ocean floor outside the platform is 2,000 to 3,000 m below the surface, the 400 m contour includes all the central and southern islands (the 200 m contour includes Fernandina, Isabela, Santiago, Santa Cruz, Rábida and Pinzón). Roca Redonda, an offshore rock only a few hectares large, is the tip of a huge mountain 20 km across at the base and 3,000 m high. The northern line of islands, Genovesa, Marchena, Pinta, Wolf and Darwin, are somewhat separated from the rest of the archipelago.

To the southwest, the archipelago shelf descends quickly to the sea floor at 3,000 m below sea level. To the north of Marchena and Pinta, the sea floor dips to 2,000 m (Fig. 2) and then continues unevenly as the Cocos Ridge, including Cocos Island, to near the coast of Costa Rica. To the east, another less well-defined saddle joins the Galápagos Platform to the Carnegie Ridge, which continues almost to the coast of Ecuador. To the northeast, the platform slopes gradually into the Panama Basin.

Only 100 km to the north of the islands is an uneven line of ridges and chasms called the Galápagos Rift. This is an area of intense geologic activity that has probably played an important role in the formation of the Galápagos. Some 1,000 km to the west is the East Pacific Rise, a chain of undersea mountains running from Mexico to the South Pacific, which is a major area of sea-floor spreading.

One hundred and fifty years ago, Charles Darwin noticed that the major volcanoes of the archipelago were arranged in a rectilinear pattern, with major axes running east-northeast and north-northwest. We now think that this alignment corresponds to lines of weakness in the earth's crust called "faults." These may be partly responsible for determining the sites where volcanoes formed in the Galápagos.

The first and now easternmost Galápagos Islands formed several (perhaps ten) million years ago (Christie et al. 1992) when volcanic eruptions began to break through the ocean floor. These eruptions began the building of underwater mountains. The mountains continued to grow with successive eruptions and their bases joined to form the Galápagos Platform. Some mountain tips emerged from the sea and the Galápagos Islands came into being as barren volcanic islets. This probably occurred in much the same

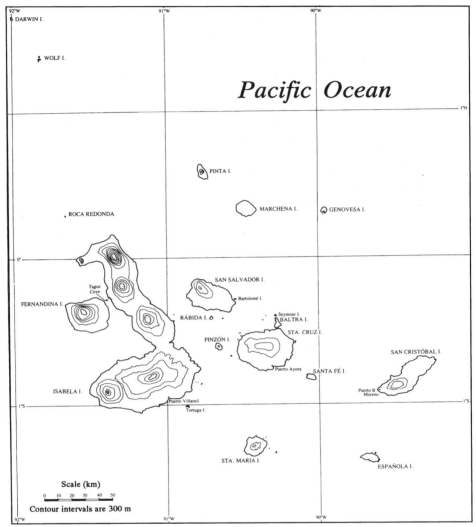

Figure 1: Map of the Galápagos Archipelago. (Based on Instituto Geografico Militar 1981.)

way as in the birth of Surtsey Island, near Iceland, in 1962 (see Chapter 3).

The process of island formation has continued off and on up to the present day and will probably continue for millions of years. Recent research (Christie et al. 1992) suggests that some of the earliest "Galápagos" islands have subsided below the waves and form extinct volcanic seamounts to the east of the archipelago.

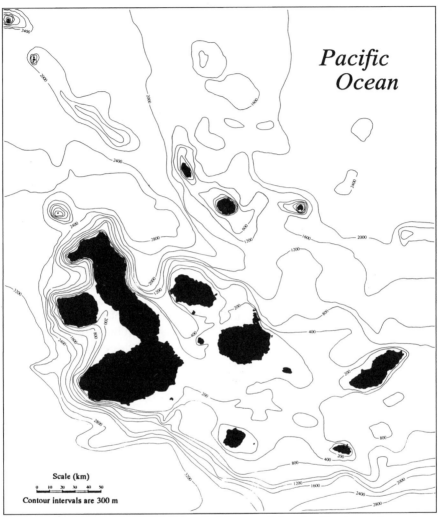

Figure 2: Bathymetric map of the Galápagos Islands. Contours in metres below sea level. (Based on Instituto Geografico Militar 1981.)

The Galápagos Islands are one of the most active oceanic volcanic regions on earth. Up to 1981, fifty-three eruptions have been recorded from eight of the Galápagos volcanoes (Simkin 1984a,b). Since then there have been several eruptions (Plate 3), the most recent of which were on Fernandina and Marchena in 1991. The eruption of Marchena was the first recorded in at least 100 years for that island. In 1968, much of Fernandina's seven km^2 caldera floor collapsed by as much as 300 m—a displacement of between 1 and 2 km^3 of material! In 1954, one and one half square kilometres of marine reef were uplifted by as much as 4 m at Urbina Bay on the west coast of Isabela. This was so rapid that much of the marine life, including fish, crabs, mollusks and lobsters, was left high and dry. Events such as these have certainly happened frequently in the past and are likely to continue occurring.

Plate Tectonics

Since the mid-1930s, when Alfred Wegener postulated the idea of continental drift, there has been a revolution in geological thought with the development of the theory of plate tectonics in the 1960s. This theory explains many diverse phenomena, including the close fit of the continental coastlines on either side of the Atlantic, the growth of such mountain ranges as the Andes, Alps and Himalayas, and many features of the geology of the Galápagos Islands.

According to the theory of plate tectonics, the earth's outer shell or "crust" is composed of several rigid pieces of continental or ocean floor, called "tectonic plates." These move in relation to one another at rates of 1 to 10 cm/yr. This is a result of processes deep in the earth. At the plate edges many important geologic processes occur. Where two sea-floor plates are moving apart, we find long underwater mountain ranges such as the Mid-Atlantic Ridge or the East Pacific Rise. At the centre of these ridges new molten rock is rising from beneath the crust and solidifying at the surface to form new sea floor. This process, which gradually causes points on the two plates to become further apart, is called sea-floor spreading. Evidence for this process comes from many sources, one being that the measured ages of rocks steadily increase as one moves away from the ridges.

Where a sea-floor plate is moving toward a continental mass, the sea-floor plate is forced under the continent. This process, called subduction, occurs on the west coast of South America where the Nazca Plate is colliding with the American continent. This process is directly responsible for the many earthquakes along this coast, the building of the Andes mountains, and the presence of volcanoes in the Andes. It is now thought that the plate movement is driven by convection currents in the mantle which drag the plates along with them.

Where two plates are moving past one another with little or no destruction or generation of plate material we find "transform faults." These occur along the ocean ridges where they join offset segments of these ridges. Another type of boundary is called a "collision zone" and occurs in areas of former subduction zones where the continents, which are transported on the sea-floor plates, are colliding. This is occurring in the Himalayas where the Indian sub-continent is in collision with the Asian continent.

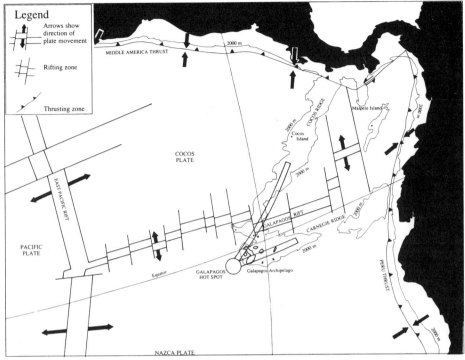

Figure 3: Galápagos tectonic situation. (Based on American Association of Petroleum Geologists 1981.)

The tectonic situation around the Galápagos is depicted in Fig. 3 where we find examples of sea-floor spreading and subduction zones as well as transform faults. The Galápagos situation is complicated because there are three plates in close proximity: the Pacific, the Nazca and the Cocos. The Galápagos Islands are on the Nazca Plate close to its junction with the Cocos Plate. As a result of the spreading of the sea floor along the Galápagos Rift and the East Pacific Rise, the islands are moving south and east at more than 7 cm/yr. This may not seem fast but would over a million years or so amount to more than 70 km of movement. One million years is a short time when compared with the estimated age of earth—four thousand six hundred million years. The oldest islands in the Galápagos are thought to be no more than five million years old, yet the first islands to appear above water could have done so as much as 350 km northwest of their present position!

Each major island consists of a single large shield volcano except for Isabela which is formed from six volcanoes that have joined above sea level. The islands are not all the same age. Española in the southeast has the oldest rock above sea level, whose age (three and one quarter million years) is accurately known, while the oldest rocks from Fernandina and Isabela in the west are less than seven hundred thousand years old.

The evidence that the crustal plate on which the islands sit is moving eastward, and that the oldest islands are in the eastern part of the archipelago, indicates that there has been some volcano-forming force near where the western islands are now. These western islands are also where all the recent volcanic activity has occurred.

Island Formation

The question remains: why should volcanoes form in the precise area of the Galápagos and not elsewhere? Only one per cent of the world's volcanoes are not associated with tectonic plate margins, and most of these are found in either the Galápagos or Hawaiian archipelagos. Geological evidence suggests that a similar island-forming process has occurred in both the Galápagos and Hawaiian archipelagos. The Hawaiian Islands stretch for thousands of kilometres in a straight line, with the volcanic islands becoming older and more eroded to the northwest. Some volcanoes in the chain are so eroded that their tips are now below sea level. The direction of aging of the islands is also parallel to that of the Pacific Plate movement.

Geologists have proposed a hot spot theory, which says that, in certain places around the earth, there are more or less stationary areas of intense heat in the mantle that wax and wane in strength. These hot spots cause the crust and mantle to melt in certain places and give rise to volcanoes (Fig. 4). We do not yet know why "hot spots" occur, nor what "drives" them, but the idea does explain much of Galápagos geology. If the hot spot theory is correct, then it explains not only the various ages of the Galápagos Islands, but also the existence of the Cocos and Carnegie ridges as "traces" of hot spot activity as the plates moved. It is now thought that these ridges indicate that the Galápagos hot spot may have been active for several tens of millions of years. Part of this hot spot trace may extend into the Caribbean.

The recent work (1992) of David Christie and his colleagues is interesting in that it supports the hot spot theory and also explains how the islands may have had more time for evolution to occur. Christie's team made detailed soundings and dredged samples from undersea mountains along the Carnegie ridge. They found round pebbles and cobbles which would likely form as a result of beach erosion. They concluded that these seamounts were once at or above sea level and have since eroded away or sunk. The oldest seamount that they found was nine million years old and about 600 km from the coast of South America. It is currently some 2,000 m below sea level!

The Galápagos and Hawaiian islands have mild volcanic eruptions by world standards. The bulk of the volcanic material comes out gently to form large lava flows rather than explosions. This is because the molten rock or magma forming these eruptions is basaltic. Basaltic lavas have a low water

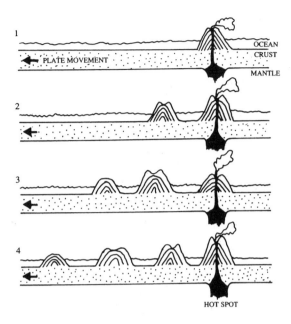

*Figure 4: Hot spots and volcano formation. The hot spot remains
        stationary while the sea-floor plate moves. Successive cycles of
        volcanic activity at the site of the hot spot leave a trail of
        volcanic peaks. These become older and more eroded in the
        direction of plate movement.*

content and flow more easily than more silica-rich lavas. The result is that
the major Galápagos volcanoes tend to have smooth shield-shaped outlines
with rounded tops rather than the elegant cones evident in Mt. Fuji in Japan,
Mt. Rainier and Mt. Baker in the U.S.A., and Volcan Cotopaxi on the
Ecuadorean mainland, which were formed by explosive eruptions. These
conical volcanoes are formed from less fluid andesitic lavas through more
explosive eruptions and are connected with the geologic activity at plate
subduction zones.

The magma that supplies a volcano rises from within the earth and
consists of molten rock and gases. As this magma rises, the pressure of
overlying rocks decreases and, in much the same way as bubbles form in a
bottle of soda water when the top is taken off, the gases come out of solution
and try to escape. With the more fluid basaltic magmas, the gas can escape
easily from the vent and the largely gas-free molten rock will flow out from
the vent to form lava flows. The less fluid magmas found in other parts of the
world prevent easy degassing; this usually leads to more explosive eruptions. Although most of the Galápagos land mass has been formed by lava

flows, there are many small cones scattered about the archipelago. The formation of these is discussed later in this chapter.

The younger Galápagos volcanoes have a characteristic overturned soup-plate outline (Plate 7) and are topped by large crater-like depressions called "calderas." These are formed by the subsidence of the upper parts of the volcano when the underlying structure has been weakened and the magma has retracted. The caldera of Sierra Negra Volcano is 7 by 10 km across and that of Fernandina is 1,120 m deep (Simkin 1984b). Calderas form by a series of dramatic collapse events. One of these occurred in 1968 on Fernandina Volcano. It was the most dramatic geologic event recorded in the Galápagos. In June of that year, the floor of the caldera, previously 800 m below the rim, and measuring 4 by 6.5 km across, collapsed a further 300 m in places. The event was accompanied by hundreds of earthquakes (over 200 in one day) as the caldera floor subsided. When the event began on 11 June, a huge explosion occurred as 1.5 km^3 of gas and magma were rapidly released from below, sending ash 25 km skyward and hundreds of kilometres away. In 1958, an eruption covered the floor of the caldera and evaporated the lake, which took two years to refill. By 1968, the lake harboured the largest population of pintail ducks to be found in the islands. After the 1968 events, there were, not surprisingly, no signs of the ducks and the lake had shifted from the northwest to the southeast end of the caldera. Since the collapse, ducks have recolonised the lake. Vegetation was killed by the ash fall as much as 8 km away from the rim. Since 1968, there have been four lava flow eruptions within the caldera.

Though most Galápagos eruptions are reasonably gentle by world standards, the following description, written in 1825 by Benjamin Morrell, about an eruption of Fernandina shows that this is not always the case:

> While the sable mantle of night was yet spread over the mighty Pacific, shrouding the neighbouring islands from our view, and while the stillness of death reigned everywhere about us, our ears were suddenly assailed by a sound that could only be equalled by ten thousand thunders bursting upon the air at once; while, at the same instant, the whole hemisphere was lighted up with a horrid glare that might have appalled the stoutest heart! I soon ascertained that one of the volcanoes of Narborough [Fernandina] Island, which had quietly slept for the last ten years, had suddenly broken forth with accumulated vengeance.
>
> The sublimity, the majesty, the terrific grandeur of this scene baffle description and set the powers of language at defiance. Had the fires of Milton's hell burst its vault of adamant, and threatened the heavens with conflagration, his description of the incident would have been appropriate to the present subject. No words that I can command will give the reader even a faint idea of the awful splendour of the great reality.
>
> . . . The heavens appeared to be one blaze of fire, intermingled with millions of falling stars and meteors; while the flames shot upward from the peak of Narborough [Fernandina] to the height of at least two thousand feet in the air.

. . . A river of melted lava was now seen rushing down the side of the mountain, pursuing a serpentine course to the sea, a distance of about three miles from the blazing orifice of the volcano. This dazzling stream descended in a gully, one fourth of a mile in width, presenting the appearance of a tremendous torrent of melted iron running from the furnace. Although the mountain was steep, and the gully capacious, the flaming river could not descend with sufficient rapidity to prevent its overflowing its banks in certain places, and forming new rivers, which branched out in almost every direction, each rushing downward as if eager to cool its temperament in the deep caverns of the neighbouring ocean. The demon of fire seemed rushing to the embraces of Neptune; and dreadful indeed was the uproar occasioned by their meeting. The ocean boiled and roared and bellowed, as if a civil war had broken out in the Tartarean gulf.

At three a.m., I ascertained the temperature of the water, by Fahrenheit's thermometer, to be 61 degrees, while that of the air was 71 degrees. At eleven a.m., the air was 113 degrees, and the water 100 degrees, the eruption still continuing with unabated fury. The Tartar's anchorage was about ten miles to the northward of the mountain, and the heat was so great that melted pitch was running from the vessel's seams, and the tar dropping from the rigging.

The mercury continued to rise til four p.m., when the temperature of the air had increased to 123 degrees, and that of the water to 105 degrees. Our respiration now became difficult, and several of the crew complained of extreme faintness.

. . . the Tartar slid along through the almost boiling ocean at the rate of about seven miles an hour. On passing the currents of melted lava, I became apprehensive that I should lose some of my men, as the influence of heat was so great that several of them were incapable of standing. At the time the mercury in the thermometer was at 147 degrees but on immersing it in water it instantly rose to 150 degrees. Had the wind deserted us here, the consequences must have been horrible.

. . . Fifty miles and more to the leeward the crater of Narborough [Fernandina] appeared like a colossal beacon-light, shooting its vengeful flames high into the gloomy atmosphere, with a rumbling noise like distant thunder. (Morrell 1832, taken from Beebe 1924)

This event occurred in February. When Morrell returned to the islands in October, the volcano was "still burning, but very moderately." He and the crew of the Tartar were fortunate in witnessing this incredible spectacle but they were also lucky to have escaped from Banks Bay (Isabela Island) with their lives.

Volcanic Features

The bulk of the Galápagos volcanoes has been formed by successive lava flows. Lava flows of various types, sizes and ages can be found throughout the archipelago and these show some interesting rock features.

When a fluid basaltic magma emerges it is very hot, usually around 1,100°C and a reddish yellow in colour. At this temperature it flows downhill like a fiery river. As it flows, it cools like treacle and becomes more viscous. The more viscous it becomes, the more slowly and steadily it flows. Near the vent the lava may flow at many kilometres per hour but it becomes slower until, at its limits, it may crawl along at a snail's pace. Because the surface is in contact with the air, it cools most rapidly and a crust forms which may be of two major types: rubbly surfaced and called "aa" (after the Hawaiian for "hurt"); or smooth, ropy surfaced, and called "pahoehoe" (after the Hawaiian for "rope"). The smooth type is thin-skinned and when it slows down and comes to rest, the movement of molten material underneath buckles the surface and causes curved rope shapes. This type of flow is not common in most parts of the world but is often found in Hawaii and the Galápagos. A fine example of a pahoehoe flow is found at Sulivan Bay on Santiago Island. Here there is an extensive flow which is the result of an eruption at the turn of the twentieth century (Plate 2).

At the edges of a pahoehoe flow the lava tends to progress by "tongues." These tongues occur when a small spurt of lava breaks out from underneath the existing crust and forms a new spur of molten rock that quickly forms a crust and from which further tongues may arise. These flow processes cause some of the truly fantastic shapes and patterns found in the lava flow at Sulivan Bay. Should the flow encounter an obstacle such as a tree, it will initially flow around it and engulf it. The tree may then vapourise, leaving a mould of its trunk and branches. even to the detail of the bark. Such tree moulds are common in Galápagos lava flows.

The aa, or rubbly surfaced, flow type occurs in many parts of the Galápagos, such as the Perry Isthmus which divides north from south Isabela. This large flow forms a barrier to many land animals. The surface is covered with sharp and loose boulders that make every step a dangerous one. This cindery layer

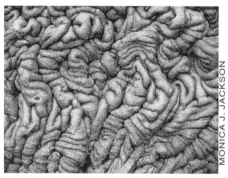

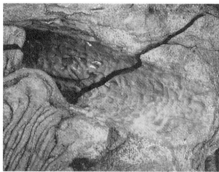

"Intestinal" pahoehoe lava, Sulivan Bay, Santiago Island.

Tree mould in lava, showing bark imprint.

The lava flow at Sulivan Bay, Santiago Island, with Bartolomé Island in the background.

is carried on top of the moving flow and appears like rocks on a conveyor belt. As the flow cools, banks of rubbly material form on the sides, channelling the flow to a canal. If, as is often the case, the volume of flow decreases, it leaves a levee. At the front of an aa flow there is usually a bank of rubble which is pushed forward by pressure from behind, as if by a bulldozer.

Solid lava is a good insulator and, in both aa and pahoehoe flows, a solid exterior often surrounds a molten interior that continues to flow. When the rate of supply of lava at the source or vent decreases there is not enough material to fill the whole cylinder and an empty space will form, called a "lava tube." These vary in diameter from less than 1 m to over 10 m. On Santa Cruz there are several large lava tunnels that run for many kilometres (Plate 1).

In the middle of some lava flows one sometimes finds small cones of glassy lava. These are called "hornitos" or "driblet cones" (Plate 15). These are caused by pockets of gas escaping from the still molten flow. The gas escaping from the lava flings small gobbets of molten rock a short distance into the air and these fall to the ground to form small "chimneys" or cones. These hornitos are usually less than 1 m high. Some are found at Sulivan Bay. These hornitos also occur at sites where the flow encountered small pockets of moisture. The water was rapidly turned to steam and bubbled up through the flow.

At the vent from which the lava emerges, a similar process to the above occurs which forms dramatic fire fountains and spatter cones. As large amounts of gas are released, large lumps of molten material are sent sky-

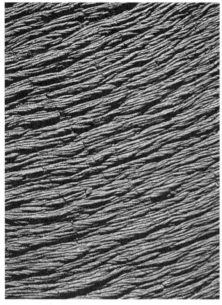

Ropy pahoehoe lava.   Tuff formations, James Bay, Santiago Island.

ward. These land and solidify to look like cow-pats, which pile up one on another to form spatter cones. One side is often broken down by the lava flow. Sometimes the eruption has insufficient material to form a lava flow, and mainly gas is vented, resulting in unbroken spatter cones such as are found on Bartolomé Island (Plate 16).

Large "scoria," or cinder, cones are common in the Galápagos. These form by explosive ejection of large amounts of solid rock which is thrown high into the air and falls to the ground at varying distances from the vent, depending on the size of particles and the force of ejection. The fragments forming these cones, and all other cones formed by explosive eruptions, are called "tephra" and may be of various sizes; particles less than 4 mm are called "ash"; particles between 4 and 32 mm are called "lapilli" and bigger lumps are called "bombs." Scoria cones are rarely more than a few hundred metres high and are composed largely of lapilli-sized fragments. An interesting feature of scoria cones is that, when young, they usually have an outer slope of about 33 degrees. This is the angle of repose of loose cinders.

Scoria cones are usually found on fissures or faults in the major volcano structure and are termed "parasitic" cones because they are fed from the main volcano. Ash rings (often called "tuff cones") are also parasitic, but are usually found near the coasts or offshore from a major volcano. These cones tend to be formed from much smaller, ash-sized, particles than are scoria cones and have a wider profile. The interaction of molten rock and water leads to violent explosions, causing highly fragmented material to be flung far and wide. Either by the heat of the eruption, or by later cementation, the particles forming an ash ring usually become agglomerated into a harder rock, called "tuff" (hence the name "tuff cone").

In the Galápagos, the shapes of ash rings and scoria cones can be used as a rough guide to direction. Charles Darwin was the first to notice that the northwest side of most cones is higher than the southeast side. This is a result of the prevailing winds that come from the southeast and have led to more erosion on that side. It is also likely that the prevailing wind would cause more material to be deposited on the northwest side during an eruption. A good example of an offshore tuff cone is Daphne Major with its dramatic bird-filled craters (Plate 9). Its little neighbour, Daphne Minor, is an eroded remnant of the same kind of cone. Fine coastal examples of tuff cones are found at James Bay and Tagus Cove (Plate 8).

When a vent of an ash ring is no longer in contact with water, the eruption will often finish by "oozing out" a pool of lava. This gives the crater a flat floor, and also a "neck" which is less easily eroded. Such lava "pools" can be seen on the coasts of Bartolomé.

Alcedo Volcano on Isabela is unusual in that the eastern flank is covered by a thick blanket of white pumice. Pumice of this type and rhyolite (also found on Alcedo) are rocks which are more typical of continental settings (McBirney 1985). The trail up to the caldera of Alcedo traverses much of this pumice blanket.

At present, the only volcanic activity that is regularly observable in the Galápagos is from fumaroles that give off volcanic gases and steam. They are usually small and may last for many years. These gases may be rich in dissolved minerals such as sulphur or carbonates that are deposited around the vent. From Elizabeth Bay on the west coast of Isabela, one can usually see wisps of fumarolic steam coming from the 1979 eruption area of Sierra Negra

Uplifted coastline of Urbina Bay, Isabela Island.

Coral skeletons at Urbina Bay.

called Volcan Chico (Plate 13). There is also a fumarole in the caldera of Alcedo Volcano whose tall column of steam is a valuable landmark for hikers (Plate 14).

Some Galápagos rocks were not formed directly from volcanic eruptions. Charles Darwin was the first to find marine fossils in the islands. Later the Ecuadorean geologist, Theodor Wolf, found some shell-bearing rock layers, as much as 100 m above sea level. Layers of fossil-bearing rocks as thick as 3 m are found between lava layers on Baltra Island and on the northeast part of Santa Cruz. These layers may be more than a million years old. A demonstration of how some of these layers formed occurred in 1954 at Urbina Bay (also called Urvina Bay), Isabela Island. Here, as was previously mentioned, 1.5 km^2 of marine reef, along a front of 5 km, was uplifted by as much as 4 m. This occurred over a very short time leaving much of the marine life, including turtles, fish and lobsters, stranded. This visitor site, with its gaunt marine skeletons, is a dramatic and unsettling monument to the forces of nature and its instability. In 1975, it was discovered that small uplifts had recently raised both sides of the Bolivar Channel between Isabela and Fernandina by about 90 cm. Some mangroves and barnacles died as a result of being raised above water level, and a landing jetty, formerly in deeper water, is now only usable at high tide. These uplifts are thought to be related to subsurface movements of magma and are often related to subsequent eruptive activity. Past events such as these have probably led to the formation of the uplifted islands of Seymour, Baltra, Plazas, and parts of the northeast coast of Santa Cruz. Santa Fé was thought to have been entirely formed as an uplifted block, but recent research suggests that this is not the case. Some parts of the island formed below sea level, but several parts show clear evidence of forming on land.

As well as uplifting, subsidence may occur. Subsidence results in the formation of calderas and pit-craters such as the Gemelos on Santa Cruz (Plate 12). These craters are the result of surface layers of lava subsiding about a fissure above a subsurface magma chamber.

Erosion

Though the most dramatic features of Galápagos geology relate to constructive volcanic processes, erosion has altered much of the Galápagos landscape and will continue to counteract the mountain-building forces. Along the coastline, the sea gnaws at cliffs and eats away at shores, causing them gradually to disintegrate and change. This process is slow in areas where solid lava forms the shore, but ash-formed rocks are weaker. Tuff cones such those found at Bartolomé show signs of rapid erosion by the sea (Plate 4).

Beaches are formed by a combination of the erosion of rocks on land and the deposition of the remains of marine creatures, especially shells and

Aerial view of North Seymour, Mosquera, Baltra and Santa Cruz Islands, showing the uplifted blocks.

Side of a pit crater, showing layered lava flows.

North-east tip of Baltra Island showing a white fossiliferous layer.

The cliffs near the albatross colony, Punta Suarez, Española Island.

corals. Coastlines exposed to the prevailing southeasterly winds and waves tend to accumulate marine material and white sand beaches often result. On more sheltered coastlines, the erosion of land material is dominant and beaches take the colour of the surrounding rocks and we find black, brown, red and even green-tinged beaches.

Away from the coast, rain and wind become the major forces that erode the land. In the dry lowlands, weathering is slow but, in the humid highlands, the landscape has been rounded by the powerful action of frequent rains. In the arid lowlands, little soil has formed, and it is only found in the cracks between rocks, whereas in the *Scalesia* and *Miconia* zones (see Chapter 3) as much as a metre of soil has formed. The soils of the Pampa zone are quite thin, however. Lowland soils tend to be reddish, while those of higher altitudes are more coffee-coloured (Black 1973).

Over aeons of time, land-forming and land-degrading processes have shaped the Galápagos to provide a unique set of ecological conditions to which life in the archipelago has had to adapt or die. Factors of relief and topography, and the soils that have formed from the rocks play a fundamental role in the "natural economy" of these islands.

Climate

The climate of the Galápagos Islands is unusually dry for the tropics. There are two main seasons, each of which has a dramatic effect on the vegetation. From January to June, air temperatures are warm and the skies are usually clear with occasional heavy rain showers. From June to December, the air is cooler, the skies are often lightly overcast, and there is virtually no precipitation in the lowlands, while the highlands are almost continually wet. The January to June season is known as the warm/wet season and the July to December as the *garúa* or cool/dry season (see Fig. 5 for a summary of climatic information). During the *garúa* season, prevailing winds are from the southeast and the sea is often choppy, while during the warm/wet season winds from the east prevail, and the sea is more gentle. Between seasons, the weather is highly variable and unpredictable. This interseasonal period may last as much as a couple of months and the dates may vary from year to year. The climate in different parts of the archipelago is also varied. Sea temperature in the islands ranges from as low as 16°C to as high as 28°C, depending on season and site.

The Galápagos Islands are distant from any other land mass, and consequently their climate is largely determined by the ocean currents which bathe the archipelago (Fig. 6). During the *garúa* season, cooler waters from the Humboldt (Peru) Current are dominant with average sea temperatures of 22°C in Academy Bay. As a result, air temperatures are cool and an inversion layer is created. The moisture evaporating from the sea is concen-

Table 3. Rainfall Variation in the Galápagos[a]

Year	C.D.R.S. (6 m) Santa Cruz Is.	Caseta (200 m) Santa Cruz Is.	Sto. Tomas (350 m) Isabela Is.	Media Luna (620 m) Santa Cruz Is.
1969[b]	470	1586	(1902)[c]	2656
1970[b]	84	402	(426)[c]	1155
1979	170	877	732	1855
1980	256	859	1029	1378
1981	370	1174	–	–
1982	640	1068	1506	–
1983	2769	–	5295	–
1984	157	–	824	–
1985	63	–	453	365
1986	278	835[d]	1300	1396[d]
1987	1254	2029	2824	2001[d]

[a]Rainfall (in millimetres) based on C.D.R.S. meteorological reports.
[b]Data for 1969 and 1970 are from Black (1973).
[c]Data from Devine Ranch 320 m (Santa Cruz Island).
[d]Data incomplete or uncertain.
– no data available.

trated in this inversion layer (300 to 600 m above sea level) and only the higher parts of islands, which intercept this layer, receive rain. The lowland areas remain dry, though cool (Plate 6).

The variation in rainfall with altitude (see Table 3) is a result of this inversion layer and has important consequences for the zonation of vegetation. These are discussed in Chapter 3. Not only do higher parts of the islands receive more rain but this rain is concentrated on the southern and eastern slopes. The northern slopes of islands, and islands in the rain shadow of other islands, remain much drier.

During the warm season, the southeast trade winds, which drive the cool currents, diminish in strength and warmer waters from the Panama Basin flow through the islands. The average sea temperature in Academy Bay rises to 25°C. The warmer waters cause the cool season inversion layer to break up and normal convective cloud-forming occurs. The islands experience a more typical tropical climate with blue skies and occasional heavy rainshowers (Plate 5).

In some years, the flow of warm waters is much greater than normal, and an "El Niño" year results. Surface water temperatures are higher and rainfall can increase greatly. Life on land burgeons but seabirds, which depend on the productive cooler waters, may experience dramatic breeding failures.

Average Monthly Temperatures - CDRS

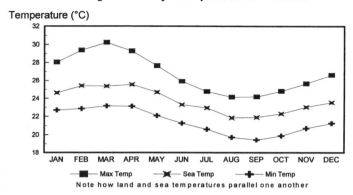

Note how land and sea temperatures parallel one another

Average Monthly Rainfall and Sunshine - CDRS

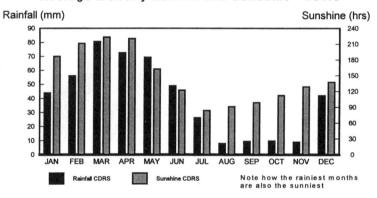

Note how the rainiest months are also the sunniest

Annual Rainfall - CDRS

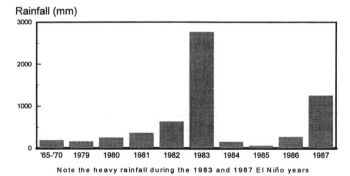

Note the heavy rainfall during the 1983 and 1987 El Niño years

Figure 5: Galápagos climate. (Based on data from Harris 1974 and C.D.R.S. meteorological reports 1978–87.)

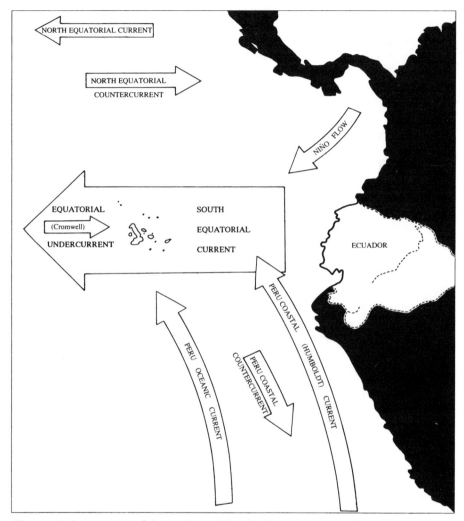

Figure 6: Oceanographic setting of the Galápagos. (Based on C.D.R.S. museum exhibit.)

The causes of the El Niño phenomenon are not well understood but are currently under intensive study, as El Niño seriously affects Peruvian and other fisheries in the eastern Pacific. In late 1982, the most dramatic El Niño on record occurred. It began when the easterly trade winds failed. These winds usually blow steadily and cause the surface waters of the Pacific to be pushed westwards, resulting in a bulge on the western edge of the ocean. When the winds fail, the bulge of warm water "sloshes" back eastwards along the Equator. The warm water reaches the coasts of Central and South

America by late September, and by April 1983 the El Niño had raised surface water temperatures in the eastern Pacific by 10°C. During the winter, warm water had spread north and south through the temperate zones, causing drastic changes in the weather patterns of both North and South America (Levenson 1983) and possibly worldwide. El Niño effects are evident near my home in British Columbia as the water becomes noticeably warmer and several species of warm-water fish appear. The effects in the Galápagos were dramatic. Seabird colonies, such as the blue-footed booby colony on Española, temporarily vanished, sea lions and the fur seals died of hunger, vegetation went rampant and Darwin's finches were able to breed at an unusually high rate. The amount of rainfall, too, was unprecedented. During the eight months of "El Niño" from December 1982 to July 1983, the Charles Darwin Research Station (C.D.R.S.) on Santa Cruz Island received 3,224 mm of rain (403 mm/month), and Santo Tomás, Isabela, received 5,528 mm (691 mm/month)! For comparison, the mean annual rainfall at the C.D.R.S. during the years 1965 to 1970 was less than 200 mm (Harris 1974). It has not taken long, however, for most of the biota to return to something like its normal state, but an event as drastic as this one is bound to have had important evolutionary consequences for some populations.

There is a great variability in rainfall from year to year, as well as from place to place, and with altitude. Climatic records have been maintained for several years by the Charles Darwin Research Station and National Park personnel. A sample of these records which illustrates the trends and variability in rainfall is provided in Table 3.

The Galápagos climate is unpredictable and often severe, especially in the lowlands. The severity of the environment and its unpredictability are in part responsible for the fact that so few species can survive in the Galápagos. The occasional drought years place strong natural selective pressures on plant and animal species that live in the islands. These droughts have probably played an important role in shaping the evolution of these species. Plants, animals, geology and climate have all interacted, and continue to interact, in a multitude of ways to create the Galápagos as we know them now. It is only through an understanding of these various factors, and how they interrelate, that we can begin to understand the mysterious ways of nature.

Ice Ages and the Galápagos

For the last two million years, a most important factor in shaping the landscape of much of North America and elsewhere has been the advances and retreats of the great ice sheets. Today, ice covers about 10 per cent of the Earth's land surface, but, at their maximum extent in the Pleistocene Epoch (20,000 B.P.), the ice sheets covered more than three times this area. The causes of ice ages are still unclear, but we know that they were accompanied by major global climatic changes. What effects might these changes have had on the equatorial Galápagos Islands?

Glacial advances and retreats appear to have occurred in cycles of about 100,000 years—there may have been as many as twenty cycles in the last two million years. The Galápagos are at most five million years old with many islands much younger than this. It follows, then, that glacial dry periods have been a recurrent feature of the Galápagos environment. Climatologists agree that the Galápagos were much drier during periods of glacial advance. Conditions for life would have been much more severe than the already tough ones we see now.

Currently, about 26 million km³ of ice remain on the continents. If all the present glaciers were to melt, the water released could raise the world's sea level by 65 m. This would greatly change the outline of the world's land areas and would completely submerge many large coastal cities. The water that was locked up in the ice of the Pleistocene glaciers originally came from the oceans. It was evaporated, transported landward by winds, precipitated as snow, and compacted into ice. At their maximum extent, the Pleistocene ice sheets had volume of about 77 million km³. This conversion of sea water to ice would have lowered the sea level to some 120 m below the present level. The significance of this change to the shape of the Galápagos archipelago can be estimated from the bathymetric map (Fig. 2). The ice age coastlines were such that many of the present islands were likely connected, especially in the central part of the archipelago. These connections have undoubtedly played an important role in the evolution and distribution of Galápagos species.

The importance of climate and isolation to the evolution of new species is discussed in the next chapter. Biologists studying the speciation of plants and animals in the Galápagos must remember that the islands and their climates may have been different in the past. Major changes in the climate of one part of the world are usually accompanied by related changes in other parts. Because of this we can use information gained about past climates in North America to tell us about the past climates of the Galápagos. Not even islands are truly isolated.

Colonisation, Evolution and Ecology

Islands and island life fascinate biologists. The way in which islands so clearly depict the results of evolutionary and ecological processes has caused them to be the focus of much research. One need only glance at a biology textbook to see that islands have played an important role in the development of biological theory. The Galápagos Islands are scientifically one of the most interesting and best studied of the world's archipelagos; they have much to offer the naturalist.

The scientific principles that are most useful to naturalists in understanding what we find in the world about us are those of evolution and ecology. Plants and animals exist in the environmental framework of the present day, but they also have an evolutionary ancestry in which present form is related to what has happened in the past. Ecological relationships and evolutionary history form a framework for understanding the way in which our natural world functions. Many of these principles apply to plants and animals wherever they may live, but islands and archipelagos, such as the Galápagos, have some features which set them apart from mainland areas, particularly insofar as the character and distributions of organisms are concerned.

The nature of the colonisation and establishment processes have also played an important role in shaping the Galápagos biota. For most terrestrial organisms, a small barrier of water is usually impassable, allowing nearby populations to exist independently of one another, which would not be possible in most mainland areas. Because of these barriers, the results of ecological and evolutionary processes occurring in island situations are much easier to study.

A feature that sets the Galápagos apart from all other archipelagos is its unique geographic position. Situated on the equator under the tropical sun, and yet bathed for much of the year by the cool waters of the Humboldt and Cromwell currents, the islands have a special mix of tropical and temperate environments which is reflected in the ecology of its unusual plants and animals.

Colonisation

When the tips of the Galápagos volcanoes first appeared above the sea's surface, some five to ten million years ago, they were devoid of life. The ancestors of every plant and animal species native to the islands must have arrived there from some other part of the world. We will never know how colonisation occurred, as such events do not leave records for us, but the circumstantial evidence allows us to make reasoned guesses about what probably happened.

Almost 1,000 km of ocean separates the Galápagos from the mainland. Despite this considerable barrier, a seemingly haphazard collection of species has made it to the islands. If we look more closely at the types of creatures that live in the islands, and consider the ways in which they may have reached the islands, we can piece together the fascinating process that has shaped the fundamental nature of life in the Galápagos. How did they get there? Where did they come from? Why some species and not others? These are some of the questions that this chapter attempts to answer.

Dispersal to the Islands

Oceanic volcanic islands, such as the Galápagos, differ from continental islands in that they have never had contact with continental land masses. Continental islands (e.g., many of the Caribbean islands) have at some time in their history been connected with the mainland and have since been separated therefrom by rising sea levels or by land subsidence. Continental islands thus start off their island existence fully vegetated and with a representative selection of mainland organisms. Over time they may lose some of these by extinction and gain others by long-distance dispersal.

Oceanic islands, on the other hand, start off sterile and must gain their biota by long-distance dispersal alone (Carlquist 1966a,b; 1981). In Chapter 2, the geological evidence suggested that the Galápagos have never been connected to the mainland and, as we shall see later, the range of plant and animal species found on the islands, and their distributions, support this conclusion.

Any plant or animal now native to the Galápagos must have originally been dispersed to the islands by some means or other. If the organism survived the hazardous journey and was able to survive in the unfamiliar and probably inimicable environment, and if there were enough individuals for successful reproduction to occur, then the kernel of a coloniser population would exist. This population would have to grow, adapt to, and compete with, other immigrants.

Scientists have been repeatedly struck by the unbalanced nature of the Galápagos fauna and flora. By *unbalanced* we mean that only a small

Table 4. Plant Disharmony in the Galápagos

Over-represented groups:
    ferns .... (Pteridophyta)
    grasses .... (Poaceae)
    sunflower family .... (Asteraceae)
    pigweed family .... (Amaranthaceae)
    bean family .... (Fabaceae)
    sedge family .... (Cyperaceae)
    lichens
    mosses and liverworts

Under- or non-represented groups:
    palms .... (Palmaceae)
    cashew family .... (Anacardiaceae)
    mahogany family .... (Meliaceae)
    mint family .... (Labiatae)
    figwort family .... (Scrophulariaceae)
    orchid family .... (Orchidaceae)
    acanthus family .... (Acanthaceae)
    melastoma family .... (Melastomaceae)
    pineapple family .... (Bromeliaceae)

selection of the groups of plants and animals found on nearby continents are represented in the islands. For example, the islands have a preponderance of reptiles but no amphibians; many birds but few mammals. From the plant kingdom, palms, conifers, and other plant groups that typically have large flowers or heavy seeds are absent, while such groups as ferns, grasses, and composites (sunflower and dandelion family) are more abundant than would be expected (see Table 4).

The dispersal process acts like a sieve, screening out some species while letting through others. Species vary in their dispersal abilities; this variation plays a most important role in determining whether a species occurs in the Galápagos or not. Apart from the hand of man, there are two ways for organisms to travel to the islands—by sea or by air. Some animals arrived swimming or flying under their own steam, others may have been blown by strong winds, still others floated or were carried across the sea on rafts of vegetation. Some plant seeds and spores were carried by air currents, others were carried out by ocean currents, most were brought by birds. The Galápagos are in a fortunate position with respect to receiving immigrants by these means. Both the northeast and southeast trade winds blow toward the Galápagos from the American mainland, and similarly, ocean currents wash out from the coasts of South America in a way that increases the chances of organisms reaching the islands.

Transport by Sea

Sea lions, fur seals, sea turtles, and penguins are all good swimmers, and almost certainly made their way to the islands with the help of favourable currents. Giant tortoises are known to float for some time and could possibly have been carried out by the same currents.

During the rainy season on the mainland, rafts of vegetation are broken loose from river banks by floods and these are carried out to sea and some may reach the islands. Most of the reptiles must have arrived in this manner, as must the only terrestrial mammals (the rice rats) and many of the insects. A raft might consist of a single log or tree but could have been large—rafts of a few hectares have been recorded elsewhere in the world and a number have been recorded with animals on them. In 1911, a floating island of vegetation, some 30 m square and with trees 9 m high on it, was reported as travelling for one thousand miles in the North Atlantic (Thornton 1971). In 1827, a large boa constrictor was reported as arriving on the island of St. Vincent in the West Indies, wrapped around the trunk of a cedar tree. It was so little injured by its journey of at least two hundred miles that it was able to kill a few sheep before it was destroyed (Thornton 1971).

MONICA J. JACKSON

Mainland iguanas, such as this one, could reach the islands by rafting.

Red mangrove seedlings, such as this one, are transported by the sea.

Most natural rafts would become water-logged and sink well before they could reach the islands, but rafts certainly do occur and have been recorded dispersing long distances elsewhere. The Galápagos have been in existence for some five million years or more and, for example, it would only require half a dozen successful introductions to account for the present reptile species.

The problems of rafting also offer an explanation of why there is such a preponderance of reptiles in the islands, few mammals, and no amphibians. Reptiles have a relatively water-impermeable skin and need little water, whereas an amphibian's skin would not resist the desiccation of a long journey at sea. Nor would most mammals be able to survive a few weeks at sea under the hot tropical sun. Ian Thornton (1971) has calculated that, based on the speed of the currents and winds of the area, it would take about two weeks for a raft to reach the islands.

Most beach plants are well-adapted to dispersal by sea. Mangroves, sea grapes (*Scaevola plumeri*), saltbushes, and others have seeds that float well and are salt tolerant. About 10 per cent of the Galápagos plants are thought to have arrived by sea dispersal.

Transport by Air

The small light spores of many lower plants, such as bacteria and moulds, and of ferns, mosses and lichens are easily dispersed by the wind. Wind is thought to have been the major agent of transport for these plant groups. However, though most vascular plants have heavier seeds, some have plumes or parachute-like appendages that enable them to be dispersed by wind. Many species of the large and weedy composite (dandelion) family were likely dispersed to the Galápagos in this manner by prevailing winds from Central or South America. Rains are more likely to occur over islands rather than at sea and would thus encourage seed deposition by removing them from the air.

Small insects, spiders, and tiny land snails are frequently transported passively by winds. Samples of the "aerial plankton" taken by aircraft show a surprising range of small animals being transported.

The land birds and bats, excepting the migratory species, are generally weak fliers and most likely were blown to the islands by strong winds. This may be why the diversity of land birds is so low and only a tiny proportion of the vast range of species found on the mainland are represented in the Galápagos. Similarly, only two bat species occur in the Galápagos (one of which is migratory), whereas hundreds occur on the mainland.

The arrival of seabirds poses little problem as most of them are excellent long-distance fliers. Endemic species, such as the gulls and the cormorant, are not habitual long-distance fliers.

Transport by Birds

Transportation of seeds, or plant propagules, by birds is thought to have been the most important mechanism of dispersal to the islands. The waters surrounding the islands were probably shallow and productive for some time before the land was colonisable, and marine life would have provided a food source for seabirds and migratory shore birds. These long-distance fliers could have brought many plant colonists attached to their feet or feathers, or in their guts. Some of these "hitch-hikers," with their juicy fruits, sticky or burred seeds were deposited in places where it was possible for them to grow and begin the process of colonisation.

I have frequently seen ducks, turnstones and plovers at many different altitudes in the islands. Boobies have been reported plucking plant material from the surface of the sea and carrying it to land. Owls are known to have killed finches with bellies full of seeds on one island and to regurgitate these in pellets on another island (Grant et al. 1975).

Ingested seeds and fruits may be digested and never make it, but many seeds have hard, resistant coatings, and some, such as those of the Galápagos tomato, have improved germination after passing through the guts of mock-ingbirds or giant tortoises (Rick and Bowman 1961). Ingested seeds may be excreted before reaching the islands. This depends on the time it takes for seeds to pass through the gut and how long it takes a bird to reach the islands. Birds flying at 50 to 80 km/hr would take thirteen to twenty hours to reach the islands from the nearest Ecuadorean coast. Many must have flown much further than this.

Charles Darwin was very interested in the dispersal of plants and how this related to geographical distribution and evolution. He carried out some interesting experiments, as reported in *The Origin of Species*:

> I have never seen an instance of nutritious seeds passing through the intestines of a bird; but hard seeds of fruit will pass uninjured through even the digestive organs of a turkey. In the course of two months, I picked up in my garden 12 kinds of seeds, out of the excrement of small birds, and these seemed perfect, and some of them, which I tried, germinated. But the following fact is more important: the crops of birds do not secrete gastric juice, and do not in the least injure, as I know by trial, the germination of seeds; now after a bird has found and devoured a large supply of food, it is positively asserted that all the grains do not pass into the gizzard for 12 or even 18 hours. A bird in this interval might easily be blown to the distance of 500 miles, and hawks are known to look out for tired birds, and the contents of their torn crops might thus readily get scattered. Mr Brent informs me that a friend of his had to give up flying carrier pigeons from France to England, as the hawks on the English coast destroyed so many on their arrival. Some hawks and owls bolt their prey whole, and after an interval of from twelve to twenty hours, disgorge pellets, which, as I know from experiments made in the Zoological Gardens, include seeds capable of

germination. Some seeds of the oat, wheat, millet, canary, hemp, clover, and beet germinated after having been twelve to twenty-one hours in the stomachs of different birds of prey; and two seeds of beet grew after having been thus retained for two days and fourteen hours. Freshwater fish, I find, eat seeds of many land and water plants: fish are frequently devoured by birds, and thus the seeds might be transported from place to place.

Observations such as these show the quality and depth of Darwin's logic. The above arguments for dispersal of seeds by birds can hardly be bettered. Peregrine falcons and ospreys are occasionally reported as vagrants in the Galápagos and might have helped dispersal in the above way. Seeds deposited on beaches by ocean currents could reach other parts of the islands by birds eating them at the coast and excreting them elsewhere. Migrant and vagrant birds are likely to seek out a similar environment to that which they left, thus increasing the chances of seed deposition in a favourable site.

Bristly, barbed or sticky seeds may be transported on the feathers of birds. Many plants have remarkable adaptations for this type of transport and you will surely encounter some of these while walking the trails of the Galápagos. Please be sure not to transport these yourself from island to island. Seeds may easily be dislodged from feathers during flight by preening before or during the flight. The importance of mud on birds' feet as a potential means of arrival was shown by an experiment made by Charles Darwin. He was able to germinate eighty-two seedlings of five plant species, all from a ball of earth attached to a partridge's foot that had been stored in a museum drawer for three years.

Duncan Porter (1976;1979;1983;1984) has attempted to deduce the most likely dispersal methods for the various Galápagos plants. He estimates that 378 original introductions could account for 522 indigenous species known from the islands. Of these natural introductions, 59 per cent were a result of transport by birds, 32 per cent by wind transport, and 9 per cent by drifting on the ocean surface. These figures are only estimates; other authorities may disagree over the percentages, but not over the importance of birds in the transportation of plants to the islands. Of the 225 (59%) species introduced by birds, Porter estimates 64 per cent arrived internally, 15 per cent in mud attached to birds, 12 per cent attached by sticky structures of seeds or fruits, and 8 per cent attached mechanically. Amongst the flowering plants, birds account for 77 per cent of the arrivals.

For the Galápagos Islands, long-distance dispersal has been essential to the development of the species of flora and fauna and their communities. Figure 7 shows the source regions of some Galápagos species and how they have probably reached the islands. After hearing about the difficulties involved, one may be surprised that any organisms occur at all in these islands but, given enough time, anything possible becomes probable. The Galápagos Islands have far fewer species than a comparable area on main-

Figure 7: Source regions of some Galápagos animal species. (Based on C.D.R.S. museum exhibit.)

land South America would have but more than many other Pacific oceanic islands, especially considering their age.

An event similar to what must have occurred frequently in the Galápagos happened near Iceland in November, 1963. Volcanic eruptions beneath the sea gave birth to the island of Surtsey some 40 km southwest of Iceland. Six months after the eruption, bacteria, fungi, seabirds, and seeds had all reached the new islands (Einarsson 1967). By June, 1965, a clump of the beach plant Cakile edentulata (sea rocket) was thriving. In 1967, the first moss colony was found. By 1973, thirteen species of vascular plants and sixty-six species of mosses had become established. Work on Surtsey has shown that the rate of dispersal of biota to the island is directly proportional to the abundance of available material and roughly inversely proportional to the distances from the sources of available colonisers. The mobility of life forms is also an important factor.

Surtsey is much closer to Iceland than the Galápagos are to Ecuador and thus it very soon began to receive colonists. The differences are only of degree; given more time, the same processes would be expected to occur in the Galápagos. We cannot prove that such events took place in the past because there are no records, but we can infer conclusions that make what we believe consistent with what we see. As stated earlier, the oldest Galápagos Islands are some five to ten million years old. Thus, for 378 introductions to account for the present flora, it would require only one species to arrive and become established every eight to ten thousand years (Porter 1976).

Establishment

For a vagrant species to become established, it must find itself in a suitable habitat where it can at least eke out a living and survive to reproduce. A plant propagule must be deposited in a suitable environment for growth and reproduction. It is likely that many plant propagules must have been deposited on the Galápagos in unfavourable places, only to perish. Species brought by birds have an advantage in that birds tend to seek out a similar environment to that from which they came. The plant types most likely to succeed in colonising are weedy species with wide ecological tolerances. Not surprisingly, the Galápagos flora is characterised by weedy species. Animals are able to move to more favourable areas, if such exist and thus have an advantage over plants in the establishment business.

In the beginning, there would have been no soil for plants to grow in. Soil formation is a slow process, especially in arid areas. Soils form as a result of weather, plants, and animals all acting to erode the rocks. Bacteria, fungi, algae and beach plants are likely to be the first colonists of dry land, as is shown by the Surtsey example. Lichens and other plants that need little or no soil and little moisture follow shortly.

The lava cactus, *Brachycereus*, is a coloniser of bare lava.

Higher plants could not establish until enough soil was available, though some are remarkable in their ability to do almost without. *Brachycereus* cacti and *Mollugo* are plants that today are the first colonists of new lava flows. Their ancestors may have been amongst the first plants to share the Galápagos with the lichens. Gradually the lava was broken down, with soil accumulating in the cracks, and more and more plant species could find a home.

A further problem facing colonising plants is that of pollination. Many plants need insects or other animals to ensure their fertilisation; without pollinators there is no reproduction and no colonisation. Plants from many families have evolved such close relationships with their pollinators that they cannot survive without them. This explains, in part, why plants with large attractive flowers are conspicuous by their absence in the Galápagos. It is much less likely that both plant and insect will be carried to the islands at the same time than that either species would make it on its own.

Orchids, which are so famous for their flowers, have very small seeds that could easily be carried out to the islands. Yet the Galápagos have only eleven orchid species while Ecuador has thousands. Orchid colonisation is made unlikely by the need for special pollinators. Many species also need certain fungi to help their germination.

On the Galápagos there are few pollinating insects. Only one species of bee, the carpenter bee, a few butterflies, and some moths occur in the islands, and these are not very abundant. It does not surprise us, then, that most Galápagos flowers are small and not very colourful. Many of the more abundant plant groups are wind-pollinated.

Seabirds that nest on the ground need no vegetation, and thus may have been among the first colonists. Animals need food, water, nesting materials and would not be able to establish until there was enough vegetation to support them. Red-footed boobies, pelicans, and frigatebirds, which nest in trees, would have had to await these, even though there may have been food available. Insects, iguanas, and seed-eating finches had to await their respective food plants, while hawks, flycatchers, snakes, and lava lizards needed suitable prey before they could live in the Galápagos.

An arriving organism will also have a greater chance if its niche is not already occupied. Competition for food and resources will place a greater stress on colonising individuals, though if the new arrival is a good competitor, it may out-compete the native species and drive it to extinction or a new niche.

Once a species has found a suitable home, it must reproduce and create a reasonably stable population before it can be considered established. For a sexually reproducing species, both sexes must arrive within each other's reproductive lifespan so that reproduction can occur. A single individual (apart from a pregnant female, a self-fertile or vegetatively reproducing plant) will eventually die, leaving no progeny. This is yet another constraint on the colonisation of islands by long-distance dispersal.

In the last few centuries, humans have become an important factor in the introduction of plants and animals. Porter (1976) states that "*Homo sapiens* has replaced birds as the most important factor in the dissemination of plants to the Galápagos." Humans have introduced 195 weeds and cultivated exotic plants (comprising 39% of the flora) and numerous domestic animals that have gone wild. They have also introduced other noisome creatures, such as fire ants. Many of these introduced organisms are disrupting the natural balance and are now the focus of the National Park Service eradication or control programs.

It should be evident, from the above examples and arguments, that most of the animals and all of the plants that colonised the islands did so by accident. They did not set out to colonise the islands but rather arrived because they were carried there by forces beyond their control. There are certainly many species of potential colonists that have not made it to the Galápagos. The problems of long-distance dispersal to, and establishment on, islands are responsible for much of the character of the flora and fauna of these islands. This provides the material on which evolutionary processes may act to give us the assemblage of plants and animals that we see today.

Diversity and Species Numbers

When comparing the biota of different areas, scientists frequently consider the relative species diversities of the areas. The simplest measure of the diversity of an area is the number of species found in that area. (Other more complex measures take into account the relative abundance of the species found as well.) The Galápagos Islands are by and large "species poor," that is to say, they have a low diversity when compared to similar environments on the South American mainland. The foregoing discussions of colonisation and establishment give us some clues as to why this is so.

When the islands first appeared, they were devoid of life. The species that are found there now are the result of the processes of arrival, establishment and extinction. These processes determine the presence or absence of species on islands and elsewhere, but on islands the results of these processes are more easily discernable. Several factors affect the immigration rate to an island: the size of the island (a large island is much more likely to receive immigrants than a small island); the distance of that island from a source of colonisers (the further away the island is, the less likely it is to receive immigrants); and the pool of species available for colonisation. Similarly, the factors that determine the extinction rate of species on an island are: island area (a larger area can support more species than a smaller island); and island physical diversity such as elevation (higher islands tend to support more species than lower ones, because of the greater range of life zones found). The number of species that are able to coexist in a particular area may thus be considered to be the result of the balance between the rates of immigration and extinction of species.

These generalisations explain in part why large islands, which have a diversity of habitats and are relatively close to sources of colonisers, tend to have more species than simple, small and distant islands. For example, Santa Cruz is a large island with several life zones (because of its elevation) and is close to several other islands, while Española Island is smaller, lower and more isolated in the southeastern part of the archipelago. It should not surprise us then to find that Santa Cruz has nine species of Darwin's finches, whereas Española has only three. Results are similar when the biotas as a whole or subgroups are considered.

Evolution

The Galápagos Islands have often been called a "laboratory of evolution." There are few places in the world where it has been possible to find such a variety of species, both plant and animal, which show so many degrees of evolutionary change, in such a restricted area. Here, scientists have been able to study in detail many of the processes that have shaped the face of life on earth.

Once organisms reach oceanic islands, they are isolated from other land masses. If the islands are distant enough from a source to make colonisation a rare event, they may be thought of as almost independent biological units—more or less self-contained ecosystems. Oceanic islands can have species which, though related to mainland forms, have evolved in ways different from their mainland relatives as a result of isolation in a different environment. This is a key factor in island evolution.

Not only are the Galápagos distant from the mainland, but within them are a multitude of islands, islets and rocks, each in its own way an independent unit, yet the relationships within the archipelago are closer than those with the mainland. There is an internal "harmony" in the distribution of species within the archipelago, reflecting their proximity to one another, even though each island is often inhabited by different species within a genus.

In the following pages, we will look at how species are classified on the basis of supposed evolutionary relationships, how natural selection acts as a primary force leading to evolutionary change, and how evolution on islands like the Galápagos has occurred.

Classification of Species

Over two million species of plants and animals are known to science, and it is estimated that at least as many again remain to be discovered and described. To grasp this immense diversity of species, scientists have classified them on the basis of similarities and differences. Our present system of plant classification was developed by Carl von Linné (Linnaeus) in 1753—over a hundred years before evolution was accepted as a fact. (Animal classification dates from 1758.)

When the system of classification was devised, there was little belief in evolution; nevertheless, species were classified on the basis of similarities and differences in structure and form. Only later was it realised that most of these similarities and differences reflected evolutionary relationships and common ancestries. The system is hierarchical, like a family tree, and is supposed to reflect, as closely as possible, the evolutionary relationships between species. Thus, closely related *species* are grouped together in a *genus*. Related genera are grouped together within a *family;* related families within an *order;* orders within a *class;* classes into a *phylum* (*division* for plants); and phyla within a *kingdom* (plant or animal). It is usually necessary (and convenient) to recognise intermediate levels to the above seven tiers— subclasses, superorders, suborders, superfamilies and others—as these reflect the fact that not all groups of organisms have evolved at the same rate, nor have they diverged down the same number of branches.

Table 5. Classification of the Giant Tortoise

Kingdom:	Animalia (animals)
Phylum:	Chordata (animals with "notochord")
Subphylum:	Vertebrata (animals with a backbone)
Class:	Reptilia (reptiles)
Subclass:	Anapsida (reptiles with closed-in-type skull)
Order:	Chelonia (all turtles, tortoises and terrapins)
Suborder:	Cryptodyra (group containing most living chelonians)
Family:	Testudinae (major group of land tortoises)
Genus:	Geochelone (genus of large dry area land tortoises)
Species:	elephantopus (Galápagos species)

In the Linnaean system, all species are given two names, a generic one and a specific one, so that no two species, plant or animal, may have the same combination of names. For example, the Galápagos giant tortoise is the species *elephantopus* of the genus *Geochelone*, thus *Geochelone elephantopus* is its proper scientific, binomial, name. Other closely related species in the same genus (pl. genera) exist and carry the same generic name but different specific epithets (e.g., *Geochelone gigantea* on Aldabra in the Seychelles, and *Geochelone radiata* on Madagascar). A classification of the giant tortoise is shown above in Table 5. In technical works, the name of the authority who classified the species is usually also given to avoid confusions with mis-classifications (e.g., *Geochelone elephantopus* Harlan 1827).

Scientific names are often unpronounceable or foreign-sounding. This reflects their derivation from Latin or Greek adjectives, mythological figures, names of persons, geographical place names, and others. These names, though difficult for many to grasp, comprise a coherent international no-menclature. This is essential, as species tend not to pay any attention to international boundaries, and vernacular names are often imprecise, even within one language. In this book, scientific names will be mentioned frequently together with common names since both have their advantages. With plants and invertebrates especially, there are often no common names; in such cases, only scientific names will be used. In Appendix 1 there is a checklist of English and scientific names to help in recording the species that you see. Taxonomists (classifiers of organisms) cannot be correct all the time and, as new evidence appears and relationships are better understood, classifications change and names may be altered to reflect these changes. These name changes are carefully recorded in the scientific literature and (compared to the huge number of organisms classified) are few in number.

Though species are the fundamental units of taxonomy, they are neither fixed nor absolute. A species is a population of organisms distributed over

Giant tortoise, *Geochelone elephantopus.*

certain geographical areas and which occurs in certain habitats within the geographical area. Although members of a species can breed with one another, they normally cannot breed with a member of another species. This is usually because they are incompatible structurally, have different ranges, occupy different habitats, have different breeding times or incompatible breeding behaviour, or are genetically incompatible. Some species that do not interbreed in the wild (because of such isolating mechanisms), occasionally interbreed in captivity (lions and tigers may interbreed to form hybrids, as may donkeys and horses). These hybrids are usually infertile; however, Darwin's finch hybrids are fertile (Grant and Grant 1992).

Because species are dynamic evolving populations, there are frequently taxonomic problems at levels below that of the species. Hence names such as subspecies, varieties and races, are given to those subspecific taxa (a taxon is any definable unit) and, as one would expect, the status of these taxa are the subject of much dispute by taxonomists and others. We should remember that the classification of plants and animals into species is a human artifact, and that the lines drawn between taxa are occasionally matters of opinion, especially in areas where evolution is actively occurring. In the Galápagos, the fact that there are so many subspecific/specific taxonomic problems, indicates the evolutionary uniqueness of the area. In particular, its geological youth has not allowed enough time for populations within the archipelago to diverge as much as in other areas.

Natural Selection

Species populations are not static; they are continually changing with each new generation and thus not only have a dimension in present-day space, but one in time too. A species population has a history extending back through time during which changes have occurred. These changes have occurred primarily by the acquisition of genetic modifications that are passed on from parent to offspring. As traits are acquired and become characteristics of a population, the character of a species at one point in time may become noticeably different from those of its ancestors. At some, usually undefinable, point, a new species comes into being. This "descent with modification" is the basis of biological evolution. It is not possible to draw a line between two generations and say that before was species *A* and after is species *B*, but over an interval of many tens or hundreds of generations, it becomes possible to say that *B* is different from, though obviously a direct descendant of, *A*. This change in a single lineage is called "phylogenetic change." As well as a single lineage changing through time, a lineage may diversify into several species, for reasons discussed later. This is called "cladistic speciation" and is the basis of evolutionary trees such as the one shown in Fig. 8 for Darwin's finches.

In the previous section, we saw that organisms are classified in a hierarchical manner based on supposed evolutionary relationships which reflect a common ancestry. In this section, we will take a look at the ways in which this common ancestry has come about.

On July 1, 1858, two scientific papers were read to the Linnaean Society of London. One paper was authored by Charles Darwin and the other was by Alfred Wallace. These two great naturalists had independently arrived at a mechanism for the evolution of new species. The mechanism was called "natural selection." At the time of reading, neither of these papers made much impression on the distinguished scientists to whom they were read, but, a little over a year later, Darwin published *The Origin of Species*. this classic book contained a consistent and convincing set of arguments that began to persuade the western world that evolution had occurred by natural selection.

The time was right for the acceptance of this theory, which was so contrary to the widely held beliefs of special creation. Geologists such as Sir Charles Lyell (1830–33) had shown that the earth was much older than the literal interpretation of the Bible would have people believe and that the fossil record was filled with examples of species changing more or less gradually over time. Various attempts had been made to explain this by postulating numerous acts of creation or by proposing that individuals of a species change themselves in response to their environment (as Lamarck had claimed). Darwin had much to thank his predecessors for—most of all,

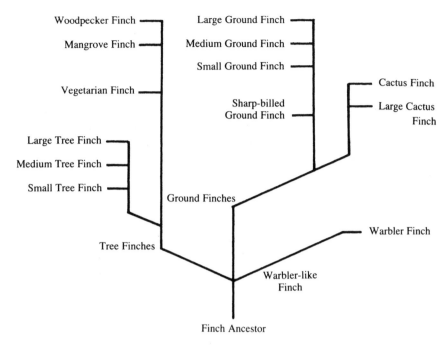

Figure 8: Tentative evolutionary tree for Galápagos finches. (Based on Lack 1947.)

Malthus (the eighteenth-century economist), for his doctrine of population growth.

Though both Darwin and Wallace had independently come up with a theory of natural selection, Darwin had developed the basics of the theory in 1837, right after his experiences during the voyage of the *Beagle*, while Wallace was still a teenager. In the meantime, he had accumulated a wealth of circumstantial evidence from nature and from artificial breeding of species for human use. In 1858, based on his observations in the Malay Archipelago, Wallace wrote to Darwin with a theory almost identical to the one that had been brewing in Darwin's mind for twenty years. This caused Darwin, with the help of his colleagues, to publish his ideas jointly with Wallace. Wallace must be credited with independently arriving at the same theory, but it is Darwin whose name is connected with natural selection by virtue of priority and of the mass of evidence that he had collected.

Darwin and his contemporaries understood that variations occurred and that there was a "strong principle of inheritance." These two facts together with the "high geometrical powers of increase" and the consequent "struggle for existence," were enough to argue the principle of natural selection but not to explain it. The theory assumes that heritable variations arise by some means or other, but in Darwin's time no method was known by which these variations might arise nor was there an understanding of how these "traits" might be inherited. (Gregor Mendel had discovered the basics of genetic inheritance, but this was not known to Darwin or most of his contemporaries.) After Darwin's death, geneticists showed that the inheritance of traits was through the action of genes and that genes were mixed and re-shuffled during recombination in sexual reproduction. Later, it was discovered that genes could spontaneously change or mutate at low rates under natural conditions. (Higher rates occur under unnatural conditions, such as with X-rays.) These discoveries have convinced most biologists that Darwin's and Wallace's arguments are in essence correct:

> If during the long course of ages and under varying conditions of life, organic beings vary at all in the several parts of their organisation, and I think this cannot be disputed; if there be, owing to the high geometrical powers of increase of each species, at some age, season, or year, a severe struggle for life, and this certainly cannot be disputed; then, considering the infinite complexity of the relations of all organic beings to each other and to their conditions of existence, causing an infinite diversity in structure, constitution and habits, to be advantageous to them, I think it would be a most extraordinary fact if no variation had occurred useful to each being's own welfare, in the same way as so many variations have occurred useful to man. But if variations useful to any organic being do occur, assuredly individuals thus characterised will have the best chance of being preserved in the struggle for life; and from the strong principle of inheritance, they will tend to produce offspring similarly characterised. This principle of preservation, I have called, for the sake of brevity, Natural Selection. (Darwin 1859)

The theory of evolution by natural selection has been a foundation of biology ever since Darwin's time and, with few modifications, has stood the test of time. Mutations, genetic inheritance, and natural selection have since been the basis of our understanding of the processes of evolution. The continued action of the natural selection process is normally a stabilising force in nature, tending to keep species much the same from one generation to another in a stable environment. It also allows the gradual accumulation of new or changed characteristics over many generations to modify the species. In a normal population under stable environmental conditions, one would not expect great changes to occur. When conditions change, however, the creative effects of the natural selection process will be demonstrated.

In a changing environment, those individuals that are best suited to the new circumstances will be more likely to survive and to produce offspring carrying their inheritance. If there is not enough variability amongst the individuals of the population to cope with the changes, that population will become extinct, perhaps providing new opportunities for the descendants of another species.

Many palaeontologists believe that the continuous gradual action of natural selection is insufficient to explain fully the diversification of species as seen in the fossil record. The record shows that, on the whole, species remain much the same for considerable periods of time and then suddenly (geologically speaking) appear changed in younger strata with few or no transitional forms being found. Often, the times at which these changes occur are the same for many groups of species and also coincide with large-scale extinctions of species, suggesting that dramatic environmental upheavals may have occurred. These upheavals may have been the result of major changes in the rates of geological processes such as sea-floor spreading or perhaps because of meteoritic impacts. Whatever the direct causes of these ecological changes, it is certain that they have occurred. It is likely that the populations (individuals) that survived these changes would find themselves in an environment where most of the competitive constraints on life were reduced. Under such conditions, the full genetic potential of these populations would have had a chance of expression. Once the environmental carrying capacity was reached, competitive natural selection would resume its action on the new variability created. In the time it had taken for the environment to fill up, it is possible that certain individuals, or groups of individuals, may have diverged sufficiently from their ancestral roots to be classed as new species. These would have created a new niche for themselves. The role that the above-mentioned processes have played in the main lines of evolution has not yet been fully evaluated, but similar processes will have occurred during the colonisation of oceanic islands. However rapidly or slowly these changes occurred, they were still governed by natural selection.

Charles Darwin should be remembered as the person who, more than a century ago, gave evolution credibility by providing a wealth of evidence and a plausible mechanism. The Galápagos—"Darwin's Islands" as they have been called—have a place in the history of ideas as one of the seeds of what has been such a great conceptual change in human thought. One has only to read the Galápagos chapter of *The Voyage of the Beagle* to realise how struck Darwin was with the natural history of these "eminently curious" islands. His observations in the islands helped him to discard the straitjacket that the notion of special creation and permanence of species imposed upon the study of natural phenomena. During the *Beagle*'s voyage, Darwin believed in the permanence of species, but as he wrote in a letter later in his life "vague doubts occasionally flitted across my mind." In 1837, almost a year after his return, he entered the following note in his diary:

In July opened the first notebook on Transmutation of Species. Had been greatly struck from about the previous March on character of South American fossils and species on Galápagos Archipelago. These facts (especially the latter) origin all my views.

In *The Voyage of the Beagle* he wrote the following about South American fossils:

This wonderful relationship between the dead and the living will, I do not doubt, hereafter throw more light on the appearance of organic beings on our earth and their disappearance from it than any other class of facts.

and about the Galápagos Islands :

Hence, both in space and time, we seem to be brought somewhat near to that great fact—that mystery of mysteries—the first appearance of new beings on this earth.

Evolution in the Galápagos

It is not surprising that Darwin was so struck by the life he found in these islands. There are unique species or varieties and examples of divergence in almost every group of plants and animals. Archipelagos, such as the Galápagos, show, in a microcosm, the results of the processes of evolution in a way that is much clearer than is possible in the confusing array of species on the mainland. In these islands, we can see the results of two types of evolutionary process. One is the descent with modification, the change of individuals in a single lineage to form a single new species; the other is the multiplication of species. These two processes are not essentially different from one another, except in the degree to which isolation and chance have played an important role.

Because of the problems of arrival, colonising populations are likely to be small. This results in the genetic variety of the establishing population being both small and also not necessarily a representative selection of the genes of the parent population. This "genetic bottleneck" effect gives a new island population a tendency to be different from its parent population without any natural selection occurring. This is often referred to as the "founder effect."

A further characteristic of small populations is their tendency towards "genetic drift." Random mutations can spread more easily through a small population and become stable features of a new population, than if the same changes occurred in a large population. Populations of new colonists are usually small and thus more susceptible to change. Chance will play a major part in determining which changes become fixed in the young population. A coloniser species may, within a few generations, become noticeably distinct from the mainland population and even be classified as a new subspecies. Examples of species that have become different enough to merit subspecific status include the sea lion, the short-eared owl, the barn owl, the flamingo, the yellow-crowned night heron and the great blue heron, to name a few.

All the change would amount to nought if the islands were not distant enough from the colonising source for immigration to be a rare event. If it was the case that new individuals of a species arrived frequently by one or other means of dispersal, the ability of the island population to change would be hampered by a continual influx of genes "diluting" the changes.

Thus, species that are good long-distance colonisers, such as mangroves and saltbushes, would not be expected to form new races or species, while those species arriving at the limits of their dispersal capability are more likely to form endemic varieties (ones unique to the archipelago). This is why islands close to mainlands have few unique species. Isolation is of great importance in the formation of new and unique species.

A major factor leading to the formation of new species is that of a new environment, different from that of the source region. Though the Galápagos have climatic and other similarities to the major source region (coastal Ecuador and Peru) these areas are by no means the same, and colonising organisms must adapt themselves to this new environment. Not only is the physical environment unique in its hot and cold nature, but also the biotic environment may be dramatically different: few competitors, few predators, and for animals, few food plants.

If isolation continues, the population may, under the continued action of natural selection, evolve into an endemic species. Such has occurred with the flightless cormorant, the Galápagos hawk, the Galápagos fur seal, the Galápagos penguin and many others.

It has often been pointed out that there is a tendency for island species to become generalists (e.g., consume a wider variety of food). Galápagos examples include the hawk and the mockingbirds. A species may be a generalist as a result of having individuals that are genetically similar but which have a great flexibility in their ecological requirements, or it may be a species that has considerable genetic variability between individuals. These latter types are the starters for adaptive radiation (speciation) in islands or the formation of two or more species from one ancestral stock.

Because of the genetic mixing effect of sexual reproduction, populations of a species must be separated from one another to be able to diverge. This may be ecological or geographic isolation. Both types have played important roles in the evolution of Galápagos species, but geographic isolation has been the major force.

Figure 9 shows one explanation of how thirteen species of Darwin's finches could have evolved. In step 1, immigrants from the mainland reach and colonise an island. Later, in step 2, dispersal to other islands takes place,

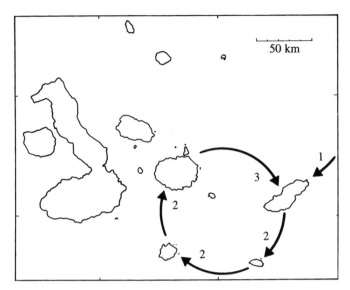

Figure 9: Tentative model for the evolution of Galápagos finches.
(See text. Based on Grant 1981; courtesy of **American Scientist.***)*

perhaps several times, and several new populations are formed. With each of these new colonisation events, genetic drift, the founder effect, and the new environment will play a part in causing these satellite populations to diverge from their ancestors. This step in itself may lead to the formation of new island races or species, and the speciation process may stop here. For groups such as the finches, a further step may have occurred. In step 3, members of the derived populations recolonise the original island and may become established as separate species if the differences between the populations are large enough. If there is insufficient difference and little selection against intermediates, then the populations will mix and return to being one species. The cycle of events may be repeated several times until three or more species have evolved from one ancestral stock. The islands used to illustrate this model were chosen arbitrarily; not all dispersal events lead to speciation.

The scenario outlined above applies equally well to the speciation of mockingbirds, giant tortoises, *Opuntia* cacti, *Scalesia* plants, lava lizards, and *Bulimulus* (*Naesiotus*) land snails. However, in many of these groups, step 3 has not occurred or has not been successful, and the distributions are characterised by only one species on any given island.

Within an archipelago like the Galápagos, there have been opportunities for island colonisation, and also for environmental specialisation, so it is not surprising that many unique groups of plants and animals have evolved. It was this diversity of unique forms, and their distribution, that captured

Darwin's attention and led him to doubt the biblical truth of special creation and which placed him upon a track that eventually led to the formulation of the theory of evolution by natural selection:

> The distribution of the tenants of this archipelago would not be nearly so wonderful, if, for instance, one island had a mocking-thrush, and a second island some other quite distinct genus. . . . But it is the circumstance, that several of the islands possess their own species of the tortoise, mocking-thrush, finches, and numerous plants, these species having the same general habits, occupying analogous situations, and obviously filling the same place in the natural economy of this archipelago, that strikes me with wonder. . . . Reviewing the facts here given, one is astonished at the amount of creative force, if such an expression may be used, displayed on these small, barren, and rocky islands; and still more so, at its diverse yet analogous action on points so near each other. I have said that the Galápagos Archipelago might be called a satellite attached to America, but it should rather be called a group of satellites, physically similar, organically distinct, yet intimately related to each other, and all related in a marked, though much lesser degree, to the great American continent. (Darwin 1845)

Ecology

Daphne Major is a small island, only 34 hectares in area, and is some 120 m high. It is a tuff cone, formed by eruptions of volcanic ash, and includes two craters (Plate 9). The smaller crater is about 30 m above the main one and forms part of the main crater rim. This barren-looking islet, some eight kilometres from the nearest major island, Santa Cruz, is the home of at least forty species of plants and twelve breeding bird species. (A further ten species are regular visitors and twenty-two others have been recorded as vagrants; Price and Millington 1982.) Though most of the island is surrounded by cliffs, there is a small wave-cut beach where sea-lions bask. Lava lizards are abundant and many types of insect may be found. How do all these species occur together, and how do they interact? Some species are more abundant than others. In some years, the same species is much more numerous than in other years.

On Daphne Major, the blue-footed boobies nest mainly on the crater floors, while the masked boobies nest on the outer slopes. Tropicbirds nest on both inside and outside slopes, while frigate birds perch on the few palo santo trees and chase returning tropicbirds and boobies. Galápagos martins are found mainly around the rim. Palo santos are found mainly on a small plateau on the western rim. *Opuntia* cacti occur thickly on the inner slopes as well as elsewhere. Goat's head (*Tribulus cistoides*) are found patchily.

Why are these plant and animal species distributed in these ways? Finch numbers vary greatly between dry years and wet years. The two closely related Darwin's finches found on Daphne Major differ in their feeding habits. How does this allow them to co-exist? Why is it that other species do not also occur on the island (except as occasional visitors)? Some species, like the sea birds, are dependent on the sea for their livelihood, while others, such as the finches, are wholly reliant upon the products of the land. What factors regulate the numbers of these species? How does the vegetation and animal life of the island change from year to year? What happens to an area that has been disturbed; how is it recolonised? Only a few of these questions can be answered at this time. All fall within the field of ecology.

Natural history and ecology are inevitably intertwined. Charles Elton (1927), in his pioneering book, *Animal Ecology*, defined ecology as "scientific natural history" implying that, it is a more systematic and formalised study of the subject. The distinctions between the two are blurred and it should suffice to say that ecology developed from natural history, a more or less amateur pursuit, to become a scientific profession. Ecology is the science of the interrelationships of whole organisms to one another and to their environment. This is a broad definition, indicating that there is little that does not come within the field of ecology. In contrast with many other biological disciplines, ecology looks at entire organisms and their environment in a holistic manner. Ecology is more precisely defined as the study of the interactions that determine the distribution and abundance of organisms (Krebs 1978).

An isolated archipelago, such as the Galápagos Islands, is especially interesting to ecologists because islands, in contrast with continental areas, are discrete units with distinct boundaries. This makes it much easier for the scientist to pick out and classify relationships. In many respects, islands are special natural laboratories in which the results of ecological processes can be seen with greater clarity than is possible elsewhere.

Studies of islands as ecological laboratories started with the works of Charles Darwin and Alfred Wallace, whose observations of the fauna, flora, and geology of islands were important in leading them to the theory of evolution by natural selection. These two great naturalists are the fathers of island ecology, and much of what they discovered and deduced remains true today with few modifications.

Distribution and Abundance

Through the process of evolution, plants and animals are adapted to ranges of environmental conditions. There are certain conditions or combinations of conditions, under which individuals of a species will be best able to grow, survive, and reproduce successfully and thus maintain viable populations. The adaptations that a species needs to live in one environment can make it difficult or impossible for it to maintain a viable population in a different environment.

The life cycles or life strategies of species have evolved as a trade-off between the contrasting environmental requirements and constraints of the habitat in which they live. For example, the marine iguana, having adapted to the intertidal, subtidal and coastal environments of the Galápagos, seems less able to live inland, where it could not compete successfully with the land iguanas or giant tortoises (which probably could not survive on a diet of seaweed). The marine iguana is well-suited to a special environment: the cool waters allow an abundant growth of suitable seaweeds, and the terrestrial environment is warm enough that they can recover their favoured body temperature after diving. There are no native mammalian predators. Within the geographic range occupied by members of the iguana family, the combination of physical and biological circumstances found in the Galápagos is unique (Dawson et al. 1977). Nowhere else can this combination of cool water, warm land and no predators be found. It is difficult to conceive of other localities where the marine iguana might have evolved nor to where it might expand its range if given the opportunity to disperse.

Birds, such as the peregrine falcon, are regularly reported from these islands but have not been known to breed. It is probable that there is insufficient suitable prey or territory for a viable population of specialised hunters such as the peregrine to have established. The top native predator in the islands is the Galápagos hawk, whose generalised predatory habits allow it to maintain a small but viable population.

The above examples indicate some ways in which the distribution of a species may be restricted. A reasonably complete list of these factors might include: dispersal abilities of the species and barriers to it; moisture availability; temperature regimes; light conditions; food, nutrients and other chemicals; predation by other organisms; and competition with other organisms. The roles that such factors play for different species varies greatly and forms a substantial part of the study of ecology. Any textbook on the subject will provide many contrasting examples.

In his introduction to *The Origin of Species,* Darwin wrote:

> Who can explain why one species ranges widely and is very numerous, and why another allied species has a narrow range and is rare? Yet those relations are of the highest importance, for they determine the present welfare, and as I believe, the future success and modification of every inhabitant of this world.

The factors that control population size have been the subject of much research by ecologists, but the picture is complex. Populations of plants and animals do not increase without limit but show more or less restricted fluctuations. This gives rise to two questions: What stops population growth, and what determines average abundance? It turns out that not any one factor is responsible, but that population changes are controlled by a complex of biotic and physical factors varying in space and time.

If we return to Daphne Major to look at the ecology of the two finch species that breed there—the cactus finch and the medium ground finch—we see that numbers fluctuate considerably but remain within limits. These birds have been intensively studied by Peter Grant and his co-workers for over twenty years (1992) with a view to understanding evolutionary processes. They have come up with much ecological information as a result. Two other species—the small ground finch and the large ground finch—regularly spend much of the dry season on the island but do not regularly breed there. In wet years, more than 200 mm of rain falls, allowing a high production of plants, insects, and finches. In 1977, however, only 24 mm of rain fell and as a result the population of the medium ground finch fell from around 1,400 individuals to only 200—an 85 per cent decline (Boag and Grant 1981). The cactus finch population fell a little less than this. Here, food availability, as determined by climate, is an important factor in determining the finch numbers on Daphne.

The variation in climate from year to year is clearly important. In 1988 and 1989 there were two dry years in a row (4 mm rain total!), resulting in no recorded breeding. In contrast, the 1982–83 El Niño event delivered 1,360 mm of rain and the finches bred continuously for eight months. Birds that hatched early in the season were breeding three months later (Grant pers. comm.).

Predation is not thought to be a significant factor on Daphne, but elsewhere it may well be. Concomitant with the drastic reduction of finch numbers, the scientists on Daphne discovered that, with the medium ground finch, the larger-billed individuals, especially males, survived best because of their greater ability to crack harder and larger seeds. The smaller-billed individuals, which are abundant in wet years, died out disproportionately. This intensive natural selection shows how evolutionary processes can happen rapidly and probably frequently. Occasional strong selection of heritable characters in a variable environment may be one key to explaining the evolutionary diversification of Darwin's finches.

Population numbers are determined by changes in reproduction, mortality, or dispersal. In some populations, one of these three parameters may be most important, but, in others, all may play a role. Some factors that might act on these parameters include: predators, parasites, diseases, food supply, shelter, nesting site availability, and the physical and chemical environment. Physiological and behavioural factors may also be involved. As we observe the world of nature about us, we realise that no species exists on its own, and that all populations exist as members of intimately interrelated communities. By gaining an understanding of the ecological relationships of organisms in their environments, we may hope to be better able to manage these communities to our advantage and yet prevent the wide-spread destruction that usually follows in the wake of man.

Communities and Vegetation Zones

Travelling about the islands, we find that there are similarities and differences in the natural inhabitants of different areas that seem to conform to a pattern. Marine iguanas are found mostly on certain types of well-exposed shores that harbour a very different flora and fauna from mangrove lagoons or sandy beaches. The plants and animals found at an altitude of 300 m on Santa Cruz are different from those found near sea level. Observations such as these have led scientists to propose the concept of "communities." A "community" is an assemblage of populations of living organisms in a prescribed area or habitat. Communities are not discrete, but grade continuously in both space and time and, though communities may have certain characteristics that seem constant, the species groups that form them are not necessarily consistent from place to place. In spite of this continuity of variation, communities can be classified, but it should be remembered that such classifications, and the notion of species themselves, are for human convenience and do not necessarily reflect the fundamental structure of nature.

The vegetation zones of the Galápagos are an example of the concept of communities, and these zones display many features of community organisation. Varying amounts of rainfall with altitude, and from island to island, have led to the formation of vegetation zones ranging from desert to lush cloud-forest and moorland (See Fig. 10). As was mentioned earlier, plant and animal species are found as members of communities or associations that live together under similar environmental conditions. The assemblage of species that we find in any one area are all more or less adapted to the range of environmental conditions found in that particular area.

An important environmental factor for plants is moisture: how much do they get and how much do they lose? On Santa Cruz there is a definite increase in precipitation with altitude because the highlands intercept the cloud-carried moisture. Rainfall in the arid lowlands ranges from 0 to 300 mm annually, while in the highlands the range is between 300 and 1,700 mm (Hamann 1981). The climate also becomes cooler and more cloudy with altitude. There is, therefore, a gradation of zonation of plant species, and, to a lesser extent, of animal species, with elevation. This change in vegetation from seashore to summit has led botanists to propose various zones. The classification of zones varies from one authority to another, but is generally according to the scheme shown in Fig. 10 (see also Table 6). Figure 10 is an idealised representation of the vegetation zones of Santa Cruz Island. This

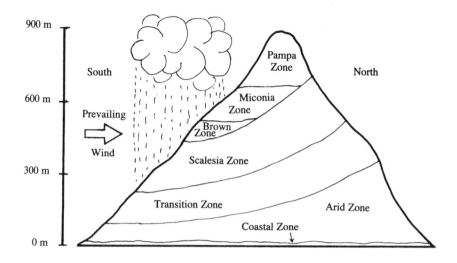

Figure 10: Vegetation zones of Santa Cruz Island. (Based on C.D.R.S.
museum exhibit.)

illustrates the concept of zones, but belies the true complexity which is as yet
poorly understood. When these zones are delimited on diagrams by hard
lines this does not reflect their true intergrading and interdigitating nature.
Because of rainshadow effects and effects of aspect on moisture relationships, there can be large variations in vegetation type at any one elevation:
one need only compare the open dry forest of Seymour Island with the
much denser deciduous woodland of the Academy Bay area. Because the
northern sides of islands receive less rain than the southern, the vegetation
zones on the northern side extend correspondingly higher.

Not all the islands show the same vegetation zonation with altitude. Many
of the lower islands have only an arid vegetation zone and a coastal strip. The
highest volcanoes of Isabela (V. Wolf and V. Cerro Azul) project above the
cloud cover and are arid at the top. The vegetation of the less eroded cinder
soils of Isabela and Fernandina does not fit into the scheme for the older
central islands such as Santa Cruz. As well as the main climatic vegetation
zones, there are vegetation types that result from local variations in the
climate. These variations have been studied in some detail by Hamann
(1981) and Van der Werff (1979).

Vegetation zones are primarily a result of the different adaptive strategies
of the species concerned to cope with specific environmental factors, and
thus it is only to be expected that some species are zone-specific (narrow in
their tolerances). These may reach dominance in their own zone, while

Table 6. Plants Typical of the Vegetation Zones

Coastal Zone	Transition Zone	Miconia Zone
Avicennia germinans	Chiococca alba	Darwiniothamnus
Atriplex peruviana	Clerodendrum molle	tenuifolius
Batis maritima	Cordia lutea	Dicranopterus flexuosus
Conocarpus erecta	Momordica charantia	Lycopodium spp.
Cryptocarpus pyriformis	Piscidia carthagenensis	Miconia robinsoniana
Heliotropium currasavicum	Pisonia floribunda	Panicum spp.
Ipomoea pes-caprae	Plumbago scandens	Pteridium aquilinum
Laguncularia racemosa	Psidium galapageium	
Lycium minimum	Psychotria rufipes	**Pampa Zone**
Maytenus octogona	Tournefortia psilostachya	
Nolana galapagensis	Tournefortia pubescens	Cyathea weatherbyana
Rhizophora mangle	Zanthoxylum fagara	Habenaria monorrhiza
Sesuvium spp.		Jaegeria gracilis
Sporobulus virginicus	**Scalesia Zone**	Lycopodium spp.
		Pernettya howelli
Arid Zone	Darwiniothamnus	Pteridium aquilinum
	tenuifolius	
Acacia spp.	Epidendrum spicatum	
Alternanthera	Lycopodium spp.	
echinocephala	Peperomia galapagensis	
Brachycereus nesioticus	Phoradendron henslovii	
Bursera graveolens	Pisonia floribunda	
Castela galapageia	Psidium galapageium	
Chamaesyce spp.	Psychotria rufipes	
Cordia lutea	Scalesia pedunculata	
Croton scouleri	Tillandsia insularis	
Erythrina velutina	Zanthoxylum fagara	
Gossypium barbadense–		
var. darwinii	**Zanthoxylum**	
Jasminocereus thouarsii	**or Brown Zone**	
Lantana peduncularis		
Mentzelia aspera	Acnistus ellipticus	
Opuntia spp.	Tournefortia pubescens	
Parkinsonia aculeata	Zanthoxylum fagara	
Passiflora foetida		
Piscidia carthagenensis		
Prosopis juliflora		
Scalesia affinis		
Scutia pauciflora		
Tiquilia spp.		
Tribulus spp.		
Waltheria ovata		

Source: Wiggins and Porter (1971).

Evergreen mangroves of the Littoral zone and deciduous palo santo trees of the Arid zone. Turtle Cove, Santa Cruz Island.

others are more tolerant and may occur in all zones but never become dominant in any zone. There are also species that are adapted to other factors and whose distributions do not reflect the general zonation with altitude and moisture. A good example of such species is *Hippomane mancinella*, the poison apple, which occurs from sea level to the Scalesia zone, primarily near ponds and clearings. *Zanthoxylum* occurs in a wide range of communities, but only reaches tree size in the upper Scalesia zone.

The Littoral (Coastal) Zone

In sharp contrast with the adjacent Arid zone, the coastal strip of the Galápagos is mainly evergreen. This zone is not strictly a climatic vegetation type but is an ecological one based on salt tolerance abilities of certain species at the land/sea interface. The type of vegetation found varies greatly and depends on the type of coast. In sheltered coves, mangroves form forests, while on sandy beaches and dunes there are creeping vines, grasses, and succulent shrubs. The saltbush, *Cryptocarpus pyriformis*, is found near most shores, where it forms a dense low shrubby tangle. Many plants in this zone are adapted to dispersal by the sea, especially the mangroves. Few of the plants found in this zone are endemic as a result of the unstable nature of the environment.

The Arid zone of Seymour Island during the dry season.

The Arid Zone

Just inland from the coast is the archipelago's major vegetation zone—a semi-desert forest dominated by deciduous trees and shrubs such as *Bursera*, and evergreen drought-tolerant species such as *Croton scouleri* and the *Opuntia* and *Jasminocereus* cacti. The deciduous plants lose their leaves during the dry season. The plants that live in this zone have adaptations to withstand drought such as small leaves, deep roots, and a deciduous habit, or are annual herbs which can survive the dry season as seeds. Because of competition for water, plants in this zone often exhibit an almost regular spacing. This is best seen on a palo santo covered hillside, or a slope with only *Tiquilia* growing on it, such as on Bartolomé (Plate 24).

The Arid zone is the most extensive vegetation zone and has by far the greatest number of endemic species. Lichens are abundant in this zone because they are tolerant of dry conditions and are capable of absorbing moisture from the occasional *garúa* mist.

The Transition Zone

The Transition zone is intermediate in character between the Scalesia and Arid zones, but it is dominated by different species than either of the adjacent zones. The characteristic *Bursera*, *Opuntia* and *Croton* of the lower elevations become less abundant or disappear. The forest is still mainly deciduous and is dominated by the "Pega-pega" (*Pisonia floribunda*) and

Lush Scalesia forest surrounds a
pit crater on Santa Cruz Island.

The Miconia zone of Santa Cruz Island.

the "Guayabillo" (*Pisidium galapagensis*), both of which are endemic and
also the "Matazarno" (*Piscidia carthagenensis*). It is much more dense and
diverse than the forest of the Arid zone and it is often difficult to say whether
any species is dominant. There are many tangled shrubs and perennial
herbs. There are also more epiphytes, especially lichens, in this zone.

The Scalesia Zone

At its upper limit, the Transition zone merges into the evergreen Scalesia
forest which is a lush cloud-forest dominated by *Scalesia pedunculata* on
Santa Cruz (Plate 12). The trunks and branches of trees in this zone are
covered with epiphytes, mostly mosses and liverworts, but also ferns, orchids, some *Peperomia* species and the bromeliad *Tillandsia*. There are
fewer shrubs in this zone, and herbaceous plants, including ferns and
lycopods, abound.

This type of forest occurs only on the higher islands and, (being the
richest zone in terms of soil fertility and productivity) has been extensively
cut down for agricultural and cattle-ranching purposes. On Santa Cruz, San
Cristóbal, and southern Isabela, only fragments of this once extensive zone
remain. On Santiago Island, goats have destroyed much of the moist Scalesia
zone vegetation.

The Scalesia forest is diverse and also has many endemic species. During
the lowland dry season, it is almost continually drenched by *garúa* mist.

Scalesia pedunculata trees dominate this high-land forest on Santa Cruz Island.

The Zanthoxylum or Brown Zone

Little of this zone remains on Santa Cruz, but the few remnants indicate that it is an intermediate between the dense Scalesia forest and the Miconia shrub vegetation. It is an open forest dominated by cat's claw (*Zanthoxylum fagara*), *Tournefortia pubescens*, and *Acnistus ellipticus*. Trees are heavily draped with epiphytes, especially mosses, liverworts and ferns, which give this zone a brown appearance during the dry season. This zone has to a large extent disappeared because of human colonisation.

The Miconia Zone

The southern slopes of San Cristóbal and Santa Cruz are the only places where there is a dense shrubby belt of *Miconia robinsoniana*. Native trees are absent from this zone and ferns are abundant in the herb layer. There are also many more liverworts than elsewhere.

The Pampa Zone

Above the Miconia zone there are virtually no trees or shrubs and the vegetation consists largely of ferns, grasses and sedges (Plate 10). The tallest plant is the tree-fern *Cyathea weatherbyana,* which has fronds 2 to 3 m long and grows to 3 m tall. This is the wettest zone, especially during the *garúa* season, receiving as much as 2.5 m of rain in some years.

The Pampa, or Fern-sedge, zone of Santa Cruz Island.

Historical Ecology

The Zanthoxylum, Miconia and Pampas zones have the lowest occurrence of endemism. This is surprising since these zones receive much moisture and could be much richer. Research into the historical ecology of plants in the Galápagos by Paul Colinvaux and Eileen Schofield (1976a,b) has shown that the lack of highland endemics may be explained as a result of climatic changes in the past. Flowers shed pollen, and this pollen may be blown into areas such as lakes, where it may be preserved in sediments. These sediments accumulate year by year and so, by taking a core of the sediments and dating the layers using radio-carbon methods, one can obtain an idea of what types of plants grew at different times in the past and also infer the past climate. The above-mentioned workers showed that, since the Ice Age (about 9,000 years ago), the climate and vegetation of the islands has been relatively constant and similar to the present. Between 10,000 and 9,000 years before the present the pollen types changed dramatically and show that, for 15,000 years before then, the climate was much drier than it has been for the last 9,000 years or so. A drier climate would have caused vegetation zone limits to be pushed higher, and possibly the higher zones were absent from the islands. It is only speculation, but the above evidence and the low endemism and species numbers indicate that the upper vegetation zones may only be a relatively recent development (less than 10,000 years old). Most of the species found in these zones are good long-distance dispersers, which

Hardy *Mollugo* plants are among the first to colonise bare lava fields.

supports the supposition that the upper zones are young. The Arid and Transition zones would have had a much greater extent, especially because the sea level during the Ice Ages is known to have dropped by as much as 120 m when much of the earth's water supply was frozen into the polar ice caps.

Community Change

From season to season, or year to year, climatic and other fluctuations profoundly affect the individual species making up a community, causing its composition to change. Many of these changes are cyclic or are fluctuations about a norm. Wet years and dry years can alter the sizes of populations and even the presence of species in any area, but these changes are reversible or non-directional. Non-directional changes are often small and not easily perceptible.

Another type of change occurs when the system is disturbed by some external force, such as humans, or by rare geological events, such as volcanic eruptions. When the lava has cooled down after an eruption, it is barren of life and must be colonised anew. Certain species are rapid colonisers and can survive the harsh environment of a new flow, and these are the ones that start the successional process. On a young lava flow in the lower regions, one is likely to find plants such as *Brachycereus* and *Mollugo*, while on a fresh ash or cinder slope, plants such as *Tribulus* and *Tiquilia* grow. Over time, these plants act together with the weather to erode the new rock sufficiently to provide a home for less pioneering species and, in time, the new flow will become fully vegetated. The rate at which this occurs depends on many factors, such as climate and availability of colonising organisms, and is a dynamic process resulting from a balance between the colonising ability of some species and the competitive ability of others. In the arid lowlands, this process is slow. The flow at Sulivan Bay which occurred at the turn of this century has only a few scattered *Mollugo* and *Brachycereus* plants. In this harsh environment, it may take a thousand years or more for a palo santo

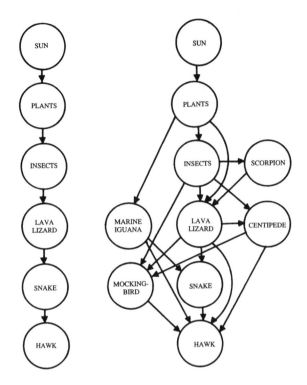

Figure 11: Food chain and food web. (Arrows indicate flow of energy.)

forest to form. Succession proceeds through a series of stages from pioneering ones to climax stage. The climax type of community is the one that would occur in an area given enough time.

Ecosystem Processes

Ecologists view the plant and animal populations within a given area as a community in which different organisms perform different roles. A community of living things, together with the non-living parts of their environment, form a ecosystem, which is characterised by the flow of energy and a constant exchange of materials. The whole earth is an ecosystem; so are the Galápagos; so is an island, a forest, a pond—any unit with definable boundaries. The living things in any ecosystem can be classified according to their functions: producers, consumers, and decomposers. Many communities have evolved in such a way that nutrients are efficiently cycled, especially when they are in short supply. The cycling of nutrients and the flow of energy from producers to consumers and decomposers are two of the most important ecological processes. These processes must occur for a system to persist in time, and this underlies the interrelatedness of organisms with their biotic and abiotic environment.

All the energy in an ecosystem comes originally from the sun and this radiant energy is converted by green plants into chemical energy or food. Some of this chemical energy is consumed by vegetarian animals, tortoises, land iguanas, finches, and insects and is converted into animal biomass. Some of this animal biomass is converted again by such predators as hawks, snakes, and lava lizards to predator biomass. This flow of energy from producers to top predator is idealised as a food chain (see Fig. 11). However, nature is not this simple. At all stages in the "chain," energy is lost through respiration and waste. Also, most of the production of any level in the chain goes directly to the decomposer organisms (e.g., bacteria) and is recycled. Most organisms are fed on by or feed on more than one species, resulting in our food chain becoming a complex food web.

Plant Life

The desert vegetation of Baltra Island comes as a shock to most visitors arriving at the archipelago's major airstrip. After the lush greens of mainland Ecuador, the browns, greys, and only occasional greens of this island seem inappropriate as an introduction to one of the world's most famous wildlife paradises. Baltra is one of the driest islands, but, even so, most of the archipelago's land area is covered by semi-desert or desert vegetation. The islands lie in the Pacific Dry Belt and only the higher parts of the larger islands receive enough rain to be considered tropically lush.

The plants of the Galápagos Islands had a great influence on Charles Darwin's work. His interest in plant geography and dispersal mechanisms was closely tied to the results of his collections on the islands. The first scientific guide to the flora of the archipelago was prepared by Joseph Dalton Hooker (1846), an eminent botanist, and was based mostly on Darwin's specimens.

Field work in the Galápagos is not easy. Lack of water and tough terrain make it difficult for botanists to undertake extensive collecting trips. The flora is still not as well known as we would like, especially that of the uninhabited islands. The number of plant species known from any island was recently shown to be strongly related to the number of collecting trips made to that island, rather than to any ecological factors. Recent collecting trips have continued to discover numerous new species and records. However, as a result of Ira Wiggins' and Duncan Porter's *Flora of the Galápagos* (1971), the plants of the Galápagos are relatively well known.

By virtue of their isolation for thousands to millions of years, many Galápagos plants differ from mainland relatives and frequently from those of neighbouring islands. The islands are young geologically and many plants seem to be in the process of evolving into new species and forms. Under these circumstances, it is often difficult for botanists to decide whether a plant is a new species, subspecies, or variety. Consequently, there is often confusion about the status of Galápagos plant populations. This in itself indicates the interesting evolutionary status of the Galápagos flora rather than of botanical inadequacies.

There are roughly 600 native taxa (species, subspecies, and varieties) of vascular plants and some 190 species introduced by humans. The large margin of error reflects the questionable distinctness of some species and the fact that some species have only been collected once. By most standards, this is a species-poor flora. By comparison, mainland Ecuador may have about 20,000 species. This fact highlights the problems of colonisation and establishment in the islands, as well as the severity of the environment. That the flora is so species-poor makes it easier to identify most plant species and also makes it easier to understand ecological and evolutionary relationships.

Duncan Porter has calculated that less than 400 original colonists could account for the 550 or so indigenous species. (The 250 or so endemics are thought to have arisen from about 110 arrivals.) To botanists it is not the number of species that is most important in the Galápagos but their nature. Leaving aside the plants introduced by humans (which will be discussed in Chapter 12), 34 per cent of the vascular plant species are endemic, while if varieties and subspecies are considered, 42 per cent of the taxa are endemic (Porter 1984). Compared to the flora of the other well-known Pacific archipelago, the Hawaiian Islands, with 95 per cent of their flowering plant species endemic, this is not a high rate of endemism. This is because the Galápagos are much younger, much closer to the mainland, and much drier than the Hawaiian Islands. Considering these factors, the amount of endemism is strikingly high. Thus, a most notable characteristic of the Galápagos flora is what is *not* there rather than what is. This disharmony, or unbalanced taxonomic composition, is shown clearly by the animals as well as the plants.

One feature of the flora that most surprised Darwin was how close the relationships between species are with those found on the American mainland, even though many of the island species are unique. The geographical origins of the Galápagos flora have recently been carefully analysed by Duncan Porter (1983) whose results are summarised in Table 7. This shows that a high proportion of the plants, 87 per cent of the endemics and 97 per cent of the non-endemic indigenous species, are descendants of either widespread tropical species or are otherwise restricted to the South American mainland nearest the islands. The plants of lowland Galápagos are closely related to those of the semi-desert area bordering the Gulf of Guayaquil in southern Ecuador and northern Peru. These areas all have similar climates, largely as a result of the cool Peruvian coastal currents.

It was mentioned earlier that some 40 per cent of the native Galápagos plants are endemic to the archipelago. The five to ten million years that the islands have existed have provided plenty of time for evolutionary change to

Table 7. Origins of Galápagos Flora[a]

	Indigenous non-endemic		Endemic		Total taxa		Introductions leading to endemics	
Neotropical	150	(48%)	61	(27%)	211	(39%)	31	(27%)
Pantropical	77	(25%)	18	(8%)	95	(17.5%)	10	(9%)
Andean	66	(21%)	128	(56%)	194	(36%)	60	(52%)
Mexico and Central America	3	(1%)	6	(3%)	9	(1.5%)	5	(4%)
South America	–		4	(2%)	4	(1%)	1	(1%)
Caribbean	16	(5%)	9	(4%)	25	(4.5%)	6	(5%)
North America	–		3	(1%)	3	(0.5%)	3	(3%)
Total	312		229		541		116	

Geographical areas are defined as follows: *Neotropical* – distributed generally in American tropics; *Pantropical* – distributed in both Old and New World tropics; *Andean* – occurs only in western South America from Venezuela to Chile; *Mexico and Central America* – occurs only in Mexico and/or Central America; *South America* – occurs only in extra-Andean South America; *Caribbean* – occurs in West Indies and often on edges of surrounding continents; *North America* – occurs in south-western United States and adjacent northern Mexico.

[a]Numbers in table refer to total taxa (species, subspecies and varieties).

Source: Porter (1984a).

occur. The mechanisms of evolution on oceanic islands are essentially the same as on continents, but are often more rapid and clear cut. Not only are there two hundred or so endemic species but, also, seven genera from three families are endemic (Porter 1979). These are: *Darwiniothamnus* (four taxa), *Lecocarpus* (three taxa), *Macraea* (one taxon), and *Scalesia* (twenty taxa) from the Compositae (Asteraceae or dandelion family); *Brachycereus* (one taxon) and *Jasminocereus* (three taxa) from the Cactaceae (cactus family); *Sicyocaulis* (one taxon) from the Curcurbitaceae (cucumber family). That these species have become sufficiently different from mainland relatives to be distinguished at the genus level indicates the great amount of evolutionary change that has occurred in these islands.

Less well known than Darwin's finches, which have undergone the evolution of several divergent forms from a single ancestral form, are the nineteen genera of Galápagos vascular plants that have undergone adaptive radiations. Those that have led to the evolution of three or more endemic taxa are listed in Table 8. In addition to these nineteen genera, ten others have evolved two indigenous taxa. The genera *Alternanthera, Scalesia,*

Table 8. Plant Groups that have Undergone Extensive Adaptive Radiation

Genus	Taxa in Genus	Family
Froelichia	5	Amaranthaceae
Darwiniothamnus	4	Asteraceae
Lecocarpus	3	Asteraceae
Scalesia	20	Asteraceae
Cordia	3	Boraginaceae
Tiquilia	3	Boraginaceae
Jasminocereus	3	Cactaceae
Opuntia	14	Cactaceae
Acalypha	6	Euphorbiaceae
Chamaesyce	9	Euphorbiaceae
Croton	4	Euphorbiaceae
Salvia	3	Lamiaceae
Mollugo	9	Molluginaceae
Peperomia	4	Piperaceae
Aristida	4	Poaceae
Paspalum	3	Poaceae
Polygala	5	Polygalaceae
Borreria	6	Rubiaceae

Source: Porter (1979).

Opuntia, Chamaesyce, and *Mollugo* are notable in having developed eight or more taxa in the archipelago. The most common difference leading to the speciation within these groups is that each species is on a different island. Ecological separation on a single island, however, has played an important role in the development of some species of *Scalesia* and *Darwiniothamnus.* The genus *Scalesia* shows the greatest evolutionary changes of any Galápagos plant group and can be compared with Darwin's finches and the giant tortoises as excellent examples of how ecological and geographic isolation have led to the development of new species.

Though most of the islands have broadly similar environments, the species composition of plant communities are often different. These differences are often a reflection of isolation and the lack of inter-island colonisation. Some species have a broad distribution over much of the archipelago but are not present in certain parts. For example, *Jasminocereus thouarsii* has three subspecies which occur in almost all the central and western islands but not in the northern islands; *Lecocarpus pinnatifidus* is found only on Floreana, while *L. lecocarpoides* is found on Española and San

Cristóbal—the genus is not found elsewhere in the archipelago; *Alternanthera galapagensis* is found on the satellite islets of Floreana but not on Floreana itself; the non-endemic Palo Santo, *Bursera graveolens*, is a widespread and common plant in the islands and occurs in the Arid and Transition zones. Surprisingly though, on Seymour, Baltra, and Daphne islands it is replaced by *B.malacophylla* (which is endemic), and neither is found on Pinzón (one tree has recently been reported there!).

Plants are the foundation of most biological communities. The Galápagos are no exception. Tortoises and land iguanas depend to a great extent on the juicy pads of the *Opuntia*, or prickly pear cactus. Darwin's ground finches are adapted to feed on the variety of seeds produced by Galápagos plants while other finches feed largely on the insects that live off the plants. I have seen lava lizards lying in wait by flowers to prey upon the flies and other insects that visit them. Even the most avid zoologist must pay attention to the plants to appreciate the lives of animals. Plants are often disregarded in favour of animals with their interesting behaviour patterns, but the world of plants has a special interest. The minuscule beauty and many hidden relationships are all the more satisfying once discovered by amateur and professional alike.

Common Galápagos Plants

In the rest of this chapter we will look at the natural history of a few dozen of the more common and better known plant genera and species. In this section the plant types are grouped together according to three major ecological zones: coastal area (Littoral zone), dry area (Arid and Transition zones), and humid area (Scalesia, Miconia, Brown and Pampa zones). The reader interested in further help with identification of Galápagos plants should consult one of the guides listed in the bibliography, on which the descriptions given here are largely based (Wiggins and Porter 1971; Schoenitzer 1975; Schofield 1970). I also recommend Eileen Schofield's *Plants of the Galápagos: Field Guide and Travel Journal* as a portable and useful field guide.

Coastal Area Plants

The plants of the coastal areas occur in a narrow zone near the shore and are characterised by their tolerance of salty conditions. Many of the plants found in this zone, especially the mangroves, provide breeding sites for such birds as pelicans, frigatebirds and herons, or provide shade for other animals such as sea lions and marine iguanas. The calm lagoons fringed by mangroves are used as refuges by turtles.

Fruit/seedling of the red mangrove.   Red mangrove trees with prop roots.

Trees and Shrubs

Red Mangrove; *Rhizophora mangle* **(Rhizophoraceae):** Shrub or tree (3–7 m), with stilt or prop roots. Large waxy-looking leaves on brownish twigs. Cream-coloured small flower in small groups. Characteristic long pendant fruit/seedling.

This pioneer of the coasts is found along sheltered shores and the edges of lagoons. It sends down rooting branches from its limbs making a tangled mass of prop-roots that anchor the tree to the rocks. Its roots are in the intertidal zone and accumulate organic and other debris that helps to

Black mangrove flowers.   White mangrove foliage.

Button mangrove.

Maytenus leaves.

stabilise shores. It is dispersed by the sea, by having seedlings that develop on the parent tree and drop off into the water, where they are taken and deposited elsewhere. These usually take root when they are washed into a crack between rocks. Oysters are often found attached to the roots. Red mangrove wood is hard and resistant to rot.

Black Mangrove; *Avicennia germinans* (**Avicenniaceae**): Shrub or tree to 25 m. Leaves darker above and lighter below with grey tinge, smaller than those of red mangrove. Small white flowers in dense clusters. Large broad-bean-like fuzzy fruits.

This species is usually found on sandy beaches and near brackish lagoons. Its roots spread under the sand, helping to stabilise the beach, and send up finger-like breathing roots (pneumatophores). The fruits of this species float on water and are dispersed by the sea.

White Mangrove; *Laguncularia racemosa* (**Combretaceae**): Shrub or tree (3–8 m). Leaves paler than above species, with "dots" on underside. Usually small glands in leaf stalk. Leaves same colour above and below, rounder. Inconspicuous white flower cluster. Fruits pale green, flask-shaped.

This species frequently occurs with the red mangrove in brackish water swamps but is usually on the landward side where there is more sand or mud to take root in.

Saltbush foliage with flower clusters.   Flower of *Sesuvium portulacastrum.*

Button Mangrove; *Conocarpus erectus* (Combretaceae): Shrub or small tree (2–10 m). Leaves thinner and smaller than other Galápagos mangroves, on brown twigs. Flowers found in small ball-shaped stalked clusters. Fruits same globular shape as flowers but brown.

This mangrove species is not as widespread as the previous three and is found predominately on sandy beaches and near lagoons.

***Maytenus octogona* (Celastraceae):** Shrub or small tree to 8 m. Fissured dark grey bark. Leaves usually thick and waxy, irregular shape. Tiny inconspicuous green flowers. Fruit is a capsule which opens to reveal a red berry.

This shrub occurs on beaches and dunes as well as inland. It is highly resistant to dry conditions. Most of its leaves orient vertically so that the mid-day sun causes less overheating and drying.

Saltbush; *Cryptocarpus pyriformis* (Nyctaginaceae): Straggling shrub, often forming dense thickets along shorelines. Green all year with fleshy, formless, oppositely arranged leaves. Flowers small and green, clustered at ends of branches.

This is a popular plant for frigatebirds and pelicans to nest in. It is salt tolerant and its leaves are salty-tasting.

Herbaceous Plants

Sesuvium spp. **(Aizoaceae):** Perennial herb with fleshy leaves. Colour varies from green through yellow to red with changing seasons. Small star-shaped flowers (purplish—*S. portulacastrum*, whitish—*S. edmonstonei* (endemic)).

The two species of *Sesuvium* in the Galápagos are typical drought- and salt-tolerant, fleshy plants. Towards the end of the dry season these two species form bright red mats in areas near the shore (Plate 22). When moisture is available the plants become greener. Like those of the saltbush, the leaves of *Sesuvium* are salty.

Beach morning glory.   Scorpion weed.

Beach morning glory; *Ipomoea pes-caprae* (**Convolvulaceae**): Creeping perennial with stout stems to 10 m long. Bitter milky sap. Funnel-like purplish-mauve flower (2.5 cm diameter).

This creeping vine is common on most dune areas. The morning-glory flowers are amongst the largest in the Galápagos Islands. This species is important in stabilising sand dunes. There are other species of morning glory in the genus Ipomoea that have similar-shaped flowers.

Scorpion weed; *Heliotropium curassavicum* (**Boraginaceae**): Low dense matted herb. Leaves long, greyish to blue-green. White flowers on long curled stalk. Common on saline soils.

Salt sage; *Atriplex peruviana* (**Chenopodiaceae**): Small perennial herb, usually forming mats, but occasionally forming small shrubs. Leathery pale wrinkled leaves. Small yellow-brown flowers in clusters at ends of branches. Common at Punta Suarez, Española.

Salt sage.   *Cacabus miersii.*

Cacabus Miersii (**Solanaceae**): Annual herb, frequently forming mats. Usually sticky stems and leaves, covered with hairs. Large trumpet-shaped white flowers.

Dry Area Plants

The dry zone is the most extensive and widely visited zone in the Galápagos. The environment is primarily semi-desert or dry forest, and the plant species are adapted to drought.

Trees and Shrubs

Palo santo; *Bursera graveolens* (**Burseraceae**): Tree to 12 m. Trunk and branches usually white or grey. Twigs thick with terminal leaf, flower and fruit clusters. Loses leaves during dry season. Leaves compound with five to seven leaflets. Small cream-coloured flowers. Fleshy brown fruits that dry up. (Plate 17)

This relative of frankincense and myrrh is the best known tree in the Galápagos dry zone. Its Spanish name "palo santo" means "holy stick" and originates from its habit of coming into flower and leaf around Christmas-time (the beginning of the rainy season). During the dry season, it is gaunt and leafless with pale grey bark. Its leaves appear, together with the fragrant pale flowers, for a brief time during the rainy period. When injured it exudes a turpentine-smelling resinous sap and its fragrant smoke repels insects. Its fruits are like small cherries and are eaten and dispersed by land iguanas, endemic rats, and several bird species. There is also a smaller species of Palo Santo, *B. malacophylla*, which occurs only on Seymour, Baltra and Daphne islands. Its leaves are greyer and more hairy.

The pale grey-coloured bark is due to a covering of crustose lichens. Close to the shore, the lichens are usually not able to survive and the purple-tinged bark is visible. Often a green alga covers many of the branches on coastal trees.

Palo santo flowers and foliage.

Matazarno.

Pega pega.   Guayabillo.

Matazarno; *Piscidia carthagenensis* (**Leguminosae**): Tree or shrub to 15 m. Leaves pinnately compound with seven to thirteen oval leaflets. Leaflets velvety and light-coloured underneath. Flowers pale pink to lavender. Winged seed pod.

This species is the tallest tree of the Arid zone. It is used locally for timber.

Pega pega; *Pisonia floribunda* (**Nyctaginaceae**): Tree to 15 m. Leaves medium-sized, elliptical, with dense brown woolliness on underside of young leaves. Flowers inconspicuous in clusters.

This endemic tree is a common species in the Transition zone. It is usually covered with lichens. The fruits have sticky glands that aid in their dispersal by birds.

Guayabillo; *Psidium galapageium* (**Myrtaceae**): Shrub or small tree to 8 m. Smooth pinkish grey bark. Leaves leathery, sometimes with reddish bloom. Flowers white, 15–20 mm diameter, fruits like small guava.

This species occurs in the Transition and Scalesia zones. It is endemic to the islands and is similar to the cultivated guava.

Cacti: In the arid parts of the islands the most conspicuous plants are the cacti. Cacti are succulent plants capable of storing much moisture in their stems when water is available and can thus survive periods of drought. They are also characteristically spiny. The spines have evolved from leaves, which most cacti no longer have. The green pads are really the stem. The cactus genera *Jasminocereus* and *Brachycereus* are endemic to the islands, as are all the Galápagos species of the genus *Opuntia*, which is widespread elsewhere in the Americas.

Lava cactus.

Candelabra cactus,
Punta Moreno, Isabela Island.

Candelabra cactus; *Jasminocereus thouarsii* **(Cactaceae)**: Large candelabra-like cactus to 7 m. Formed of green-ribbed cylinders with spines, resembling organ pipes. Flowers greenish or reddish, 2–6 cm broad. Fruit greenish to reddish-purple and fleshy.

Three subspecies of this tall cactus are found in the Galápagos. The pale flowers usually open before dawn and are probably pollinated by night-flying insects, especially moths. The fruits are edible.

Lava cactus; *Brachycereus nesioticus* **(Cactaceae)**: Small cylindrical cactus in clumps to 60 cm. Many spines, younger parts with yellow spines, darkening grey or black with age. Flower creamy white.

On young lava flows, the only plant visible is often this small cactus. Each stem is unbranched and usually only lasts a few years. Each year's growth is paler and yellower than older parts because of the colour of young spines. Like those of *Jasminocereus*, the flowers of this species open before dawn and have usually shrivelled by seven or eight o'clock in the morning.

Prickly pear cactus; *Opuntia spp.* **(Cactaceae)**: Cactus to 12 m, with flat pads. Spines in groups on pads. Yellow flowers and greenish "prickly pear" fruits. Several species, many with a trunk which is spiny when young and with reddish bark when old (Plate 18).

The *Opuntias* are an interesting group in the Galápagos, not only because they have diverged to form a total of fourteen types, but because some have also evolved into tall trees. On Santa Cruz, specimens of *Opuntia echios var.*

A Candelabra cactus with
fruit and withered flower.

gigantea may reach 12 m in height, while on Santa Fé *O. echios var
barringtonensis* has a trunk up to 1.25 m in diameter. The flowers of the
Galápagos species are mainly yellow, though some flowers become
red-tinged on their second day of opening. The Galápagos species are
thought to have evolved from two ancestral stocks forming five and nine
types, respectively, which range from low shrubby forms to tall tree-like
forms. The tree-like forms have a reddish flaky bark and heavy spines while
the shrubby forms tend to have softer spines and a sprawling form. The taller
types occur on islands that have denser vegetation and usually tortoises as
well. The opposite is the case for the lower shrubby forms. The shrubby
species are also primarily vegetatively reproducing. The trunks of tall species are usually heavily armed below the browsing line of herbivores, and
less so above. These observations suggest that competition for light with the
surrounding vegetation and predation by tortoises may both have been
important factors in the evolution of Galápagos *Opuntias* (Arp 1973; Dawson
1966). The work of Peter and Thalia Grant (1981) on the ecology of Galápagos
doves suggests that the lack of stiff spines on the *O.helleri* of the northern
islands may be an adaption by the plants to encourage pollination by birds.
The usual pollinator, the carpenter bee, is absent from these islands. Doves
in particular do not damage the stigma when they feed on the rest of the
flower.

There are some 300 species of prickly pear in the Americas. When compared to the tiny *Opuntia fragilis* of the Canadian prairies, Galápagos

Shrubby prickly pear cactus, North Seymour Island.

Giant prickly pear cactus, Santa Fé Island.

A prickly pear pad with stiff spines.

Prickly pear pad with soft spines.

Opuntias seem like true giants—as much as 200 times taller. The *Opuntias* are also interesting in that, like many other tropical plants, they have a metabolism which is more efficient than most in high light conditions. They also take in carbon dioxide at night to minimise water loss through their pores, which remain closed during the day. Most plants must have their pores open during the day to be able to photosynthesise.

The *Opuntia* cactus is a key species in the ecology of lowland Galápagos. Its pads form a major food source for tortoises and land iguanas. Its fruits are favoured by iguanas, doves, and mockingbirds. The two species of cactus

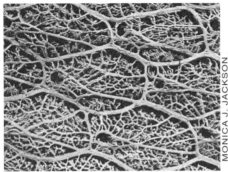

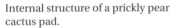

Internal structure of a prickly pear cactus pad.

Flower of *Opuntia echios.*

finches are dependent on the flowers, fruits and seeds of *Opuntia* species. The cactus finches also gain water by pecking at the pads. It never ceases to amaze me how these species negotiate the armoury of spines that the cactus presents. As well as eating the plant, these herbivores help to disperse the seeds and ensure the cactus' survival.

Manzanillo (Poison apple); *Hippomane mancinella* **(Euphorbiaceae):** Tree to 10 m with rounded crown. Leaves dark green with light mid-vein. Tiny flowers on a terminal spike. Fruits like green apples.

This tree has a poisonous milky sap (latex) and poisonous apple-like fruits. No part is safe to touch because it can cause severe dermatitis.

Espino; *Scutia pauciflora* **(Rhamnaceae):** Shrub to 2.5 m. Green spiny twigs with few inconspicuous leaves. Inconspicuous greenish flowers. Dark red or brown fruits.

The sour fruits are eaten by finches and by children living around Academy Bay.

Manzanillo (Poison apple).

Espino.

Muyuyo; *Cordia lutea* **(Boraginaceae)**: Low shrub or tree to 8 m. Hairy twigs with light grey bark. Leaves dark green, rough and also hairy. Large bright yellow trumpet-shaped flowers. Whitish round fruit. (Plate 19)

The large yellow, funnel-shaped flowers of this small tree or shrub are characteristic. The flowers have a *Syringa* (lilac)-like fragrance that is sometimes very noticeable. The fleshy parts of the fruit are sticky and are used as glue for sealing letters. In Peru, a decoction from this plant is used as a cure for jaundice.

Castela galapageia; **Simaroubaceae)**: Shrub to 5 m. Densely branched, spiny twigs. Leaves darker above than below. Small red and yellow male and female flowers on separate plants. Bright red fruits on female plants.

This small, densely-branched, spiny shrub is endemic. It is common, especially at James Bay where goats have eaten the other more palatable species.

Lecocarpus pinnatifidus **(Compositae)**: Erect shrub to 2 m. Leaves deeply lobed and succulent-looking. Large yellow composite flowers. Green and in flower for most of year.

Lecocarpus is one of the Galápagos' endemic plant genera. Three species are found on San Cristóbal, Española, and Floreana. *L. pinnatifidus* is common at Punta Cormorant, Floreana, where it is a pioneer on lava and cinders at low elevations.

Lechoso; *Scalesia spp.* **(Compositae)**: Woody shrubs or trees from a few dm to 15 m. Leaves of various sizes in clusters at ends of twigs, with dead leaves of previous season below. Leaves usually hairy. Flowers are variable composite white heads at ends of twigs.

Though the best known species in this genus is *S. pedunculata* from the moist regions, the genus occurs predominantly in the Arid and Transition zones. There are fifteen species and six subspecies and varieties that occur

Castela galapageia.   *Lecocarpus pinnatifidus.*

Scalesia affinis, Isabela Island.

Scalesia retroflexa, Santa Cruz Island.

on different islands and zones (Hamann and Andersen 1986) (see Table 9). All its species are believed to have descended from a single ancestral stock, yet there is a great diversity within the genus, including those with divided, undivided, and toothed leaves (Fig. 12) and those of shrub and tree form. Flower shape and size varies considerably too from species to species, ranging from fifteen florets in *S. cordata* to as much as 300 in *S. villosa*. Most species have flowers that lack ray florets but *S. gummifera* and *S. affinis* do have such distinctive outer florets.

Scalesia villosa, Floreana Island.

Scalesia helleri, Santa Fé Island.

Table 9. *Scalesia* Species and their Distribution

Species	Islands and zones	Growth types
S. affinis ssp. *affinis*	Floreana(W), Ar	Shrub, large flower
S. affinis ssp. *brachyloba*	Santa Cruz(S), Ar, Tr	Shrub, large flower
S. affinis ssp. *gummifera*	Fernandina, Isabela, Ar	Shrub, large flower
S. aspera	Santa Cruz(NW), Eden, Ar, Tr	Shrub, large flower
S. atractyloides var. *atractyloides*	Santiago, Tr	Shrub, narrow hairy leaves
S. atractyloides var. *darwinii*	Santiago, Tr	Shrub, narrow hairy leaves
S. baurii ssp. *baurii*	Pinzón, Sc	Shrub, divided leaves
S. baurii ssp. *hopkinsii*	Pinta, Wolf, Ar, Tr	Shrub, divided leaves
S. cordata	Isabela, Ar	Small tree to 10 m, small flowers
S. crockeri	Baltra, Seymour, Santa Cruz(N), Ar	Shrub, large flower
S. divisa	San Cristóbal, Ar	Shrub, divided leaves
S. helleri ssp. *helleri*	Santa Cruz(S), Santa Fé, Ar	Shrub, divided leaves
S. helleri ssp. *santacruziana*	Santa Cruz(S), Ar	Shrub, divided leaves
S. incisa	Santa Cruz(N), Ar	Shrub, large flower
S. microcephala var. *microcephala*	Fernandina, Isabela, Sc	Small tree, small flowers
S. microcephala var. *cordifolia*	Isabela(N), middle elevations	Small tree, small flowers
S. pedunculata	Santa Cruz, Floreana, San Cristóbal, Santiago, Sc	Tree to 20 m, small flowers
S. retroflexa	Santa Cruz(SE), Ar	Shrub, large flower
S. stewartii	Bartolomé, Santiago(E), Ar	Shrub, narrow leaves
S. villosa	Floreana and islets, Ar	Shrub, hairy leaves, large flower

Source: Porter (1979).

Notes: Ar = mainly Arid zone; Tr = mainly Transition zone; Sc = mainly Scalesia zone. Letters in parentheses indicate that the taxon is mainly distributed in one part of the island, e.g., (N) = north side.

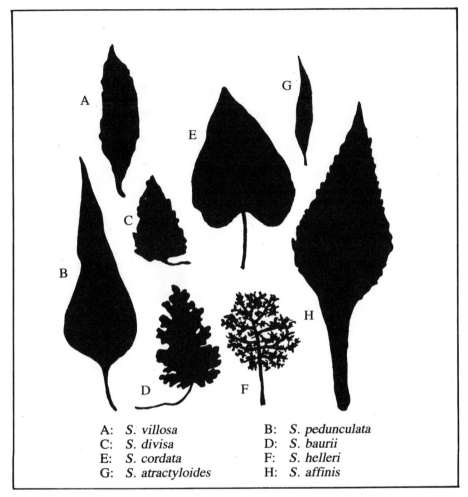

Figure 12: Leaf shapes of some Scalesia species. (Based on Eliasson 1984.)

A:	*S. villosa*	B:	*S. pedunculata*
C:	*S. divisa*	D:	*S. baurii*
E:	*S. cordata*	F:	*S. helleri*
G:	*S. atractyloides*	H:	*S. affinis*

The lowland species most likely to be seen by the visitor are *S. affinis*, *S. helleri*, and *S. villosa*. The hairy leaves and stems of *S. villosa* and *S. helleri* are able to catch the moisture that comes in the *garúa* mist.

A new species of *Scalesia*, *Scalesia gordilloi*, was recently discovered by a local teacher and naturalist, Jacinto Gordillo (Hamann and Andersen 1986). This brings San Cristóbal's tally of *Scalesias* to four.

Chala; *Croton scouleri* (Euphorbiaceae): Shrub or small tree to 6 m. Bark pale. Leaves and seeds vary considerably in shape and size. Leaves grey-green and clustered near ends of twigs. Small cream-coloured flowers in spikes at ends of twigs.

Croton scouleri.

Palo verde, *Parkinsonia aculeata.*

Croton scouleri is an abundant dry zone shrub species. The variation in shape and size of the leaves is related to the types of environments found on the various islands (Hamann 1979). The sap of this species stains clothes dark brown. Many Galápagos scientists wear Croton-stained clothes as a result of brushing with vegetation. *C. scouleri* is a dioecious plant, that is to say, individual plants are male or female and have only one type of flower. Dioecious plants are dependent on insects transferring pollen from one plant to another. This species is pollinated by a small moth at dusk.

Palo Verde; *Parkinsonia aculeata* **(Leguminosae):** Shrub or tree, 2–10 m tall, usually branching near ground. Bark thin and greenish, becoming brown when old. Many hooked spines. Leaves compound long spikes with up to thirty small oval opposite leaflets (these often missing during dry season). Flowers, yellow with some red spotting. Seeds in long pods.

Small scale insects (Coccidae) are often found on this tree. These are related to aphids and exude a sugary sap, much loved by certain ants. These ants are often found "tending" the scale insects and probably give them some measure of protection.

Flame Tree; *Erythrina velutina* **(Leguminosae):** Tree to 12 m with stout spines. Leafless at start of flowering. Young twigs hairy. Leaves alternately compound with three spade-shaped leaflets. Flowers large, red to orange. Seeds in pods (Plate 53).

Flame tree.

Acacia rorudiana.

This red-flowered tree is not common but is widespread. Its flowers add a much-needed splash of colour to the environment. The flowers are favoured by finches.

Thorn tree; *Acacia* **(Leguminosae):** Small trees to 8 m. Stems have straight paired thorns. Leaves are compound with small paired leaflets or pinnae. Flowers yellow or orange in balls. Seeds in pods.

Four species of small acacias are found in the islands. *A. rorudiana*: very small pinnate leaves with leaflets less than 1 mm long. *A. macrantha*: leaflets 1–3 mm long. *A. insulae-iacobi, A. nilotica*: leaflets 3–15 mm long; the former has leaves with one to five pairs of pinnae, each pinna with five to ten pairs of leaflets; latter has three to sixteen pairs of pinnae, each pinna with ten to thirty pairs of leaflets.

Prosopis juliflora **(Leguminosae):** Shrub or tree to 10 m. Leaves and twigs similar to A. insulae-iacobi, with one or two pairs of pinnae each with six to twenty leaflets. Flowers form a long yellow spike. Seeds carried in a long pod.

Grabowskia boerhaaviaefolia **(Solanaceae):** Stiffly branched shrub to 2.5 m with smooth whitish bark on young twigs, brownish on old. Light green leaves on new twigs. Usually without leaves during dry season. Flowers white, fruit a blue-black berry. Common on Punta Suarez, Española.

Lycium minimum **(Solanaceae):** Stiffly branching spiny shrub to 3 m. Leaves club-shaped in clusters of two to five. Usually without leaves in dry season. Flowers small and white. Fruit a small red-orange berry. Common on Punta Suarez, Española.

Galápagos Cotton; *Gossypium barbadense var. darwinii* **(Malvaceae):** Shrub to 3 m. Twigs and leaves with black spots. Leaves usually three-lobed. Large yellow flower with purple centre. Fruits are capsules with white lint (cotton) and seeds.

Prosopis juliflora.   *Grabowskia boerhaaviaefolia.*

This species has the largest flower of native Galápagos plants. The seeds of Galápagos cotton are buoyant and seawater resistant, and thus probably arrived by sea. Darwin's finches are known to use the lint for nest building. A second species, *G. klotzchianum*, is endemic and less common. Its leaves are unlobed.

Lantana; *Lantana peduncularis* **(Verbenaceae):** Small shrub to 2 m with slender tetragonal stems and branches. Leaves thin and dropped during dry season. Small white flowers with yellow centres in compact heads at ends of branches. Endemic with two varieties: var. peduncularis has leaves 4–10 mm long; var. macrophylla has leaves up to 7 cm long.

Clerodendrum molle **(Verbenaceae):** Shrub to 5 m with slender twigs. Underside of leaves lighter than upper side. White trumpet-shaped flowers with 1 cm long tube and protruding filaments (sexual parts). Flowers often in small clusters.

The flowers of this species are properly pollinated by moth species which have a long proboscis (tongue). However, the carpenter bee often bites at the flower base to reach the nectar but does not pollinate the flower.

Lycium minimum.   Galápagos cotton.

Lantana.   *Clerodendrum molle.*

Waltheria ovata (**Sterculiaceae**): Branching shrub to 2 m. Bark reddish-brown to dark grey. Leaves paler below than above, with prominent veins. Small yellow flowers in groups.

Herbaceous Plants

Galápagos tomato; *Lycopersicon cheesmanii* (**Solanaceae**): Much branched low herb. Leaves spear-shaped, compound. Flowers yellow, fruits small green, yellow or red tomato (Plate 21).

The endemic tomato is variable within the archipelago, but each population is uniform. This is because *L. cheesmanii* is usually self-fertilised, leading to little gene exchange between plants. Different varieties may grow side by side without cross fertilisation. The seeds of this tomato have a thick coat which leads to low germination rates unless it passes through the gut of a tortoise or mockingbird. These animals aid the germination and dispersal of the plant.

Alternanthera spp. (**Amaranthaceae**): Herbs or shrubs to 2 m. Leaves opposite, various sizes. Flowers white in terminal heads.

Waltheria ovata.   Galápagos tomato.

Momordica charantia.

Alternanthera echinocephala.

There are nine species, one with seven subspecies, in the archipelago. *A. echinocephala* has a larger flower head and broader leaves than the also common *A. filifolia*. Many of the species are endemic.

Passion flower; *Passiflora foetida* **(Passifloraceae):** Vine, climbing over shrubs, trees or rocks. Stems hairy with tendrils. Leaves three-lobed. Characteristic white flowers (Plate 20). Fruits in feathery bracts, green when unripe, later orange.

This vine is found from near sea level upward into the Scalesia zone. It has the characteristically complex flower of the family and has small "passion fruits." They are not the same as the cultivated type. Two other species of Passiflora are found in the islands, but these are not as common.

Momordica charantia **(Curcurbitaceae):** Slender herbaceous vine with single or branched tendrils. Leaves five-lobed, kidney-shaped. Pale five-lobed yellow flower. Bright orange-red fleshy fruit, 4–8 cm long with red seeds inside.

This palmate-leaved vine is found in the Arid and Transition zones. The pulp around the seeds is eaten by some locals, but the seeds themselves are violently purgative and toxic. An extract of the roots in alcohol is claimed to be an aphrodisiac in small doses.

Goat's head (puncture-vine); *Tribulus spp.* **(Zygophyllaceae):** Low creeping herbs. Compound leaves with six to eight leaflets, somewhat hairy, often

Goat's head (puncture vine).

Tiquilia nesiotica.

silvery-grey. Yellow flowers and distinctive spiked fruits (like a goat's head).

The two species of this attractive yellow-flowered herb are the bane of anyone who walks about with bare feet. The small spiked fruits are capable of puncturing the toughest skin. They are transported in the webbed feet of birds. *T. cistoides* has larger flowers (15–25 mm in diameter) and is perennial while *T. terrestris* has smaller flowers (5–10 mm) and is annual.

Tiquilia spp. **(Boraginaceae)**: Small herbs, forming mats or shrubs. Small leaves in clusters at ends and joints of twigs, usually covered with hairs giving grey colour. Appear more green during rainy season. Tiny white flowers. *T. nesiotica* is the shrubby species (Plate 24).

The four endemic species of this genus of grey-green herbs are wide-spread in the Arid zone, especially in sandy areas. They are often the only species of plant found on ash-covered talus slopes, such as on Bartolomé. These plants live in very dry conditions and they are often regularly spaced. On Bartolomé, lava lizards frequently eat the flowers of *Tiquilia spp.* and the insects that visit them.

Chamaesyce spp. **(Euphorbiaceae)**: Herbs or small shrubs with milky latex in all parts. Leaves opposite. Tiny flowers. Several species. *C. amplexicaulis*: little green shrub with small broad leaves (common on Bartolomé and Genovesa). *C. punctulata*: small reddish stemmed shrub with small narrow leaves (common on Isabela and Santiago).

Several endemic species of *Chamaesyce* are found in the arid parts of the Galápagos. They usually exude a white latex on injury. On Bartolomé the flowers and seeds of *C. amplexicaulis* are eaten by finches.

Galápagos milkwort; *Polygala spp.* **(Polygalaceae)**: Small erect herb to 1 m with few small green leaves. Stems golden yellow to reddish. Small white flowers with yellow centres in clusters at ends of stems. Three endemic species, two with two subspecies.

Chamaesyce amplexicaulis.   Galápagos milkwort.

Lichens: Lichens are an unusual group of plants. They are a symbiosis of two plant types: a fungus and an alga. As a group they are tolerant of desiccation and require little or no soil in which to grow. They may be found growing on trees, rocks, soil and even tortoises. There are many different forms; over 300 species are thought to occur in the islands (Weber 1966). Most of the lichen species are found in the Arid zone where they are best able to survive dry conditions and absorb moisture from the occasional *garúa* mist. Crustose lichens have given the Palo santo its white bark; the true bark colour is purplish. The colours of lichens are variable, ranging from red to

Transition zone tree festooned with lichens.   Rock lichens.

orange to green and grey. On a single small rock on South Plaza Island, I was able to distinguish seven species with different colours and shapes. Dyer's moss, *Roccella babingtonii*, was harvested at various times for its colouring properties but this was never very profitable.

Humid Area Plants

Above the dry zones are the Scalesia, Brown, Miconia and Pampa zones which receive much moisture from the *garúa* mist. These zones are much smaller in extent than the drier zones but are lush and verdant.

Trees and Shrubs

Lechoso; *Scalesia pedunculata* (Compositae): Tree to 15 m with rounded crown, leaves 3–30 cm long, 1–12 cm wide. White composite flower head.

This species of *Scalesia* forms a dense forest in the Scalesia zone. It is one of the tallest members of the daisy and sunflower family. Its crown is dome-shaped and the branches are festooned with epiphytes. Other species of the *Scalesia* occur in the humid zones of Isabela and Pinzón but these are rarely seen by visitors. The twenty forms of *Scalesia*, which are found in various environments and on various islands, are a remarkable example of how one kind of plant can be modified by natural selection to occupy many

Scalesia pedunculata trees.

Cacaotillo, *Miconia robinsoniana*.

Cat's claw.

Tree fern.

different niches. This genus is the plant kingdom's equivalent of Darwin's finches.

Cacaotillo; *Miconia robinsoniana* **(Melastomaceae):** Shrub 2–5 m high with tetragonal branchlets. Leaves opposite, usually three-veined, 10–30 cm long, 4–8 cm wide. Leaves take reddish-orange tinge during dry season. Flowers pink or purple in clusters at ends of branches. Fruit a blue-black berry.

This is an endemic shrub and occurs only on Santa Cruz and San Cristóbal islands, where it forms a distinct zone of dense thicket above the Scalesia forest.

Cat's Claw; *Zanthoxylum fagara* **(Rutaceae):** Shrub or small tree to 10 m, bark light grey, branches armed with sharply hooked spines. Leaves compound, 4–11 cm long with five to eleven leaflets. Flowers inconspicuous, fruit black, about 4 mm in diameter.

This widespread species is most abundant between the Scalesia and Miconia zones, where it is usually covered with mosses and liverworts.

MONICA J. JACKSON

Doryopteris fern.

Galápagos mistletoe.

Pernettya howellii.   Bromeliad growing on a tree trunk.

Ferns; (Polypodiaceae): There are some ninety species of fern in the Galápagos, most of which occur in the humid zones. Bracken (*Pteridium aquilinum*) is a common species, as is the tree fern (*Cyathea weatherbyana*). This latter species grows to 3 m in height and has huge fronds. Ferns reproduce by minute spores and are good long-distance dispersers.

Herbaceous Plants

Galápagos mistletoe; *Phoradendron henslovii* **(Visaceae):** Parasitic shrub on other woody plants. In humid areas it has large thick leaves. Small whitish berries.

This parasitic plant is endemic to the islands and is found virtually wherever there are woody plants, but it favours Zanthoxylum.

Pernettya howellii **(Ericaceae):** Small much-branched shrub to 3 dm. Small leaves clustered around stem. Flowers small, white and bell-shaped, Fruits pale pink.

This small attractive heather-like shrub is found in the Pampa zone.

Bromeliad; *Tillandsia insularis* **(Bromeliaceae):** Plant 20–150 cm tall, rosette form like the "head" of a pineapple. Leaf blades 13–45 cm long, greenish with some purple or red.

This relative of the pineapple and Spanish moss is the only member of its family found in the Galápagos. It is an epiphyte, growing on trees and shrubs and using them for support. It is not parasitic.

Clubmoss; *Lycopodium spp.* **(Lycopodiaceae):** Lycopods are a primitive group of plants related to the ferns. Six species are found in the Galápagos. These plants are neither ferns nor mosses. It is the club-shaped fruiting body that has given it the misleading name of clubmoss.

Clubmoss, *Lycopodium sp.*

Highland tree covered with liverworts
and mosses, Santa Cruz Island.

Mosses and Liverworts; Bryophytes: Mosses and liverworts festoon the trees and shrubs in the moist zones, and are abundant on the ground. One hundred and ten species of liverwort are known and they are most abundant in the Miconia zone. Ninety species of mosses occur in the islands. These are most abundant in the Scalesia zone.

BARRIE BAPTIE

Plate 1:
Tourists in a lava tube, Santa
Cruz Island.

Plate 2:
New lava overlying old.
Sulivan Bay, Santiago Island.

Plate 3:
Volcanic eruption, Volcan
Cerro Azul, Isabela Island in
1979.

TUI de ROY

Plate 4:
Pinnacle rock,
Bartolomé Island.

Plate 5:
The "sugarloaf"
during the wet
season, Santiago
Island.

Plate 6:
The "sugarloaf"
during the dry
season.

Plate 7:
Fernandina Volcano, showing the classic profile. Sea lions in the foreground.

Plate 8:
Tagus cove, Isabela, showing the crater lake.

Plate 9:
The craters and vegetation of Daphne Major Island.

Plate 10:
Highland cinder cone, showing scalesia and pampa zones.

Plate 11:
Highland cinder cone, "puntudo", in the pampa zone.

Plate 12:
Lush highland vegetation and pit crater, Los Gemelos, Santa Cruz Island.

Plate 13:
Fumarole vent in
the recent eruption
area of Sierra Negra
Volcano, Isabela
Island.

Plate 14:
Fumarole on the
rim of Alcedo
volcano.

Plate 15:
*Driblet cone or "hornito,"
Sulivan Bay, Santiago Island.*

Plate 16:
*Spatter cones on the slopes of
Bartolomé Island.*

Plate 17:
*Palo santo trees, Santiago
Island.*

MONICA J. JACKSON

Plate 18:
Tall Opuntia *cactus, Santa Fé Island.*

Plate 19:
Flowers of muyuyo, Cordia lutea.

Plate 20:
Passion flower, Passiflora foetida.

Plate 21:
Galápagos tomato, showing flowers and fruit.

Plate 22:
Sesuvium *vegetation, South Plaza Island.*

21

BARRIE BAPTIE

22

Plate 23:
South Plazas Island at the end of the wet season.

Plate 24:
Tiquilia vegetation, on cinder slope, Bartolomé Island.

Plate 25:
Giant tortoises in a mud wallow, Alcedo
volcano.

Plate 26:
Resting giant tortoise, Alcedo volcano,
Isabela Island.

Plate 27:
Land iguana, Fernandina Island.

Plate 28:
Land iguana, South Plaza Island.

Plate 29:
Male land iguana, South Plaza Island.

Plate 30:
Female lava lizard, Española Island.

Plate 31:
Male lava lizard, Española Island.

Plate 32:
Male lava lizard, Fernandina Island.

33

Plate 33:
Male lava lizard, Santa Cruz Island.

Plate 34:
Male lava lizard, San Cristóbal Island.

Plate 35
Marine iguana, Española Island.

34

35

Plate 36:
Green sea turtle resting on underwater ledge.

Plate 37:
Marine iguana feeding underwater off Punta Espinoza, Fernandina Island.

PAUL HUMANN

36

PAUL HUMANN

3

Plate 38:
Skypointing blue-footed boobies, Española Island.

Plate 39: Blue-footed boobies circling and diving in
pursuit of a shoal of small fish, Santiago Island.

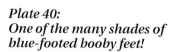

Plate 40:
One of the many shades of
blue-footed booby feet!

Plate 41:
Brown pelican plunge-diving,
Las Bachas, Santa Cruz Island.

Plate 42:
Adult brown pelican, Rábida Island.

Plate 43:
Waved albatross, Española Island.

Plates 44a to h:
Waved albatross courtship,
Española Island.

44a

44b

44c

44d

44e

44f

44g

44h

Plate 45:
White phase red-footed booby,
Genovesa Island.

Plate 46:
Red-footed booby, Genovesa
Island.

Plate 49:
Red-billed tropicbird, Daphne Major Island.

Plate 50:
The frigatebird colony, Genovesa Island.

Plate 51:
Greater flamingos in a lagoon, Rábida Island.

Plate 52:
American oystercatchers calling, Española Island.

51

52

Plate 53:
Male Darwin's finch in flame tree, Erythrina velutina, *Santiago Island.*

Plate 54:
Sanderlings on the beach at Villamil, Isabela

53

54

Plate 55:
Large cactus finch on a prickly pear cactus, Genovesa Island.

Plate 56:
Galápagos hawk feeding on carrion, Santiago Island.

57

Plate 57:
Young Galápagos hawk in
flight.

Plate 58:
Galápagos dove, Española
Island.

58

Plate 59:
Hood mockingbird, Española
Island.

Plate 60:
Male vermilion flycatcher,
Santa Cruz Island.

Plate 61:
Female vermilion flycatcher,
Santa Cruz Island.

60

MONICA J. JACKSON

59

61

Plate 62:
Sea lions resting on
a beach, Rábida
Island.

Plate 63:
Female sea lion,
Fernandina Island

Plate 64:
Painted locust,
Schistocerca
melanocera,
Santiago Island.

Plate 65:
Sally lightfoot crab
on lava shore,
Santiago Island.

PAUL HUMANN

Plate 66:
Hermit crab
underwater.

Plate 67:
Green sea urchins
(Lytechinus) on the
olivine-rich "green"
beach, Punta
Cormorant,
Floreana Island.

Plate 68:
Gulf star on pebble coral bed near Devil's Crown, Floreana Island.

Plate 69:
Red-lipped batfish, Tagus Cove, Isabela Island.

PAUL HUMANN

68

PAUL HUMANN

69

Plate 70:
The tourist trail, South Plaza Island.

Plate 71:
Tourists observing a nesting sea turtle, Sulivan Bay, Santiago Island.

*Plate 72:
Tourist
photographing a
land iguana, South
Plaza Island.*

*Plate 73:
What is this? Turn
to page 125 for
further
information.*

Reptiles

These islands appear paradises for the whole family of reptiles. (Darwin 1845)

On land, the unusual reptiles of the Galápagos dominate the animal scene. Giant tortoises and large land iguanas play the ecological role of larger mammals elsewhere. These supposedly antediluvian creatures are not relics of "the Age of Dinosaurs" but are creations of past and present selective forces in the Galápagos. As the thriving introduced mammals show, many mammals can do well in the Galápagos. However, the problems of arrival, especially a long ocean journey, have prevented them establishing here naturally. Thus, the predominance of reptiles in the fauna is less surprising.

Reptiles are "ectothermic" creatures (frequently and incorrectly called "cold-blooded"). They cannot regulate their body temperature physiologically by sweating or panting but are generally more tolerant of changes in body temperature. After the cold night, they must soak up the warmth of the sun until they have absorbed enough heat to become active, but during the heat of mid-day they must take action to prevent overheating. The options open to them are mainly behavioural, such as seeking shade and remaining inactive in positions that allow what breeze there is to cool them. The giant tortoise is able, by virtue of its great body mass, to keep a more even body temperature, but even it must "take a siesta" on the hottest days.

Because of their ectothermic metabolism, reptiles are more energy efficient than mammals and need less food and water than a comparable mammal counterpart. They get much of their water requirements from the vegetation they eat and are also capable of fasting for long periods. Reptiles are also tolerant of salt in their diet and environment, as most species have salt excreting glands as well as kidneys.

The twenty-two species of Galápagos reptiles belong to five families; Testudinidae (tortoises), Cheloniidae (marine turtles), Iguanidae (lizards and iguanas), Gekkonidae (geckos) and Colubridae (snakes). Twenty of these species are endemic to the archipelago, and many are endemic to

Domed giant tortoise from Alcedo Volcano, Isabela Island.

individual islands. Table 10 provides a list of the reptile species and their distribution within the archipelago.

Giant Tortoise

These huge reptiles, surrounded by the black lava, the leafless shrubs and large cacti, seemed to my fancy like some antediluvian animals. (Darwin 1845)

These islands have been famed for their giant tortoises ever since their discovery, and these enormous creatures continue to be the best known of the Galápagos animals (Plates 25 and 26). The name "Galápagos" originates from the Spanish word "galapago" meaning "saddle," after the saddle-backed tortoises. A Galápagos giant tortoise (*Geochelone elephantopus*) may weigh up to 250 kg and measure 150 cm over the curve of the carapace. Together with the Aldabra tortoise of the Seychelles, they are the largest living tortoises: "Some grow to an immense size . . . several so large that it required six or eight men to lift them from the ground" (Darwin 1845).

The giant tortoises of the Galápagos played an important role in the development of Charles Darwin's theory of evolution, even though he did not pursue the matter during his visit. The then vice-governor's claim that he could tell with certainty which island any tortoise came from is perhaps a little exaggerated, but is by and large true. Though some individuals from one island may look very similar to those from another, the typical fully

Table 10. Distribution of Reptile Species

	Isabela	Santa Cruz	Fernandina	Santiago	San Cristóbal	Floreana	Marchena	Española	Pinta	Baltra	Sante Fe	Pinzón	Genovesa	Rábida	N. Seymour	Wolf	Darwin	Daphne Major	Plaza Sur	Comments
Giant tortoise *Geochelone elephantopus*	5	+	x	+	+	x		+	?		x	+								11 subspecies
Green sea turtle *Chelonia mydas*	widespread – offshore																			
Snakes: *Philodryas biserialis*					+	+		+												3 subspecies
Alsophis slevini	+	+	+	+				+		+				+	+					2 subspecies
Alsophis dorsalis	+	+	+	+					+	+				+	+					3 subspecies
Leaf-toed geckoes: *Phyllodactylus leei*				+																
Phyllodactylus gilberti																+				
Phyllodactylus barringtonensis											+									
Phyllodactylus galapagoensis	+	+	+	+									+					+		
Phyllodactylus bauri						+		+												
Phyllodactylus tuberculosus				+																
Lava lizards: *Tropidurus grayi*					+															
Tropidurus bivittatus				+																
Tropidurus pacificus							+													
Tropidurus habellii						+														
Tropidurus delanonis						+														
Tropidurus albemarlensis	+	+	+	+					+	+				+	+			+	+	
Tropidurus duncanensis												+								
Land iguana *Conolophus subcristatus*	+	+	+	x						?					i				+	
Conolophus pallidus											+									
Marine iguana *Amblyrhynchus cristatus*	widespread on coastal rocks																			7 subspecies

Notes:
+ – present on this island.
5 – five subspecies of tortoise on Isabela.
x – extinct on this island.
i – introduced to this island.
? – status uncertain.

grown tortoises from one island are different from those of most other islands:

> The inhabitants . . . state that they can distinguish the tortoises from the different islands; and that they differ not only in size, but in other characters. Captain Porter has described those from Charles and from the nearest island to it, namely, Hood [Española] Island, as having their shells in front thick and turned up like a Spanish saddle, whilst the tortoises from James [Santiago] Island are rounder, blacker, and have a better taste when cooked. (Darwin 1845)

Research has shown that there were probably fourteen races or subspecies of *Geochelone elephantopus*. Now only ten viable races remain. Tortoises were common on Floreana in the early 1800s but as a result of hunting by whalers, sealers, and settlers, they were extinct by the turn of the twentieth century. The Santa Fé tortoise is known only from skeletal remains. Only one giant tortoise has ever been found on Fernandina and, aptly named *G. elephantopus phantastica*, this individual was skinned on the spot by a member of the California Academy of Sciences' 1905–6 expedition and now rests in their museum in San Francisco. Whether a population ever existed on this island is not certain; droppings and a half-eaten cactus pad were reported in 1964, but despite much searching, no tortoises have been seen. A fifteenth race has been proposed for Rábida Island, but it is most unlikely that the one individual discovered there belonged to a different race. It is more likely that it reached the island with man's help as there is evidence that the beach area of Rábida was used as a holding area for tortoises captured elsewhere.

Five of the remaining eleven surviving races are found on the five main volcanoes of Isabela, while the other six are found on James, Santa Cruz, San Cristóbal, Pinzón, Española, and Pinta, respectively. The five separate volcanoes of Isabela appear to have been isolated enough, as far as tortoises are concerned, to have allowed the formation of distinct races. Lava flows and perhaps previously higher sea levels may have formed impassable barriers.

On Pinta, the depredations of sailors, fishermen, and collectors have perhaps caused the extinction of the race. Only a single male, Lonesome George, is known to be alive and he resides at the Charles Darwin Research Station while the world is searching for a captive female of his race. A reward of $10,000 has been offered for a true Pinta female, but there is now little hope of finding one in zoos. In 1981, a tortoise dropping was discovered on Pinta which indicated the exciting possibility of there being another individual on the island itself.

Many of the giant tortoise populations in the Galápagos are not large and are still at risk from introduced mammals. These are in danger of extinction, unless man helps to redress the balance. Fortunately much has been done to improve the status of these populations over the last fifteen years (see Chapter 12).

The main way in which tortoises vary from island to island is in the shape of their carapaces. These range from the smaller "saddle-backed" types from Española and Pinta to the larger "dome-shaped" types from Santa Cruz and Alcedo Volcano, with many intermediates. The different carapace shapes and sizes are thought to have evolved, at least partly, as adaptations to the different environments of the various islands. The saddle-backed types with their long necks and limbs, and raised carapace-front, are found only on the lower drier islands, where the vegetation is not so dense and is more difficult to reach. On the higher, lusher, islands the dome-shaped types are found. These races do not need to reach so high for their food and must be able to push their way through dense vegetation where a protected front end could be useful. Tortoises also vary noticeably in such features as skin colouration and scute striations (Fritts 1984).

Recent genetic studies have shown that the races of giant tortoises have evolved from a common ancestor that probably first colonised San Cristóbal Island. From this island, they succeeded in dispersing to other islands, where they diverged from their parent populations. It is also thought that the saddle-backed type carapace evolved independently several times as a reaction to dry environments.

Tortoises are famed for their longevity but reliable records are scarce, as these animals may easily outlive a person. A specimen of the Madagascar Tortoise (*G. radiata*) was reputedly presented to the Queen of Tonga by Captain Cook in the 1770s. This individual apparently lived until 1966. However, there are no certain records for tortoises living more than 100 years, despite repeated claims in the literature. Many of the older Galápagos tortoises have extensive lichen and fungal growths on their carapaces, indicating their great age.

The giant tortoises are vegetarian, eating a wide variety of plants. Linda Cayot (1981) recently found that tortoises in the Santa Cruz tortoise reserve ate well over fifty different plant species. Some items appear to be relished, including the poison apple (*Hippomane mancinella*), which is highly poisonous to humans, the endemic "guava" (*Psidium galapageium*), the water fern (*Azolla microphylla*), and the bromeliad (*Tillandsia insularis*). In the drier areas, fallen *Opuntia* cactus pads and fruits are an important element in the diet of tortoises. Galápagos tortoises eat a large quantity of food when it is available and do not digest it thoroughly. It takes one to three weeks for food to pass through the inefficient digestive system, and, even so, most ingested plant species are still easily identifiable in the large droppings.

Galápagos giant tortoises are well known for their water storage abilities and drought resistance. Their ability to survive for long periods without water is in large part due to their ability to metabolise fat stored in their tissues which leads to water production (De Vries 1984). In whaling times, tortoises were popular as a source of fresh meat as they could remain alive

Giant tortoises wallowing in a mud hole, Alcedo Volcano.

on board ship for as much as a year without food or water. Though capable of withstanding long periods of drought, tortoises are fond of water and of wallowing in the mud of the moist highlands of some islands (Plate 25). Darwin, in *The Voyage of the Beagle*, describes the scene at a pool thus:

> Near the springs it was a curious spectacle to behold many of these huge creatures, one set eagerly travelling onwards with outstretched necks, and another set returning, after having drunk their fill. When the tortoise arrives at the spring, quite regardless of any spectator, he buries his head in the water above his eyes, and greedily swallows great mouthfuls, at the rate of about ten in a minute. (Darwin 1845)

In the moister highland areas of Alcedo Volcano and Santa Cruz Island one often finds groups of tortoises wallowing in rain-formed pools or even the dew ponds formed by *garúa*-moisture dripping off trees. These pools tend to be churned up into veritable mud baths. The reasons for this behaviour are not clear but may relate to keeping cool, reducing the number of ticks and mites, or avoiding mosquito bites.

In spite of their extensive body armour, their areas of exposed skin are vulnerable to attacks by ecto-parasites. These can be a considerable nuisance to the tortoises as the animals are not able themselves to remove such parasites. Fortunately, tortoises and other large reptiles have developed mutually beneficial cleaning relationships with mocking birds and finches. When a tortoise wished to be cleaned, after being approached by a finch or mockingbird, it stands up on all fours and stretches its neck fully. This exposes all its skin to the ministrations of these small birds which hop about looking for succulent morsels. Other birds, including hawks and flycatchers, often use tortoises as observation posts from which to sight their prey.

Tortoises, and other members of the turtle order, are unique amongst the vertebrates in having a bony shell or carapace, which is an integral part of the skeleton. The bony plates of the shell are fused with the ribs and other bones to form a rigid protective structure. To compensate for this rigidity tortoises have long, flexible necks that can be withdrawn, together with the legs, until all are almost hidden by the carapace. The legs have hard scales that provide an effective armour when withdrawn. The scutes (or scales) of the carapace are not coincident with the underlying bony plates and grow at their outer edges. Tortoises thus keep their characteristic scute pattern throughout life. These do have annual growth bands but are not useful for aging as the outer layers are rubbed off in the normal wear and tear of living.

Tortoises have no muscles to control the volume of their lungs. Breathing is controlled by the volume of the body cavity which can be altered by leg and head movements. When startled, tortoises retract their head and limbs and this is always accompanied by a dramatic hiss of escaping air. Apart from the cow-like moans of the males during the mating season, this hiss is virtually the only sound they make.

Since Aesop's fables, tortoises have been famous for their lack of speed and ponderous habits. Feeding giant tortoises move about slowly, taking a bite here and a bite there with no apparent direction; but if they have a purpose, such as moving to water or nesting grounds, they can move with surprising speed and determination:

> The tortoises, when purposely moving towards any point, travel by night and day, and arrive at their journey's end much sooner than would be expected. The inhabitants, from observing marked individuals, consider that they travel a distance of about eight miles in two or three days. One large tortoise, which I watched, walked at the rate of sixty yards in ten minutes, that is 360 yards in the hour, or four miles a day,—allowing a little time for it to eat on the road. (Darwin 1845)

Though Darwin's calculations (0.3 km/h) may be accurate over long distances, I have seen them move much faster over short distances.

Tortoises have a relaxed activity schedule; with their long life-span, they can afford to. They are usually active from about 8 a.m. (two hours after dawn) until about 4 or 5 p.m., when they will find a place to sleep. This may be in a mud wallow or pool, but is more usually in a "pallet" or "form" under shrubs or in dense vegetation. These areas are a common sight along trails where tortoises occur. On Alcedo Volcano, where there is a large population, repeated use of the same sites has resulted in the formation of small sandy pits, like golfing bunkers. These pits are of all sizes and tortoises fit snugly into them. Such "beds" probably help to reduce overnight heat loss. Galápagos tortoises have been recorded moving about at night while nesting and seeking water after a rain.

Scientists have studied the temperature regulation of Galápagos tortoises using radio-transmitting thermometers and have shown that they are capable of regulating their temperature within fairly close limits by heating or cooling the carapace through movements into sun or shade. Tortoises in the reserve on Santa Cruz island are most active when air temperatures are between 24 and 28°C. In the cool season this is mainly between noon and 2 p.m. During the warm season, temperatures are too high during the middle of the day for compensation by the tortoises' inadequate heat-control systems; thus, they may be seen taking "siestas."

Giant tortoises are now known to be sexually mature at about 20 to 25 years of age, as the first animals reintroduced to Española have nested and produced young. In captivity, they can grow rapidly—a 13 kg tortoise taken from Isabela put on 175 kg in fifteen years! There are a few records of growth rates in the wild, but growth in the wild is likely to be much slower.

For a month or so each year, usually towards the end of the warm season, the normally sedentary tortoises become occupied with the business of breeding. The males, which are much larger than the females, become aggressive and will chase and posture at each other. Posturing usually involves raising the head as high as possible, with the highest head indicating the dominant tortoise. On occasions, I have seen them behaving like "bumper-cars" at a fair, pushing and shoving in battles for dominance. After asserting their power they seek out females. Mating usually occurs during the warm/wet season. The male's shell has a concave-shaped underpart (called a plastron) and a long tail. Thus, they are able to mount females from behind and bring their penis, which is in the tail, into contact with the female's genital region. Copulation, which may last for hours and is a noisy, creaky affair, has its own hazards. Males have been known to fall off females and to have much difficulty in righting themselves. Frustrated males may attempt to mate with other males and even with boulders!

After mating, females journey to the nesting areas which are usually some distance from the feeding areas. Most eggs are laid between June and December. They require sandy and dry ground for successful nesting. Nest digging is an elaborate task and takes several hours sometimes spread out over several days. It is carried out blindly using only the hind legs to dig a 30 cm deep hole, in which she will deposit two to sixteen tennis ball-sized eggs (the number varies from one race to another). After the completion of egg-laying, the female caps the nest with a layer of mud mixed with urine to protect the eggs. The young emerge from the nest 120 to 140 days later between December and April and may weigh only 80 g (De Vries 1984). Hawks are probably the only native predator of the tortoise hatchlings.

Tortoises are much less abundant than they used to be, numbering only some 15,000 compared to an estimated 250,000 original population (MacFarland et al. 1974a,b), but they can still be seen by visitors in captivity and the wild. Several are kept at the Research Station in pens for captive-breeding purposes and for viewing and include representatives from many islands. To see tortoises in the wild one must either hike into the tortoise reserve on Santa Cruz or make an expedition to the rim of Alcedo Volcano, where tortoises are still abundant.

Marine Turtles

For much of the year these mysterious creatures are only seen when they come to the sea surface to breathe. However, late in the year the quiet lagoons of the Galápagos become the favourite mating areas for the Pacific green turtle (*Chelonia mydas agassisi*) which is the only species resident in the islands. Three other species of turtle are occasionally encountered in Galápagos waters: the leatherback (*Dermochelys coriacea*), the hawksbill (*Eretmochelys imbricata*) and the olive ridley (*Lepidochelys olivacea*).

Green sea turtles do not form pair bonds but both males and females mate with many individuals. There seems to be a fair amount of competition for females, as during the peak mating season (November to January), one almost always finds one or more males hanging around a copulating couple waiting for the current male to get off. Copulation usually occurs at the surface with the male on top of the female. Unlike the giant tortoise, the male is smaller than the female and he leaves it up to the female to do the necessary swimming during copulation as he uses his own flippers to hold on tightly.

The constant train of suitors must be exhausting for the females and it is common to see them floating with one flipper hooked around a mangrove root or hauling themselves just out of the water to rest. The male can be distinguished from the female by his longer tail which is used in copulation and by his curved plastron (underside).

Green sea turtles may weigh up to 150 kg though they are more usually in the 50 to 100 kg range. Their shell is hard and is covered by scales which vary in colour from almost black to green and rarely orange or yellow.

Though they are known to feed, mate, and nest in the Galápagos, some individuals marked in the islands have been recaptured off the coasts of Ecuador, Peru, Panama, Colombia and Costa Rica (Green 1984). It is not known how many or how frequently individuals move across the large stretch of ocean. Marked individuals were recaptured as much as 2,100 km away from their place of marking. One individual was marked in the Galápagos after nesting and was then recaptured off the coast of mainland Ecuador. It was later found renesting in the Galápagos, showing a two-way migration.

Nesting sea turtle covering her eggs, Santiago Island.

They feed primarily on seaweeds and I have seen them feeding alongside marine iguanas on sea lettuce and other seaweeds close to the shore. Their diet is not well known, however.

Turtles may spend long periods of time submerged, especially when they are inactive. They can often be found "sleeping" on shallow sandy bottoms and rocky underwater ledges (Plate 36). How they can hold their breath for so long is not clear. Some freshwater turtles have been known to survive without oxygen for over eight hours, and it is thought that they can run up a considerable oxygen debt. This does not appear to have been studied in the green turtle.

Marine turtles are not completely adapted to aquatic life and must come onto land to lay their eggs. They have also been recorded as coming ashore to bask during the day, perhaps to help digestion and fat build up (Snell and Fritts 1983). Females are thought to come to nesting beaches once every two or three years. In one season each female may come ashore at high tide as many as eight times at about two week intervals, laying seventy to eighty eggs at a time. She will climb up the beach until well above the high tide mark, leaving a characteristic trail behind her. She then digs a large "body pit" and, within it, excavates a smaller flask-shaped pit into which the eggs are laid. Like the giant tortoise, the hind limbs are the "digging tools" and she never sees the eggs. Egg-laying is a remarkably robot-like operation. A female turtle has been observed laying eggs while at the same time a feral pig was

Sea turtle, Elizabeth Bay, Isabela Island.

consuming her eggs as they were extruded from her body. She appeared to be totally unaware of this.

The nesting process takes about three hours after which the female returns to the sea. In the Galápagos, the main nesting period is from December to June with a peak around February, though nesting has been recorded at all times of year.

Nesting usually occurs at night, so all one may see in the morning is a trail to and from a depression in the sand. Sometimes one sees trails leading to some obstacle, such as a log, where the animal must have turned back without nesting. One should take care not to walk in or around nest depressions; otherwise, eggs may be destroyed. It is thought that, by and large, turtles come back to nest on the beach they hatched from, and continue to do so throughout their life. There are some nesting beaches in the Galápagos where feral pigs and rats are serious predators. The only natural predators of eggs are a beetle (*Trox suberosus*), whose larvae and adults feed on the eggs in the nest, and ghost crabs, which dig into the nests.

Small hatchlings will emerge from those nests that have survived the long incubation period. Emergence usually occurs at night but may occasionally occur in daylight. If so, the hatchlings move close to the sand's surface and wait until it gets dark. Sometimes they may be mistaken, or are fooled by dull weather and emerge during daylight, whereupon they are eaten by ghost crabs, hawks, mockingbirds and frigate birds. Those that reach the sea may become the prey of sharks and fish and possibly boobies and pelicans.

A great blue heron that I saw regularly on Bartolomé had learnt to catch the hatchlings even before they emerged. The bird would wait near a nest, detect the movements of the hatchlings, and with its long beak it would stab down into the sand and pull a hatchling out. It would then take the hatchling to the water's edge to wash it before swallowing and returning for another.

Despite the enormous risks and losses to predators, enough hatchlings make it to the open ocean and survive long enough to return to the same beach as they emerged from to nest and start the cycle again. Elsewhere, populations of marine turtles have been drastically reduced by hunting of eggs and adults, and it is fortunate that hunting is no longer allowed in the Galápagos. Turtle populations in Galápagos waters remain high and are of international importance.

Snakes

Three species of snakes, each with two or three subspecies, are endemic to the islands. All are small, slender, constrictors about a metre long. The three species are *Philodryas (Dromicus) biserialis, Alsophis (Dromicus) dorsalis* and *A. slevini.* They are mainly brown but have either yellowish stripes, or spots, on their back (irrespective of species). *Alsophis slevini* is smaller than the other two species, reaching a maximum of about 0.5 m. Snakes are not found on any of the northern chain of islands probably because they have not "made it" to these islands or failed to establish themselves. They are widespread and common on all the other main islands.

Their main prey includes lava lizards, geckos, marine iguana hatchlings, rats and grasshoppers. They catch these with their mouths and then strangle or squeeze them to death with their coils. Snakes have a unique jaw mechanism which allows them to eat unusually large prey. Galápagos snakes are probably venomous to their prey and perhaps to humans (Greene and Reynolds, in press). They may also feed on mockingbird and finch nestlings and they are often pestered by these birds. The globular shape of finch nests may be an adaption to reduce snake predation as it is easier to defend one small hole then the perimeter of a more normal cup-shaped nest. Aggregations of two or three dozen individuals have been seen and were associated with predation on hatchling marine iguanas.

Few organisms prey on the Galápagos snakes but Galápagos hawks have been observed to capture them, thus completing a long food-chain from plant to insect to lizard to snake to hawk. Feral cats are likely to be a threat to Galápagos snakes directly and also by making the snakes' lizard prey more wary.

The yellow-bellied sea snake, *Pelamis platurus,* is also found in Galápagos waters. It is a widespread venomous marine species.

Alsophis (Dromicus) snake, Fernandina Island.

Gecko, *P. galapagoensis*, Santa Cruz Island.

Geckos

Geckos are small nocturnally active lizards with large eyes which feed on small insects. During the day they hide under rocks, logs and bark or other shaded places. These attractive little lizards are rarely seen by visitors during the day but are commonly seen at night around houses in Academy Bay and Wreck Bay. Unlike the other Galápagos lizards from the family iguanidae, the geckos are soft-skinned and have toes with many minute transverse folds of skin. These pads help them to climb smooth vertical faces, including even glass, by fitting into the tiniest irregularities in the surface. Like many lizard species, geckoes can also lose their tails easily and regenerate them rapidly.

The native leaf-toed geckos belong to genus *Phyllodactylus* and are classified into at least six species, five of which are endemic (Wright 1983). Three other species, *Gonatodes caudiscutatus*, *Phyllodactylus reissi*, and *Lepidodactylus lugubris*, have been recently introduced to the islands (Hoogmoed, 1989). The latter two are widespread tropical species that are usually associated with human dwellings.

The geckoes are known to make high-pitched squeaking noises and also to cache their eggs under stones and bark and sometimes in trees (Kushlan 1981). They only lay one egg at a time but will use the same site for more than one clutch. The same nesting sites may be used by more than one female especially when good sites are in short supply.

Lava Lizards

The most ubiquitous reptiles of the arid lowlands must be the little lava lizards. Seven endemic species of *Tropidurus* are found in the archipelago and a species is found on most islands except for Genovesa, Darwin, and

Lava lizard with grasshopper prey, Santiago Island.

Wolf islands. These variously coloured lizards, which may grow to 30 cm in length, feed on a variety of small insects and other arthropods.

The distribution of these lizards and their variations in shape, colour and behaviour show the phenomenon of adaptive radiation so typical of the inhabitants of this archipelago. One species occurs on all the central and western islands (which were perhaps connected during periods of lower sea levels), while one species each occurs on six other more peripheral islands. All have most likely evolved from a single ancestral species, though perhaps two separate colonisations occurred (Wright 1983). Genovesa Island is conspicuous by its lack of land reptiles. Their absence there, along with that of land iguanas and tortoises, can be attributed to the direction of prevailing ocean currents which would not have carried them there.

Males and females of all species are markedly different. The male is usually much larger (two to three times heavier) than the female, and its body is more brightly coloured and distinctly patterned (Plates 31–34). The female has much red about its throat (Plate 30) unlike the male which usually has a black and yellow throat. The average size of lizards varies greatly from island to island as does the pattern of body markings. Markings vary considerably, even within an individual species. Like many lizards, they show changes of colour with mood and temperature. Members of the same species occurring in different habitats also show colour differences. Thus animals living mainly on dark lava are darker than ones which live in lighter, sandy environments.

"Cannibal" lava lizard, Fernandina Island.

The most dramatic example of how isolation on different islands can lead to divergence in character is the "push-up" behaviour of these lizards (Carpenter 1966). The push-up display is usually associated with terrestrial aggression or courtship and may be shown by both sexes, though males do so more often and more actively. What is unique about these displays is that for every different island population the precise pattern of push-ups is different—even for islands which harbour the same species. Both males and females are territorial but individual territories are only defended against members of the same sex. Most male territories are much larger than those of females and usually include several female ones.

Vision is the most important sense for lava lizards. Their vision is most sensitive to red and yellow and this is perhaps why the females have such bright red throats during breeding times. They are also sensitive to movement, especially of objects that are the size of small insects—it is easy to get a lizard to chase after pebbles.

These lizards are omnivorous predators and feed primarily on moths, flies, beetles, grasshoppers, ants, spiders, and even scorpions. Some plant material is eaten at all times of the year but this is more frequent during the cool dry season. On the very dry island of Bartolomé, flowers of *Tiquilia* form a major part of the lava lizard's diet. Animal carcasses, flowers and other animals are often used as places to catch prey from. I have seen lizards lying in wait for insects to land on a flower or a carcass. I have also seen a snake lying in wait under a pelican carcass to catch unwary lizards in search of flies.

Tailless lava lizard, Santiago Island.

Male lava lizard from Española Island.

The small lava lizards are vulnerable to predation by several animals. These include hawks, snakes, mockingbirds, herons, and even centipedes.

Like many other lizards, the Galápagos species can lose their tails to escape from predation, and they can regenerate them, but they rarely regain their original length.

Lava lizards have a daily rhythm that is mainly determined by temperature. On warm sunny days, they emerge at dawn and try to raise their body temperature as rapidly as possible by lying on sunny rocks. After warming up for about half an hour, they remain active until it becomes too hot around mid-day, when they seek shade. Temperatures of rocks and sand can be very high on sunny days and one often sees lizards walking, or standing, on their "ankles" with their toes raised off the ground to reduce heat transfer. When it becomes cooler around mid-afternoon, they become active again until dusk when they bury themselves under leaves or loose soil to keep warm for the night. On cool days, activity starts later and finishes earlier and there may be no mid-day "break."

Lava lizards may live up to ten years. Male lava lizards become sexually mature in about three years; females take only nine months. Breeding is mainly during the warm season during which clutches of three to six eggs are laid every three to four weeks in nests deep in the soil (Werner 1978). Many females may nest in a small area. Incubation takes about three months after which the 3 to 4 cm long, cryptically coloured, hatchlings emerge. Young

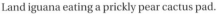

Land iguana eating a prickly pear cactus pad.   Male land iguanas contesting territory on South Plaza Island.

lizards are difficult to see. As they grow, both sexes look like small females. It is not until they reach adult female size, that males begin to take on the male colour pattern.

Land Iguanas

> Like their brothers the sea-kind, they are ugly animals, of a yellowish orange beneath, and of a brownish red colour above: from their low facial angle they have a singularly stupid appearance. (Darwin 1845)

The Galápagos land iguanas are found in the drier parts of six of the central and western islands. These large lizards may grow to more than a metre and weigh as much as 13 kg. Two species of the Galápagos endemic genus *Conolophus* occur. Both have much yellow and brown colouration in contrast with the green iguana of the Ecuadorean mainland. One species, *C. palidus*, is restricted to Santa Fé Island and is yellower with a more pronounced row of spines on its back than the other species, *C. subcristatus* (Plates 27, 28), which has much dark brown or black-coloured skin and some red on the larger adult males, but is variable from island to island (Plate 29).

Prickly pear cactus fruits and pads are the major food of land iguanas. These are supplemented by many other plants and insects. Unlike the lava lizards, the iguana is principally a herbivore. It will supplement its diet by eating carrion if given the opportunity. Land iguanas will also eat centipedes which enter their burrows looking for shade or humidity. Sylvia Harcourt reports seeing a juvenile iguana climb a bush on Plazas and take finch nestlings from the nest.

The mouths of these creatures must be incredibly tough as they may swallow cactus pads and fruits without removing the spines. They are able to remove the spines by scraping them with their claws. They sometimes

Land iguana from South Plaza Island (*C. subscristatus*).

climb shrubs to obtain food but have difficulty doing so with cacti. These either have smooth bark when they are tall or downward pointing tough spines when small so iguanas must limit themselves to fallen pads or branches that droop to within their reach. They can sit up on their hind legs to reach succulent pads but are not stable when doing so. These lizards live in the dry lowlands and see virtually no fresh water during the year. They obtain most of their liquid needs from their food, but after rain they will drink large quantities of fresh water from puddles formed in rocks and cactus pads.

Male land iguanas are much larger and more brightly coloured than the females and, like the male lava lizards, defend larger territories, which usually include more than one female's territory. Males are highly aggressive to one another and often engage in head-bashing battles in which blood is only occasionally drawn. When excited, they can brighten their colours dramatically, but this also occurs with varying body temperature. Aggressive displays involve arching the back, bloating the trunk and throat, lowering the head, and all are accompanied by head-nodding.

Land iguanas take from eight to twelve years to mature sexually and, from the survival of individuals introduced to Seymour Island from Baltra in the 1930s, it seems that they may be able to live more than sixty years. Mating appears to be a traumatic affair for the females of this genus (as it is for those of the other two types of lizard found in the islands). When a female is receptive, she lets the male in whose territory she is living know this by her

Land iguana from Santa Fé Island (*C.pallidus*).

posture and also perhaps by scent. Once interested, the male will follow the female in ever-decreasing circles until he is close enough to catch her and hold her by the neck while he hooks a leg over her and brings his tail around underneath hers so that their genital areas make contact. After mating the female often flees from the male. I have seen females evade an ardent male's ministrations by sprinting at a surprisingly fast speed out of his territory.

After mating, the females move to areas that are more suitable for nesting burrows and proceed to lay between two and twenty-five eggs, the clutch size varying from island to island (Snell et al. 1981;1984). The burrow may be up to half a metre deep. The time of breeding also varies between islands: starting in September on Santa Cruz, in January on Isabela, and in June on Fernandina. Nesting burrows are usually defended for a while after egg laying to prevent another female usurping the nest. The eggs take from three to four months to hatch and hatchlings may spend up to a week digging their way to the outside world, a world of heavy predation. Herons, egrets, hawks and owls congregate in nesting areas during emergence periods and prey on the lava lizard-sized hatchlings. This occurs mainly in the morning when the iguanas are too cold to move fast. Adults, on the other hand, have no native predators. The only recorded natural causes of death on South Plaza include a falling cactus and a rolling sea lion! The young iguanas feed mainly on insects and other arthropods and only become vegetarian as they grow larger.

Like the other Galápagos reptiles, the land iguanas are assiduous sun-bathers. Early in the morning, they soak up the sun and may take shelter in the meagre shade of a cactus or other shrub during the mid-day heat. Unlike the other reptiles they have burrows that are the centre of their territory and which are used for shelter from heat during the day as well as to conserve heat at night. It has been shown that average body temperatures for these lizards are markedly different during the two seasons (Christian et al. 1983). During the cool/dry season, the average was 32.2°C, and during the warm/wet it was 36.6°C. At night they may take shelter in small burrows to help conserve body heat.

As with the tortoises, the land iguanas have a mutualistic cleaning relationship with various small birds that remove ticks and other parasites from their hides. This relationship benefits both partners in that the iguanas are cleaned and the birds obtain a meal. The relationship involves different bird species on different islands and includes mockingbirds, the small ground finch and the medium ground finch. Typically, a bout of cleaning begins when a bird lands on or near the iguana which, if it wishes to be cleaned, takes up the "cooperative" posture, raising itself off the ground as high as possible on all fours, remaining motionless while the bird removes ticks from the exposed skin. These interactions may last up to five minutes at a time. That the land iguanas and tortoises have evolved special cooperative cleaning postures suggests the importance of cleaning in their ecology and it is notable that marine iguanas, which live in an environment which is much less conducive to parasites, take a completely passive role in cleaning.

Land iguanas were formerly widespread and abundant in the islands, and only 150 years ago Darwin wrote about these iguanas on James Island:

> I cannot give a more forcible proof of their numbers, than by stating that when we were at James Island, we could not for some time find a spot free from their burrows on which to pitch our single tent. (Darwin 1845)

Now they are gone from Santiago Island because of human activity and the animals that humans have introduced. Competition for food with goats, destruction of their eggs by rats and pigs, predation by dogs and former hunting by man have all made the land iguana an endangered species. Since 1976 animals from Baltra, Isabela and Santa Cruz have been bred at the Research Station and some have been reintroduced (see Chapter 12).

Visitors are fortunate in being able to observe Galápagos land iguanas in undisturbed situations on Fernandina, Santa Fé, and South Plaza islands. On these islands, there are either no introduced animals or these have been removed. The tiny islet of South Plaza, only 13 ha large, is an unusual natural iguana reserve. For some as yet poorly understood reason, this island is able to support a dense population of some 300 adults; on landing at South Plaza, these lizards seem to be everywhere. It is interesting that even on this small island the iguanas are confined for most of the year to the cactus forest at the west end of the island. During the nesting season in January, the females move from the cactus forest to the sandier *Sesuvium*/*Tiquilia* vegetated area near the southern cliffs where they dig their nests. A little later when the rains begin, the *Portulaca* at the east end of the island comes out in bright yellow flowers. These appear to be a delicacy for these lizards for they migrate there while these plants are in bloom. As well as being a dramatic site for visitors, South Plaza is a natural laboratory for scientists who wish to study the ecology of land iguanas.

Marine Iguanas

The rocks on the coast abounded with great black lizards, between three and four feet long; . . . It is a hideous-looking creature, of a dirty black colour, stupid, and sluggish in its movements. (Darwin 1845)

Nothing could be more characteristic of the tortured, black coastlines of the Galápagos than the marine iguana (*Amblyrhynchus cristatus*). The only sea-going lizard in the world, it is found throughout the islands wherever there are suitable shores. It may be found in densities of well over 3,000 per kilometre of coastline, though usually they are less abundant than this. They prefer exposed southern coastlines and are most abundant where shallow reefs occur and where there are extensive areas of intertidal zone.

Though these lizards are famed for their swimming and diving abilities, it is in most cases only the larger males that feed offshore by diving. The larger males are strong enough to swim through the breaking waves. The remainder, the majority of females and juveniles, feed intertidally or on exposed reefs close to shore.

The diving abilities of marine iguanas are impressive. Natural dives usually last from five to ten minutes and most are shallow (1.5–5 m), but these lizards sometimes descend to more than 12 m below the surface and can remain submerged for as long as sixty minutes. Darwin reported in *The Voyage of the Beagle*: "A seaman on board sank one, with a heavy weight attached to it, thinking thus to kill it directly; but when, an hour afterwards, he drew up the line, it was quite active."

To be able to hold its breath and make these dives for such long times in cold water the marine iguana is able to slow its heartbeat. Also, its metabolism allows it to do work without renewing its supply of oxygen for a considerable period.

The marine iguana feeds almost entirely on algae (seaweed) that it finds between the tide-lines or below the sea's surface (Plate 37). Whether above or below the sea, the food consists of small red or green algae. It does not seem to be very choosy as to which species of algae it eats, except that it

Marine iguana grazing on intertidal seaweeds.   Marine iguanas gathering for warmth.

avoids the large brown seaweed *Blossevillea*. This is an indigestible species for the marine iguana.

The algae that the marine iguana feeds on are not apparent, leading Darwin (1845) to remark: "I do not recollect having observed this sea-weed in any quantity on the tidal rocks; and I have reason to believe it grows at the bottom of the sea, at some little distance from the coast." If you take a close look at the intertidal rocks, you will find abundant small clumps of dark red-brown or green algae, mostly less than 1 cm tall. It is these insignificant-looking species that form the bulk of the marine iguana's diet (as well as that of many crabs). One may ask how so many iguanas and crabs can be feeding off such small amounts of algae; the answer lies in the fact that the algae are very fast-growing. These plants cover a large proportion of the lower intertidal zone and are known to double their length and increase their weight by up to six times, in two weeks. The barren-looking rocks are very productive, but the turnover is fast. This is why the animals appear to be more abundant than the plants. In most ecosystems, the plants usually outweigh the animals by orders of magnitude, but for the Galápagos intertidal zone this is not the case. Nagy and Shoemaker (1984) estimate that the iguanas of Punta Espinoza, Fernandina,(about 2,000 animals) consume about 28 tonnes of fresh algae each year.

As well as feeding on seaweed, these iguanas occasionally feed on the faeces of their own species and those of sea lions and red crabs. To cope with the high salt intake in its diet, the marine iguana must excrete salt. It has the most effective salt glands of any reptile. These are located above the eye and are connected via a duct to the nostrils. The salt is then forcibly expelled by frequent sneezing. This looks like spitting and results in the iguanas frequently having salt encrusted heads.

Most marine iguanas feed once a day, but some of the larger ones will feed only every second or third day. The pattern of daily activity is largely determined by the temperature and the state of the tide (Meatyard et al.

A colony of marine iguanas, Punta Espinoza, Fernandina Island. Note the orientation of individuals towards the sun.

1982). The larger males will usually wait until the middle of the day when the sun is at its hottest and they have had time to warm up before they will swim offshore and start diving to feed. The rest of the population leave the colonies a little before the tide has reached its lowest ebb and feed on the shoreline. They eat until the tide again starts to wash over them. It is remarkable that two parts of the same population have such different activity cycles. This may well be a result of the difficulties of offshore feeding for smaller individuals which cannot store much heat or swim well. They thus cannot make use of the more abundant offshore food resource. These activity patterns were elucidated from a population on Santa Cruz Island and may not be typical of all other parts of the archipelago.

Like other reptiles, the marine iguana is an ectothermic creature and must regulate its body temperature by behavioural means. After sunrise, it assumes a flat basking posture (prostrate basking) that exposes as much body area as possible to the sun's warming rays. When its body reaches an optimum temperature of 35.5°C it will change its position to prevent overheating. The most commonly assumed posture is "elevated basking," in which the lizard faces the sun and raises the front half of its body. Orienting towards the sun reduces the body area exposed to radiant heat and raising the body allows whatever breeze there is to circulate under the body and convect away heat. Reptiles cannot sweat, but if the marine iguana's body temperature rises above 39.9°C it will pant to lose heat.

Marine iguana in elevated basking position.   Nesting female marine iguana, North Seymour Island.

To be able to move about, swim, and digest efficiently, these iguanas must have a high body temperature. Before it can swim offshore, an iguana must wait until it has reached optimum. This is why offshore swimming occurs mainly in the middle of the day. During a swimming sortie, an iguana may lose as much as 10°C body temperature. After swimming, individuals will spreadeagle themselves over the rocks, and orient their bodies to receive as much sunlight as possible. They also must replenish their oxygen supplies. Toward dusk, marine iguanas try to catch the last warming rays of the sun before congregating in piles of as many as fifty individuals to conserve heat overnight. Some individuals do not congregate but attempt to conserve heat by crawling into crevices or under vegetation. The marine iguana is an excellent example of how an ectothermic animal can regulate its body temperature by behavioural means.

Most marine iguanas are colonial for much of the year. Only a few males remain outside the colonies. During the non-breeding season there is little aggression between individuals, but at the start of the breeding season, which varies from island to island (starting in January on Santa Cruz), adult males become more brightly coloured and aggressively territorial. Skin colour is usually black with a few grey, green, or reddish spots, but during the breeding season it becomes mottled red, orange, green and black. The amount of colour change varies from island to island and is most dramatic on Española Island (Plate 35). Territorial males will usually site themselves on the highest part of their territory and posture to make their bodies seem as large as possible. The aggressive display used by these iguanas is a rapid head-bobbing. Territories are contested by fighting, which usually involves head-butting and pushing. Territorial behaviour varies somewhat from island to island.

Males do not control females, but must court them as they move freely about. To court a female in his territory, a male will try to circle her and will

Prostrate marine iguana with a finch removing parasites.

Marine iguana swimming, James Bay, Santiago Island.

nod at her frequently. If the courtship is successful, the male will mount the female and hold her by the neck and twist his tail around her enabling one of his two penis-like organs to contact the female's cloacal region.

Once the mating season is over, the males lose their territorial behaviours and bright colouration, but when nesting starts the females become aggressive toward one another. The females migrate to a suitable sandy area where they set up nesting territories. They guard these vigilantly to ensure that their eggs are not dug up by another female. One to four leathery white eggs are laid in a sandy burrow. After an incubation period of three to four months (Eibl-Eibesfeldt 1984a) the hatchlings emerge. On Santa Cruz this is in mid-May. Hatchlings are preyed upon by snakes, lava gulls, and herons as well as the now feral, introduced house cat.

The marine iguana is associated with many organisms in its coastal environment. I have often seen lava lizards sitting on and running over iguanas as they search for flies. Sally Lightfoot crabs, which eat much the same food, crawl over these iguanas as if they were rocks. Both finches and mockingbirds have been observed taking ticks and mites from the skin of marine iguanas. Unlike the land iguana and giant tortoises, the marine iguanas do little to help these birds with their work. The Galápagos hawk is probably the most important native predator of older iguanas.

Plate 73 shows the trail made by a marine iguana up a beach.

Seabirds

6

Because the Galápagos Islands are surrounded by thousands of miles of open ocean, seabirds have a prominent place in the fauna of the islands. There are nineteen resident species, five of which are endemic, and most of which are likely to be seen by the visitor who spends a week in the islands, whatever the time of year. There may be as many as three-quarters of a million seabirds in the Galápagos, including 30 per cent of the world's blue-footed boobies, the world's largest red-footed booby colony and perhaps the largest concentration of masked boobies in the world (Harris 1984).

Birds must keep their plumage in good condition if they are to survive and breed. Most seabirds change or moult their feathers each year or so before they become too ragged. Between moults, birds spend much time preening their feathers, straightening them out and keeping them oiled and waterproof. The Galápagos penguin spends as much as three hours a day preening to keep even its reduced plumage in top condition (Boersma 1976). In virtually any seabird colony you visit, there will be some birds meticulously taking care of their plumage.

Visitors to the islands are able to retire to the shade during the heat of the middle of the day. Seabirds trying to raise their young must often spend hours, days, and even weeks, staying in the same spot as they incubate their egg(s) or brood their young. Nestlings must spend months in the same place with no shade. As you wander through seabird colonies in the Galápagos, look for ways in which the birds are trying to keep cool under the hot sun. Albatross chicks are often to be found sitting in the meagre shade of shrubs; boobies, pelicans, cormorants, and frigatebirds all use a form of panting, called "gular fluttering," to lose heat. The loose flaps of skin between the bill and neck are moved and the air currents generated evaporate moisture and cause evaporative cooling; boobies are frequently found with the feathers on their backs fluffed up and their bodies oriented so that the breeze comes from behind and cools the skin, and the feet are kept shaded. Red-footed boobies and frigatebirds may often be seen draped over their nest or a branch with their necks hanging down, wings drooped, and cloacal (anal) surfaces exposed to the air but in the shade of the body.

Many seabirds have a sunning behaviour. Frigatebirds and herons may be seen sitting or standing in a near vertical position with their wings turned to give a "palms up" appearance. Boobies are frequently seen with their wings outstretched behind them as they face their backs to the sun. The function of this type of behaviour is not well understood but may be connected with disturbing parasites or with Vitamin D production (Nelson 1979).

Seabirds must overcome the problem of salt accumulation. The Ancient Mariner was correct in saying "water, water everywhere, nor any drop to drink," as sea water contains about 3 per cent salt and is about three times as salty as a bird's body fluids. Most terrestrial vertebrates eliminate salts via their kidneys, but when faced with sea water they would have to excrete two litres of urine for every litre of sea water drunk. As birds conserve water by not excreting water but a paste composed of uric acid, seabirds have a special problem. In seabirds, as well as several terrestrial species, there are special glands located above the eyes which can secrete a 5 per cent salt solution. In most species, it dribbles out of the internal or external nostrils but with petrels this fluid is forcibly ejected through the tubular nostrils. Many birds have specially channelled bills so that the fluid flows to the end rather than getting into the eyes. If you watch a cormorant after it returns from the sea you will see a steady train of drips forming at the tip of its bill to drop off every ten seconds or so. One also often sees recently returned boobies shaking the drops from their bill.

In the rest of this chapter, the species of resident sea birds will be described and discussed individually. The distributions of the resident species and some of their approximate population sizes are shown in Table 11.

Galápagos Penguin

The Galápagos penguin (*Spheniscus mendiculus*) is the bird that seems most out of place in the equatorial Galápagos Islands. Standing only 35 cm tall, it is the third smallest of the eighteen species in the penguin family and the only species to occur north of the equator and nest entirely within the tropics. Penguins are a group of flightless seabirds characteristic of the Antarctic oceans and islands. It comes as a surprise to find a little penguin swimming amongst the stilt roots of tropical red mangroves.

The closest relatives of the Galápagos penguin are the Humboldt and Magellan penguins of southern South America. The Humboldt penguin occurs primarily in the cold waters of the Humboldt or Peru currents and is only rarely seen off the coast of Ecuador. The Galápagos penguin is most likely descended from stray individuals of this species that managed to find the cool upwellings of the western islands. It breeds only on the west coast

Swimming Galápagos penguins.

of Isabela and on most of Fernandina's coasts. Some are seen in other parts of the archipelago and may breed in sites such as by Pinnacle Rock on Bartolomé Island.

Recent estimates put the population of these birds at between two and five thousand individuals and they are common within their breeding range. They are frequently seen sunning or resting on rocks, especially in the early morning and late afternoon, but most often are found swimming, singly or in groups of up to fifty or more, along the shoreline.

The adults are black above and white on the underparts, with a stripe around the breast and on the face. The juveniles are greyer, without the white lines, and have a pale patch on the side of the head and chin. They rise before dawn and spend the day swimming, with a few breaks on land. In the mid-afternoon, they start returning to their colonies. On the surface, penguins swim slowly, half submerged, but underwater, they fly through the water using their wings for propulsion and their feet as rudders. They can travel quickly through the water (as much as 40 km/h), especially when they "porpoise" on the surface. They usually do so when pursuing a school of fish. The kinds of fish taken are small, ranging from 10 to 150 mm; some crustaceans are taken as well.

The penguin has different feeding strategies dependent on the water temperature. If the water is below about 23°C, they feed in large groups of twenty or more, as fish are abundant when the water is cool and rich. When the water is warmer they tend to feed in smaller groups or singly, as fish are less abundant. This indicates that group fishing is more efficient when fish are abundant.

Galápagos penguins must adapt to two environments, hot land and cool water, while their more southerly relatives need only adapt to cold. In the water, the temperature may range from a cool 16°C to a warm 28°C, while on

Table 11. Distribution and Abundance of Seabird Species

Species	Isabela	Santa Cruz	Fernandina	Santiago	San Cristóbal	Floreana	Marchena	Española	Pinta	Baltra	Santa Fe	Pinzón	Tower	Rábida	Seymour	Wolf	Darwin	Daphne Major	Plaza Sur	Population size #
Galapagos penguin (end)	o	+	o	o	o			o					o	o						2 - 5,000 pairs
Waved albatross (end)								+												12,000 pairs
Audubon's shearwater	widespread cliffs and islets																			10,000 pairs
Hawaiian petrel	+	+		+	+	+														10 - 50,000 pairs
Elliot's storm petrel	breeding distribution not known as nests have not been found																			many thousands
Madeiran storm petrel	*	*		*	*	+							+	+			+	+		15,000 pairs
Galapagos storm petrel				+									+							200,000 pairs
Red-billed tropicbird	widespread cliffs and islets, less common in west																			few thousand pairs
Brown pelican	widespread along coasts with bushes or mangroves																			few thousand pairs
Blue-footed booby	+		+	+	+	+	?	+	?		+	?	o	+	+		+	+		10,000+ pairs
Masked booby	+	*	+	+	+	*	?	+	?		+	?	+		+	+	+			25 - 50,000 pairs
Red-footed booby				+	*								+		+	+				250,000 pairs
Flightless cormorant (end)	+		+																	700 - 800 pairs
Great frigatebird				+	*		+						+	o	+	+				few thousand pairs
Magnificent frigatebird	+			+	*	?							+	+	+		+			1000 pairs
Swallow-tailed gull (end)	widespread but less common in the west of the archipelago																			10- 15,000 pairs
Lava gull (end)	+	+	?	+	?	?	+	?	?	?	?	?	+	?	+					300 - 400 pairs
Brown noddy tern	+	+	+	+					+						+	+	+			few thousand pairs
Sooty tern																+				enormous numbers

Notes:
(end) - endemic to the islands.
+   present on this island.
o   occasionally found on this island.
?   distribution uncertain.
*   present on satellite islands but not on main island.
#   population figures are very approximate, from Harris (1984).

land the temperature may rise to over 40°C. All penguins have thick layers of fat, covered by protective, waterproof, feathers. This is excellent insulation, but it keeps the heat in as well as the cold out. They can keep cool on land by holding their wings out at 45 degree angles, allowing air to pass over the less heavily feathered areas and convect away heat. On land they always shade their feet with their bodies. By keeping their feet shaded, and allowing the circulation in their feet to increase, the breeze passing over them helps in cooling (like an automobile radiator). As well as the above two methods of keeping cool, the penguin, like most other tropical seabirds, will pant rapidly when necessary and hide in shady places if these are available. It sometimes happens that these methods are not enough and the birds will take to the water. Dr. Boersma (1974), who has made a detailed study of the Galápagos penguin, has observed a case of a bird watching over its nest in the open sun, becoming overheated to the point where it had to either cool itself or die. It left the nest and took to the water—unfortunately, when it returned to the nest the eggs had heated and died.

The penguin spends much time preening, as its feathers and down have extremely important insulating properties. The value of the insulation is demonstrated by Dr. Boersma's observations of moulting birds. During the moulting period, they fast and do not enter the water at all. After a few days, the feathers all stand on end and the birds have a great aversion to entering the water. One bird that entered the water lost 6°C body temperature in thirty seconds before it managed to scramble out. During the first few days of moulting, birds often stand out in the open, but once the old feathers start to drop out and expose the new plumage, they seek cover. Heat stress would be highest at this stage because the new plumage is dark and much of the insulating fat stores have been used up. After ten to fifteen days of fasting and staying out of the water, the penguin resumes its normal life. Often they will start to breed after moulting.

The Galápagos penguin chooses a mate for life, barring accidents. It lays its one or two eggs in holes, caves, or crevices to keep them out of the sun. One parent will always stay with the eggs or young while the other will be gone for several days to feed. The parents will take turns at this for a full five weeks, after which the fluffy brown down-covered chicks appear. If there is not enough food available, the nest may be abandoned. However, if conditions are good, a pair may lay as frequently as three times in fifteen months.

Starvation is thought to be a major cause of death for these penguins; predation seems to be insignificant though at sea, sharks, fur seals, and sea lions are potential threats. On Isabela, the introduced cats, dogs, and rats are predators but their effect on the population is not known. Sometimes when the penguins feel threatened, they will turn their backs toward the perceived source of danger and thus camouflage themselves against the black lava rocks.

On land, Galápagos penguins have three methods of transportation: walking, which they do with more grace than most penguins, perhaps because of their smaller size; scrambling after a fashion over rough terrain, using both flippers and feet; and hopping or jumping which is used to get on top of a rock or places they cannot otherwise reach. To avoid missing, the penguin seems to measure the distance by putting its beak on the spot it is attempting to jump to before doing so. When entering the water it usually hops or flops in feet first.

Penguins are social birds that maintain a personal territory within the group. They have both a defended area around the nest and also an invisible curtain around themselves which must not be invaded. If this does happen, the defending penguin will screech and start bill-duelling and pecking.

Waved albatross in flight.

Galápagos penguin.

Penguins are somewhat myopic and often go to the wrong place on their way to their nest or mate, and this can get them into trouble with other penguins. Pecking and bill-duelling can do much damage, so the birds have an appeasing side-to-side head motion that seems to say "don't attack, I'm just passing by." The motion is like a continuous infinity sign drawn by the bill. No one has ever reported seeing a penguin attacked while performing this appeasement behaviour.

Penguins are quiet most of the time, but occasionally during the day and especially during the evening, they have a call that sounds peculiarly like the sound one makes when the doctor asks you to say "aaah." Some compare this sound to that made by a braying donkey.

Waved Albatross

Weighing 3 to 4 kg and with a wingspan of over 2 metres this aristo-cratic-looking creature is one of the largest birds in the islands (Plate 43). Virtually the entire world population of some 12,000 pairs nests on Española Island (a few pairs breed on the tiny Isla de la Plata off Ecuador) and the species is usually regarded as endemic to Española Island. The waved albatross (*Diomedea (Leptorhynchus) irrorata*) is also the only one of thirteen albatross species to occur entirely within the tropics; most of the others are confined to the southern oceans.

Not all visitors to Española will see the magnificent waved albatross. The colonies are deserted from January to March while the birds roam the tropical East Pacific off Ecuador and Peru where the cool waters of the Humboldt current flow. The first to arrive at the end of March are the males. The females arrive shortly afterwards and pairs will mate soon after reuniting. Albatrosses pair for life. Their lifespan could be as much as forty to fifty years. Pairs appear to return to the same area to breed year after year but do most of their spectacular courtship toward the end of the preceding breeding season so that when they return they can start straight away with the lengthy business of raising a chick.

Egg laying occurs between mid-April and the end of June, with most eggs appearing during the first two weeks of May. Each pair produces one large (285 g) white egg that is incubated by both parents for two months. Each parent may sit for up to twenty-three days at a time. Near to hatching time the incubation stints become shorter to ensure that a parent is ready to feed the newly hatched chick. There is no nest as such and the birds have a peculiar habit of moving their eggs around, as much as 40 m in a few days. This is a hazardous operation, and its function is not clearly understood, though recently it was shown that hatching success was greater for birds that moved their eggs frequently. Eggs are often deserted and are occasionally adopted by other pairs which have lost their own egg. Catherine Rechten (1981) has reported the surprising instances of three eggs being adopted by blue-footed boobies, who incubated them devotedly, together with their own smaller eggs. No albatrosses hatched, though in two cases the booby eggs did. The booby apparently feels that bigger is better when it comes to eggs!—an example of a positive response to a supernormal stimulus.

At the end of incubation, a little brown downy albatross chick hatches. For the first couple of weeks, the parents brood their chick and thereafter leave it unguarded, returning only to feed it. While parents are away, the chicks usually congregate in "nursery groups," often in the shade of shrubs, but are quick to react and go to their parents on recognition of their call to be fed. As happens when the sea lions and many colonial nesting birds, the young find their parent by mutual calling back and forth until they locate each other. They can distinguish individual calls. Once the parent finds its own chick, it will feed it large amounts of an oily liquid consisting of digested fish and squid. This is manufactured by the parent in the proventriculus—a part of the stomach. In one bout of feeding the chick may receive as much as 2 kg of oil, after which it can hardly move. As Bryan Nelson (1968) has written: "For the first four months of its life the chick is hardly more than a great, oil-filled skin, covered in matted brown down. It is grotesque with the fascination of the truly ugly." This unseemly method of feeding has its advantages. Unlike the boobies and frigatebirds, which must return to their offspring immediately, before their food is digested, the albatross can, by virtue of manufac-

Waved albatross, Española Island.

Waved albatross chick.

turing chick-oil, cover large distances over a week or two and feed until it has accumulated a great quantity of food that is probably richer than the raw fish, squid, and crustaceans from which it is made.

The young continue to grow until, by December, they are adult sized and similar in plumage to their parents. Most have left the colony by January to spend the next few years at sea. Late in the season of their fourth or fifth year, the young albatrosses will return to Española to seek a mate. Courtship of newly forming pairs and of established pairs that have failed to breed successfully in the current season, occurs in the latter half of the season, peaking around October. Pairs that have bred successfully in the current season do not seem to need to reinforce their pair-bond by much display.

The dance of the waved albatross is a wonderful display. It is complex and takes a long time to perfect. Most visitors will be lucky if they see only a fraction of the full dance, but even such fractions are magnificent to watch. The following description by Bryan Nelson (1968) gives an idea of the full beauty and complexity of the display (Plates 44a–h):

> The dance, or "ecstatic ritual" as it has been called, is one of the most extraordinary displays imaginable. It is highly entertaining, but also a complex piece of ritualised behaviour in which the dancing partners co-operate with great precision. Dancing albatrosses face each other so that when they lean forward their bills come into contact from about half way down to the tip. The basic movement is then a bill-circling in which they rapidly and irregularly

slide their bill over the top of the other's, not in a full circling movement but rather a half circle and back again. The bills are mainly in contact throughout the display, but often jump apart, then meet again making a wooden, clattering noise. Dancing "excites" the birds and a slight secretion of oil seeps from the tubular nostrils and lubricates the bills which become glossy and slippery. Time and again, whatever other movements intervene, the partners return to this rapid bill-circling. Frequently one bird, usually the male, breaks off and stands bolt upright, staring fixedly ahead with the peculiar expression imparted by the flattened head and conspicuous "eyebrows." The other may follow suit or else keep bill-circling in mid-air, too slow to react to the withdrawal of its partner's bill. With a swift forward and downward bow which takes it slightly below the level at which the pair bill-circle, each bird then returns to the circling with sustained vigour. Then suddenly, one arches its neck and, holding its head motionless, fixedly touches a spot on its flank. Even as its head sweeps down to touch its flank, the partner, still in the forward, low, bill-circling position, clappers its mandibles together so rapidly that they are just a blur, whereupon the side-touching bird stretches its neck, throws its bill vertically upwards and utters a loud, prolonged and high-pitched "whoo-ooo." Then a swift bow, and both birds fall to enthusiastic bill-circling again. In another part of this esoteric and athletic display one or both birds suddenly click into an upright position, necks fully stretched, and silently open their bills in the widest possible gape, as though advertising Bird's custard powder. Then they snap the bill closed with a resounding "clunk" which owes its quality partly to the sounding chamber formed by the mouth and return to the circling. After some time one bird turns away and, with the most ridiculous walk imaginable, a grotesque caricature of a movement in which, with the bill tucked into the chest, the head sways right over and down at each step, leads the other, also walking in the same exaggerated fashion, to some particular spot. This ludicrous "sway-walk" is a highly exaggerated version of normal locomotion; by increasing the extent of the head and foot movements a conspicuous ritualised walk has evolved. After several minutes, perhaps even half an hour, the display ends for the time being with one bird assuming a squatting position, head down, neck retracted and bill pointing between its feet, and bobbing jerkily up and down, meantime uttering a repeated low note. This "forward bobbing" is actually a special display indicating ownership of a site and it is unfailingly performed, for instance, when a bird settles down after returning to its egg or small chick. It also plays an important part in the chick's life.

When things become really hectic the various display movements and postures follow each other in rapid succession with never a moment's pause. When several pairs display simultaneously the air is full of weird noises— whoops, grunts, rattles and clunks and mad laughter. Rival males stretch to their full height and with beaks gaping widely, as in the display described above, run at each other uttering a "ha-ha-ha" call and occasionally biting at each other, although things never develop into a real fight. In dancing displays it is the male that performs this aggressive beak-gaping most often; considerably more than females. . . . The male is also mainly responsible for switching from one part of the dance to another; in a sense he directs the dance and the

Audubon's shearwater (left) and dark-rumped petrel (right) (not to scale).

female reacts to her cues. Whilst there is a highly stereotyped pattern to these dances, a certain amount of variation in the order of component parts is permissible. However, this must not go too far, and the displays of different species of albatross, though in some cases very similar, are acceptable only to their own kind.

True Petrels and Shearwaters

Only two species of the family Procellariidae are resident in the Galápagos, though some others may be seen occasionally. These residents are Audubon's shearwater and the dark-rumped (or Hawaiian) petrel. Shearwaters gain their name from the way in which they skim the waves when in flight, while the word "petrel" is thought to derive from the story of St. Peter, who walked on water.

Audubon's Shearwater

This small black and white bird is always on the move. Whether skimming the waves, pattering along the surface, or displaying at its colonies, these enigmatic birds hardly ever allow one a close look. At their nesting colonies, they fly circuits centred on their burrow or hole and call loudly as they display. Standing atop a lava cliff where these birds nest, it is fascinating to watch them circling rapidly below you, alternately showing their white underparts and black upper parts. Audubon's shearwater, *Puffinus l'herminieri*, is widespread and common in the Galápagos islands and breeds on the smaller islets and on the cliffs of larger islands (Snow 1965a).

This shearwater feeds mainly on small crustaceans and fish larvae which it catches by day on or just below the sea's surface. They will sometimes dive from the surface in pursuit of their prey. As a result of diving, they take on a glistening coat of air bubbles, giving them an all white appearance.

Dark-rumped (Hawaiian) Petrel

The dark-rumped petrel, *Pterodroma phaeopygia*, is much larger than Audubon's shearwater and has long narrow wings and a white forehead. The black upper parts and white underparts contrast sharply when in flight. This petrel is most easily identified at long range by its characteristic flight pattern of gliding and banking.

As its alternate name suggests, this petrel nests in the Hawaiian Islands as well as the Galápagos, but it is almost extinct in the former area because of the depredations of introduced predators. The same problem exists in the Galápagos, but the populations are currently much larger. Nevertheless, this species is the only endangered bird in these islands and its problems will be more fully discussed in the chapter on conservation.

Dark-rumped petrels are most frequently seen at dawn and dusk near the islands as they make their way to the feeding grounds to catch fish and squid. Nesting is in the moist highlands of the main islands, where birds select nest sites in moist soils along the banks of sinkholes, gullies and stream beds. This petrel is rarely seen on land as it is only active around the colony at night. A single white egg is laid in a deep earthy burrow between June and August on Santa Cruz (different times elsewhere) and the young fledge at the end of the year (Harris 1970). Banding recoveries suggest that adults may live for well over twenty years (Dagit 1989).

Storm Petrels

Three species of similar storm petrels or "Mother Carey's Chickens" are found in Galápagos waters. These dark little birds with white rumps are the

Feeding storm petrel.

Storm petrels.
Galápagos (top).
Madeiran (centre).
Elliot's (bottom).

smallest of oceanic seabirds, about the size of large swallows. The smallest, Elliot's storm petrel, is smaller than the largest of Darwin's finches. The storm petrels characteristically have short black bills with the distinct tubular nostrils forming a single orifice. Their flight is erratic and fluttering and they are often seen weaving across the wakes of boats, dropping their legs to the water and hopping or skipping as they search for minute crustaceans and other food particles.

Elliot's (white-vented) storm petrel, *Oceanites gracilis*, is most commonly seen around yachts at anchor as it patters its way around looking for scraps. They seem to be attracted by oily substances in food and frequently come to boats. When feeding near boats, they usually patter upwind from the stern picking up minute particles and, before reaching the bow, circle back downwind to start their search again. Look for them around the ships after your meals. This species is distinguished from the other two species by having a white line running down its breast and under its tail, and also because its feet project behind its tail. A puzzling feature of this bird is that, though it is known to be resident and no doubt breeds in the islands, no nesting places have been found to date.

The other two species, the Galápagos (wedge-rumped) and the Madeiran (band-rumped) storm petrels, are larger than Elliot's and similar to each other. The Galápagos storm petrel, *Oceanodroma tethys*, is smaller and slimmer than the Madeiran storm petrel, *O. castro*, and has a larger triangular white rump-patch. Its flight is also more twisting and erratic. The Madeiran is larger and has a distinct white band on the rump.

Both species breed on Genovesa Island, though the Madeiran also breeds on many small islets such as Plaza and Daphne. Amongst the lava above Prince Philip's Steps on the eastern horn of Darwin Bay, Genovesa Island there is a huge colony of both species whose numbers are estimated to be hundreds of thousands (Nelson 1966). Nesting amongst the cracks and crevices in the broken lava, the storm petrels flit about in their thousands above the colony like a cloud of mosquitoes. To watch them for long is a bewildering experience. They fly around in erratic circles and if you are able to fix upon an individual and keep it in sight, it will usually come round and round again to almost the same spot and eventually will disappear into a crack in the lava. Storm petrels are reputed to have a well-developed sense of smell and may use odour to locate their own nesting spot amongst the myriad burrows. These birds have not been well studied and there are many aspects of their behaviour at the colony that are not well known.

The Galápagos storm petrel differs from most other species of storm petrel in that it is active at the colony during the day. The Madeiran storm petrel is nocturnal at its colonies and if you are near a colony at night you may hear their squeaky call. This is like the sound made by rubbing a wet finger on glass. The Madeiran storm petrel has a more widespread distribution in the islands than the Galápagos storm petrel. The nesting sites are used twice a year, though the birds themselves are annual in their breeding cycle (Harris 1968a). There are two separate breeding populations which use the colonies at different times, thus allowing a much larger number of birds to nest in a limited number of nest sites. The egg-laying periods are from November to January and from May to June.

Both species appear to feed on small fish, squid, and crustaceans, but they differ from one another in that the Galápagos storm petrel is mainly a nocturnal feeder. The Madeiran storm petrel is more diurnal in its feeding habits but is also more pelagic. The former species is often attracted aboard ships at night. The short-eared owl is a predator of both species on Genovesa Island and elsewhere and takes the birds mainly from nesting burrows that are not deep enough to prevent the owl from reaching them.

Red-billed Tropicbird

The long white tail streamers, sometimes as long again as the body of the bird, and coral red bill make these magnificent white birds unmistakable (Plate 49). They are strong and direct fliers, feeding well out to sea, but at their scattered colonies I never fail to be attracted to their elegant figures as they display in groups of up to a dozen. In display, they fly back and forth along the cliffs and make wide circles out to sea. In mid-flight, displaying birds will suddenly stop their rapid flapping and glide for a few seconds, while making a dramatic staccato screaming call.

Red-billed tropicbirds fighting on Daphne
Major Island.

Red-billed tropicbird in flight.

The juvenile birds are similar to the adults but have pale yellow bills. Only this one of three tropicbird species is found in the Galápagos. It ranges through the tropical and sub-tropical east Pacific and Atlantic islands. Individuals banded in the Galápagos have been recovered near both Panama and Peru, showing that it is a highly mobile species.

Tropicbirds feed chiefly on squid and fish. They catch their food by steep plunge diving and normally feed well away from land. When on the surface of the sea, they usually swim with their long tail cocked upward.

The red-billed tropicbird, *Phaethon aethereus*, is colonial and makes its nest on over-hanging ledges or in the crevices of steep slopes and cliffs. At the nest, these dazzling birds stand out against the dark lava cliffs, but often all that is to be seen are the long tail feathers. They have short legs and have difficulty moving about on land. Often many passes at the burrow are made before landing, as positioning and timing must be just right. A single reddish-brown, speckled egg is laid in the nest hole, which may have a few feathers for lining. Both parents help incubate for six to six and one half weeks and the chick, on hatching, has a grey downy coat. It is fed by both parents and leaves the nest at around twelve to fifteen weeks of age. In most parts of the archipelago, breeding occurs throughout the year, but the population on South Plaza Island has an annual cycle with eggs laid between August and February. Only a few kilometres away on Daphne Island, the breeding season is not so restricted.

It seems that suitable nesting sites may be a limiting factor in the distribution and abundance of this species. Nesting sites are jealously guarded and disputes may result in serious fights. One such fight on Daphne Major lasted for half an hour and took place only a few metres away from my feet; I was able to observe that both birds had drawn blood.

Young brown pelican.

Adult brown pelican with nestling.

Brown Pelican

The bird most often seen around anchorages is the brown pelican, *Pelecanus occidentalis.* One or two of the all brown juveniles are usually found paddling mutely about the yachts at anchor or sitting on a dinghy where they wait for scraps to be thrown overboard from the galleys.

Though the pelican is such a large and apparently clumsy bird, it catches its food mainly by shallow plunge diving (Plate 41). When fishing, it flies with its huge bill pointing downwards and, on sighting prey, suddenly checks its flight and plunges awkwardly into the water with an enormous splash. The pelican seems almost too buoyant to be plunge diving—most of the body submerges but at least the tail and wingtips remain above water. On surfacing, the bird will drain its large distensible pouch of water and swallow the fish. These fish are usually small, although the pelicans are known to take fish as large as 35 cm. The pouch of a diving bird expands enormously and may enclose as much as two or three gallons of water as well as some fish. Often one sees a brown noddy flying around near fishing pelicans, and, when the latter are draining their pouches, the noddy will sit on the pelican's head waiting for fish scraps to wash out.

Brown pelicans are magnificent in flight. Carrying their necks tucked back and alternating strong wing beats with glides, a group flying in almost complete unison has a special charm. They are often to be seen flying low over the water, almost skimming the surface with an undulating flight.

At the start of the breeding season, the adult birds have striking white and chestnut-brown markings on their heads and necks, often with a tinge of yellow at the crown, and have a silvery look to their wings (Plate 42). Out of the breeding season, the head and neck are dull white. The young birds are light brown above and paler below and are drab when compared to the magnificent adults in breeding plumage. In the Galápagos, the brown pelican nests in small colonies in mangrove forests or on low shrubs such as the saltbush. An untidy platform of twigs is built by the pair and two or three eggs are laid. Both adults share incubation for about four weeks. In a few days, the hatchlings grow a white downy covering and will remain in the nest until fledging at around ten weeks. Both parents feed the young, allowing them to take food directly from their gular pouches. The adults usually have a high success in fledging their young, but it seems that the art of fishing pelican-style is not an easy one to master. Many juveniles are thought to die of starvation. Breeding occurs at most times of the year, but, in any one colony, most pairs will breed at the same time. However, as the breeding cycle is less than a year, breeding will not be at the same time each year at the same site. I have never heard the adults make much sound, but the young mew loudly when begging for food and also often hiss and clap their bills.

The brown pelican is widespread in the Galápagos and is found around most tropical American coasts. There are eight species of pelican worldwide; the Chilean pelican is the only similar species but is much larger. Though the brown pelican is one of the largest Galápagos birds, it is the smallest member of its family.

The Boobies

The three species of boobies in the Galápagos are certainly the commonest and most frequently seen of the seabirds. Looking similar to gannets, and in the same family (Sulidae), they are large birds, 70 to 90 cm in length, with long (1–1.5 m) narrow wings. Their long pointed beaks give rise to their local name "piquero" (lancer), but no one seems certain where their English name "booby" came from. "Bobo" is a Spanish word for clown and may be the root of the word. It is thought that their name originated in the seafarer's term for them, for they appear stupid, often showing no concern on being approached and captured. Boobies frequently perch on ships at sea, sometimes using a vantage point near the bow from which to dive on flying fish skipping away from the bow wave. The word "booby-hatch" is almost certainly derived from their habit of perching at the bow.

The boobies all have a strong, direct flight with several powerful rapid wing beats followed by a glide. When in groups, they often fly in a ragged line. All species of boobies feed by spectacular plunge diving. When hunting, they will fly with their bill pointing downwards, fifteen metres or more above the water. On sighting their prey, they check their flight and hurtle in a headlong dive to the sea. After seeing them hit the water at break-neck speed and bob back up to the surface, one wonders how they survive the shock. Boobies and gannets are well built for penetrating air and water, with a pointed, tapered bill, torpedo-shaped body, and pointed tail. Air sacs in the skull cushion the impact of the dive and closed nostrils prevent water from being forced in.

All three species are colonial but, in the Galápagos, they range from the widely distributed small colonies of the blue-foot to larger and less frequent colonies of the masked to a few huge colonies of the red-foot. An unusual feature of the breeding biology of boobies is the way in which they brood their eggs. The developing embryo needs a constant temperature, and in most bird species this is provided via the bare skin of brood patches. These are areas with few feathers and a good supply of blood vessels so as both to monitor the temperature of, and to provide heat to, the eggs. Boobies and gannets, together with cormorants, pelicans, and tropicbirds, incubate their eggs on their foot-webs which are well supplied with blood vessels. By either nestling down onto the eggs or raising the body so that cool air may circulate, boobies can maintain the temperature precisely around 39°C. Readers wishing to pursue studies of the boobies should consult Bryan Nelson's *The Sulidae* (1978).

Blue-footed Booby

No colour is more surprising amongst the drab rocks of these tropical desert islands than the intense bright blue of the blue-footed booby's feet (Plate 40). Shown off to their best in the dramatic landing "salute" and in the ritualised "parading" of courtship (Nelson 1968), the blue feet play an important part in the life of this species. How these birds got their bright blue feet continues to puzzle naturalists and perhaps the only safe answer to why is why not?

The blue-footed booby, *Sula nebouxi*, is the most commonly seen of the boobies as it nests near the coast in many places and also feeds close to shore. In flight, these birds have a characteristic shape. They can be told apart from juveniles of other species by the white nape patch. When visiting a colony, one can tell the female from the male of a pair as she appears to have a larger pupil and is also larger than the male. The difference in apparent pupil size is accounted for by a dark pigment around the female's pupil and not by any real difference in size. If you haven't already been able to tell the difference between a pair of these birds, then the first vocalisation will clinch the matter. The male has a long drawn-out beseeching whistle while the female makes a nasal honk.

If you wait for a short time at any large colony of blue-foots, such as the ones on Española or Daphne Major, you will certainly be able to watch at

Male blue-footed booby in a nest with guano ring.

least parts of the dramatic courtship display. Courtship will usually begin with a male advertising himself from a chosen site by "skypointing." (Plate 38). Once he has attracted a female, the two may parade to each other. The male in particular, waddles around with a cocked tail, alternately raising one blue foot then the other. While parading, the bird will alternately pose in the haughty-looking "bill-up–face-away" or shy-looking "pelican" postures. As courtship proceeds one or the other bird (usually the male) will skypoint; this becomes more frequent until both are skypointing to each other simultaneously or in turns. After mating, which occurs frequently , I have often seen the male pose in the bill-up–face-away posture, with his wings crossed behind his back, tail cocked, and head in the air. Frequently during the display, one or other member of the pair will pick up some twig or stone and with great ceremony place it on a non-existent nest. Ritual nest-building is a legacy of an evolutionary history in which ancestors constructed functional nests (red-footed boobies still do). This relict behaviour is important in strengthening the pair bond but has no practical value because they will scrape away all the twigs and stones when the female is ready to lay so that she may nest on the bare dusty ground. The blue-foots also have an endearing bill-touching ceremony in which they touch, or nearly do so, the pointed tips of their lance-like bills. Occasionally, this is done while holding a twig in the bill.

One to three eggs are laid on the bare ground and are incubated by both parents for a little over forty days. The eggs are laid three to five days apart,

Mating blue-footed boobies.

Blue-footed booby with hungry chicks.

and this is usually reflected in the hatching sequence. When times are good, the parents may successfully fledge all three chicks, but, in harder times, they may still lay as many eggs yet only obtain enough food to raise one. The problem is usually solved by the somewhat callous-sounding system of "opportunistic sibling murder." The first-born chick is larger and stronger than its nest mate(s) as a result of hatching a few days earlier and also because the parents feed the larger chick first. If food is scarce, the first born will get more food than its nest mate(s) and will outcompete them, causing them to starve. The above system optimises the reproductive capacity of the blue-foot in an unpredictable environment. The system ensures that, if possible, at least one chick will survive a period of shortage rather than all three dying of starvation under a more "humane" system.

At the time of hatching, the nest area is surrounded by a ring of guano produced by squirting excrement in all directions while incubating. Once the nest is deserted, these rings have the appearance of being the landing pads of some extraterrestrial being. This ring often coincides with what is an imaginary line that delineates the nest site of the booby, within which parent-chick relationships are normal (Gould 1983). If a chick should get out of this area, it will not be treated as offspring nor be allowed back. This fact may be exploited by an older sibling in a situation where food is scarce. The older chick could force the younger one out of the "ring," whereupon it would be rejected. The ring itself is not necessary for this set of behaviours but is coincidental as it is frequently present. Aggression to chicks outside the imaginary line has probably evolved as a means of preventing the parents from raising another's young.

After hatching, the male plays a major role in bringing fish home. He has a longer tail than the female in relation to his body size, which makes him able to execute shallower dives and to feed closer to shore. He can thus bring many small feeds back at a time when the young are small. The female takes a greater part as time proceeds. Sooner or later, the need to feed the young

Female blue-footed booby with egg and hatchling.

Half-feathered young blue-footed booby.

becomes greater than the need to protect them and both adults must fish to provide enough. When newly hatched, the young are naked and unable to regulate their temperature or to protect themselves. One parent must therefore remain at the nest. When the young have grown a coat of white down and are able to pant or gular-flutter, the parents may leave the chick(s) but risk a predator snatching an opportunity for a meal. Occasionally, I have observed frigatebirds and hawks taking unguarded chicks, but soon the chicks are too large for these predators. Owls, too may take booby chicks. For the parents, there must be a fine balance between leaving their offspring to fend for themselves and finding enough food for them.

The blue-foots usually feed close to the coastline and are well adapted to do so by having a longer tail in relation to their body size than other species. This enables them to turn sharply in the water and execute shallow dives. The male is particularly specialised in this manner, as mentioned above, and is able to dive headlong into less than half a metre of water, though out of the breeding season he usually feeds further out. These birds may also feed in groups. When doing so, a group of hunting birds frequently dive in unison. Sometimes, especially in the cool rich waters of the western isles, blue-foots can be seen feeding in groups consisting of thousands of birds. It is an incredible spectacle to watch such a swarm circling, wheeling, and diving in an almost continual stream after a shoal of small fish (Plate 39).

Masked booby, Genovesa Island.

Masked (White) Booby

With a wingspan of 1.5 m, this species is the largest of the boobies. Its brilliant pure white body plumage contrasts with its almost black wing markings. Bryan Nelson (1968) has called it the "whitest bird imaginable." Its stout bill is yellow-orange, set against a blue-black face mask, which distinguishes this species from the white form of the red-foot. The young birds look similar to those of the blue-foot but the white of the underparts extends well up the neck.

Like the blue-foot, the masked booby, *Sula dactylatra*, nests on the ground, but being heavier and larger it has more trouble taking off. As a result, its colonies are more usually found near cliffs and on the steep outer slopes of tuff and cinder cones, where the upward air currents make it easier to take off.

This booby differs from the other two species in that it has a more or less fixed annual breeding cycle. On any particular island, breeding occurs at about the same time year after year, but from island to island this time of year varies considerably. On Genovesa, most eggs are laid from August to November, whilst on Española to the south, most are laid from November to February. In any one colony, there is a distinct synchrony of breeding, and, as a result of the nine-month breeding period, the colonies are usually empty for nearly three months of the year while the adults are leading oceanic lives.

Masked booby feeding young.   Skypointing masked booby.

The masked booby lays two eggs, and usually both hatch, but only one ever survives to maturity. Sibling murder is apparently obligatory in this species. This seems a perverse behaviour pattern, but it has been found that birds that lay clutches of two eggs are on average more successful in raising a chick than those that lay only one. This is because the second egg acts as an insurance policy in case the first egg is lost or if the first hatchling dies in the first few days of life. Sibling murder ensures that the parents never have to feed both chicks for any length of time and allows them to raise young as frequently as possible. This occurs by the older and more powerful chick attacking and forcing its sibling out of the nest, where it is likely to die from starvation, overheating by day, or cold by night. This system is different to that of the blue-foot, where food competition rather than direct aggression may lead to the death of the weaker chick.

Booby chicks that have survived the crucial first few weeks often seem too large and overstuffed in their downy coats. Young birds usually grow as large or larger than their parents before sprouting feathers. These come first at the tail and wings, then on the back, and gradually a set of flight feathers develops. Half-feathered birds are truly comical, but fully feathered young birds are dull-looking and mainly grey or brown plumage and no colour to feet or bill. The young boobies will not become independent for some time. They must first develop flight muscles and then learn the complex skill of flying and plunge diving. They continue to be fed by their parents until they are able to look after themselves.

The behaviour of the masked booby is similar to that of the blue-foot, but in most respects it is less dramatic. The feet are a dull grey-green and there is little parading in the nesting territory. Sky-pointing is much less exaggerated and is only done by the male. The pelican posture and the bill-up–face-away are used in the same circumstances as are bill-touching and ritualised nest building. The masked booby seems more aggressive in many aspects of its behaviour than the blue-foot. Rival males jab bills and flail wings at each other in disputes. The territorial display is a "yes/no" head-shaking in which the head is nodded up and down and simultaneously turned from side to side in a rapid action. The blue-foot has a similar behaviour but leaves out the "no" part. There is also much mutual jabbing of bills between partners; this is only rarely seen with the blue and red-footed boobies. Like the blue-foot, there is a difference between the voices of the male and the female; the former has a weak whistle, while the latter has a loud raucous "quack." Unlike the blue-foot, there is no difference in apparent pupil size, but the female is again larger than the male.

The masked booby feeds further offshore than the blue-foot and is rarely seen fishing. They are occasionally seen taking off from the colony and diving immediately into the sea, after which they bathe themselves, perhaps to keep cool.

Red-footed Booby

The red-footed booby, *Sula sula*, is the smallest and least often seen of the Galápagos boobies. It is, however, the most abundant of the three species, but its colonies occur at the edges of the archipelago. Except for the one on Genovesa Island, these are not often seen by visitors. It feeds well out to sea, where it catches flying fish or squid.

This booby's most distinctive feature, its bright red feet, are often hidden from view when perching or in flight, so the best identification feature is its blue bill and usually brown plumage (Plate 46). Identification is sometimes difficult because a small proportion of the population has a white plumage similar to that of the masked booby (Plate 45). They can be told apart by the feet, if visible, or by the bill. Intermediates between the white and brown forms do occur. Why these two colour forms should occur is not understood. The juveniles of the red-footed are like the brown form adults, but lack the red feet and have a brown bill.

A major difference between this species and the other two is that the red-foot nests in trees and shrubs. They are well adapted to their arboreal life by having prehensile feet on short legs, but, as a result, shuffle awkwardly on the ground. Their territories are large, averaging 90 m² on Genovesa Island. Even at this spacing, Genovesa Island harbours the world's largest "red-footed boobery" (as Dr. Nelson has called it) of possibly 140,000 pairs.

The red-foot has the least conspicuous social behaviour of the three species; this is because they are hidden by trees in which they build rather flimsy nests and also because, having such large territories, they have fewer interactions with each other. They perform head-waving as a site ownership display and also skypoint, but no more dramatically than the masked booby. There is little difference between the two sexes; the male has a higher-pitched and more nasal quacking sound than the gruffer female.

Red-footed booby, Genovesa Island.   Flightless cormorant drying its wings.

Because of its far-ranging habits, the red-foot is a slow breeder, taking well over twelve months to complete a breeding cycle. Eggs are laid in any month when conditions are suitable, but this seems to occur in bursts. These bursts may be related to food availability, but have no seasonal pattern. When the young of a breeding burst fledge, the bay at Genovesa seems to swarm with young red-foots. The *Cryptocarpus* bushes around the beaches are laden with these brown birds, as is the rigging of yachts that enter the bay at such times.

Flightless Cormorant

The flightless cormorant, *Nannopterum (Phalacrocorax) harrisi*, is the only one of the twenty-nine species of living cormorants to have lost the ability to fly. Other seabirds that have become flightless are the penguins and the extinct great auk.

The adults are almost black above, brownish below, and have turquoise eyes. The male is noticeably larger than the female. Juveniles are glossy black all over with dull-coloured eyes. Both juveniles and adults have the long sinuous neck and hooked bill which is so typical of the cormorant family. Its small, ragged, vestigial wings could in no way lift this heavy bird off the ground. It has also lost the keel of the breastbone, that serves as a site for the attachment of strong wing muscles in other species. Even though it has lost many of the attributes of a flying cormorant, it still dries its wings after swimming at the edge of the sea in the outstretched manner so characteristic of its family.

By losing its ability to fly, the cormorant appears to have traded the advantages of being able to fly for a better (more streamlined) body for swimming. This has probably come about as a result of the lack of terrestrial predators and the proximity of its feeding grounds obviating the need to fly. Natural selection would then place individuals that invested less energy and effort in being able to fly at an advantage.

Returning cormorant brings seaweed "present" to the nest.

On the surface, these cormorants swim low in the water, using their strong feet for propulsion. When they wish to dive they make a small leap up and out of the water—a jack-knife movement—to send them down to the bottom in pursuit of bottom-living fish (such as eels), and octopuses. It is not known whether they use their vestigial wings to help manoeuvre themselves about the rocks under water. Their feeding area is restricted to within a hundred metres or so of the coast.

The courtship of this species is unusual and appealing. There is an "aquatic dance" (Snow 1966) in which both male and female swim back and forth past each other, with their necks bent into a coy-looking, snakelike form, and making low gurgling/growling sounds. At times, during the display first one then the other of the pair raises itself half out of the water, points its head and beak upward, flaps its wings and shakes itself. The aquatic dance is an early part of the courtship, and usually after aquatic dancing the male will lead the way towards the shore with his tail cocked, periodically turning his head and "snake-necking." Occasionally both birds will dive. On landing, the male throws back his head and bows. Snake-necking is also used as a greeting ceremony between a pair with eggs or young.

Flightless cormorants nest in small colonies on low rocky spits and on boulder beaches, constructing a large bulky nest of seaweed and other flotsam in which two or three whitish eggs are laid. The seaweed for the nest is brought ashore by the male and is incorporated by the female into the structure. Often the male will continue bringing seaweed "presents" throughout the incubation and brooding period, though both members of the pair share these duties. The incubation time is about thirty-five days. When raising young, the adults will often wait for some time after returning from fishing before allowing the hungry chicks to feed on the regurgitated food. Barbara Snow, who has made a study of these birds, suggests that this is a behavioural adaptation to prevent frigatebirds from stealing their food during regurgitation. By this delay in feeding, the frigatebirds are prevented from using the returning cormorant as an immediate cue to be ready to steal food. The unattractive hatchlings are fed by both parents for some time after leaving the nest. If food permits, the female may desert the male and go off with another male to breed again in the same season.

There are only some 700 to 800 pairs of the endemic flightless cormorant in the world, and these are principally found in the northern and western coasts of Isabela, and all coasts of Fernandina. It is in these areas that the cool rich waters of the Cromwell Current upwell. The cormorant is not an endangered species, but it is certainly vulnerable, and care must be taken that its status is not worsened by the depredations of introduced dogs.

Frigatebirds

To walk through a colony of frigatebirds during the courtship season is a spell-binding experience (Plate 50). On Genovesa Island, the great frigatebird colonies reverberate with eerie calls and the massed red pouches draw the eyes, as nature intended (Plate 48). The vibrant atmosphere as the males do their utmost to attract a mate can almost be felt. This spectacle alone can make a trip to the islands worthwhile.

The Galápagos Islands harbour two of the world's five species of frigatebird, the great frigatebird, *Fregata minor*, and the magnificent frigatebird, *Fregata magnificens*. The frigatebirds or "man of war" birds, so-named because of their piratical habits, are unmistakable large black birds with long wings, long hooked beaks and deeply forked tails. The great frigatebird is found in most tropical oceans and nests on some of the Galápagos Islands, including Genovesa and San Cristóbal. The magnificent frigatebird, on the other hand, has a mainly Caribbean distribution but also has a substantial population in the Galápagos, with major colonies on North Seymour and San Cristóbal.

The adult male great frigatebird is all black with a faint green sheen on its back (especially during the courtship season) and a brown band across the wings. The male magnificent is almost indistinguishable from that of the great but it lacks the brown band and has a purplish sheen on its back. A good indication as to the species seen can be obtained from where one sights the bird. The great frigatebird is more ocean-going than its cousin, which is a coastal bird more associated with colonised areas. The adult females of the species are easily distinguishable; the white feathers of the abdomen and breast extend up to the chin with the great, but only up to the throat in the magnificent. Furthermore, the female great frigatebird has a red eye-ring and the magnificent a bluish one. In their first year or so, the juveniles of the two species can be distinguished. The young great frigatebird has a rusty tinge to an otherwise all white head, whereas the magnificent does not.

The frigatebirds are best known for the bright red gular sacs that the males inflate to the size of a partly inflated soccer ball when courting. The males sit either singly or in groups in the trees or shrubs where they nest, waiting for

Female great frigatebird with nestling, Genovesa Island.

Magnificent frigatebird chasing a blue-footed booby, near North Seymour Island.

females of the right species to fly over; some of the colonies are mixed, and whether the female has a white or black throat is important for the males to identify their own species. On sighting a female, they turn their heads and wings upward and shake them vigorously, displaying their pouches to best advantage and call loudly. The courtship calls are different for the two species, the great frigatebird uttering an ululating sound similar to a child's impersonation of an American Indian warrior, whereas the magnificent has a resonant-sounding chatter. If a female is attracted by this display and lands, the pair may wave their heads together and the male sometimes puts his wing around the female.

Once the pair is established, a honeymoon of nest-building begins. An untidy small platform of twigs (often stolen from a red-footed booby or another frigatebird) is constructed by both sexes. The nests are usually found in low shrubs (the saltbush, *Cryptocarpus pyriformis*, is a favourite) or in trees such as the palo santo. A single egg is laid in the nest and both parents share the incubation period of seven to eight weeks, taking roughly one week shifts during which up to one fifth of their weight may be lost. Eggs are frequently lost because of poor nest building, whereupon the courtship process may start all over again. Different pairs may be formed. By the end of nest building, however, the male's pouch has shrunk slowly to a shrivelled line of pink flesh beneath the beak.

If the egg hatches successfully, the chick is guarded by one or other parent for the first week or so until it is safe from falling prey to another frigatebird, hawk, or owl. It must then sit on its platform for more than five months before it is able to fly. These dejected-looking youngsters have struck me as the most pitiable of the Galápagos creatures as they "endure" this forced immobility under the hot sun, with nothing to do but watch the world pass by and wait for the next feed. The growth of the young frigatebirds is slow and erratic and these chicks must be the best adapted to fasting among seabirds.

Female magnificent frigatebird feeding juvenile.

Nestling great frigatebird, Genovesa Island.

Once fledged the young bird is likely to remain dependent on its parents for over a year while it learns the complex skills of the frigatebird trade. It is thought that the great frigatebird is not mature until at least five years of age (De Vries and Hernandez 1981). Because of the long dependency of the young, it cannot breed more frequently than once every two years. Although accurate information on longevity is not available, they must be quite long-lived.

Frigatebirds are masters of the air; their wing shape and precise timing make them superlative stunt fliers, which they must be to feed in the way they do. They are also light for their size and have the highest wingspan to weight ratios amongst the birds. Their forked tails can be scissored in and out to maintain balance in flight. These characteristics, together with a long hook-tipped beak, enable them to snatch up flying and other fish, squid, and scraps from the surface of the sea, as well as to steal from other seabirds. Though frigatebirds are frequently observed robbing other birds, they catch much of their food themselves. To do so, the more pelagic great frigatebird flies great distances, often remaining away from the colony for a week or more. Observation at the colony thus gives an inaccurate impression of their foraging habits.

On catching sight of prey near the surface, a frigatebird will swoop down to within a foot of the water and flick its head down and up in a fraction of a second, plucking up its prey in a perfectly timed manoeuvre. Only its beak will touch the water, for it must avoid severely wetting its plumage, else it might become waterlogged and drown. Frigatebirds have only a small preen gland that is insufficient to oil and waterproof their feathers fully. I have seen young birds succumb to this watery fate a few times; clearly this factor limits the range of food that is available to them. The frigatebird's other method of feeding, piracy, involves stealing food from other seabirds, such as boobies and tropicbirds, which can dive beneath the surface for deeper-living fish. When doing so, they will soar around the colonies of other birds (which often coincide with their own) waiting for an opportunity to force a bird that is returning to feed its chick to disgorge the meal. If the chase is successful, the pirate will swoop down and catch the disgorged bolus of food, often before it hits the water. These bullying tactics, which often involve pulling at a wing or tail of the victim, demand great flying skills.

I have occasionally observed these manoeuvres to go wrong. Once a frigatebird forced a booby to disgorge over a beach and, before the bird could get to it, a lava gull had snatched the prize. On other occasions, I have seen the disgorged bolus disappear into a cactus forest where it formed a meal for some finches. Frigatebirds are not averse to finding their food over land and may snatch turtle hatchlings from a beach, unprotected nestlings of their own or other species, and even a meal from a parent booby regurgitating to its chick. On some occasions, they seem to take on more than they can handle. I once saw nine frigatebirds consecutively attempt to eat an over-sized scrap of fish that was thrown from a boat. Each one ended by dropping it and eventually it was taken by a young pelican. On another occasion, a frigatebird attempted to pick up a booby chick from its nesting site, but the chick was too large for the frigatebird to carry and ended up being flung about ten metres away from the nest. It managed to clamber back to the nest. The eyesight of these birds is phenomenal. The nine above-mentioned birds appeared, like vultures, from apparently empty sky within minutes after the fishermen began to clean their fish.

The best site to see the great frigatebird is at Darwin Bay, Genovesa Island, where many courting males may be seen during the first half of the year. North Seymour has one of the best magnificent frigatebird colonies, in which birds can be found displaying at virtually any time of year.

Swallow-tailed Gull

The swallow-tailed gull, *Creagrus (Larus) furcatus*, is one of the world's most beautiful gulls. It is endemic to the Galápagos islands and is also unusual in being one of the few species of gull that feeds out to sea at night (Hailman 1968;1964). This large gull has red feet and a crimson eye-ring to set off its beautifully textured black, grey, and white plumage (Plate 47).

These gulls leave their colonies at dusk, amidst much screaming and display, to feed. Their main prey are squid and fish which they catch at the

Swallow-tailed gull chick, Genovesa Island.

surface, perhaps using the phosphorescence created when these creatures move. As a nocturnal feeder, this gull has several features that set it apart from other gulls. It has large eyes with many night vision elements (rods). The gulls return at night to feed their young and have white markings on the bill which the chick pecks at to elicit feeding. Many other species have red markings on yellow bills which would not be visible to a chick at night. The chicks themselves are mottled white.

   The adults return to the colony from about midnight onwards to feed their young and continue to return until dawn at which time they are a useful navigation aid for boat captains who wish to check that they are on course for land. Birds with small chicks may wait for some time before they regurgitate to their young as they must digest the food into small enough pieces for the chicks to swallow. On several occasions, I have seen parents trying to feed their young pieces of squid which were almost as large as the chicks themselves. The parents had to reswallow the squid and try again later.

AILEEN HARMON

Adult swallow-tailed gull, South Plaza Island.

Swallow-tailed gull "foot-watching."

Pair of swallow-tailed gulls and their coral nest.

The swallow-tailed gull is colonial and is found on most small islands and on cliffs of larger islands. There do not seem to be as many in the western islands where the waters are cooler. Most gulls lay more than one egg, but this species lays a single buff-speckled egg on a collection of small stones or pieces of coral on a cliff edge or beach. Most nests are less than 10 m above sea level. Pair formation occurs at the nesting site, which is selected by the male. Pairs often remain the same from year to year but females are not averse to changing mate and site.

Like other features of the biology of this gull, the calls and displays are markedly different from those of most other species. The greatest similarities are between this species and the kittiwake or Sabine's gull (which only nests north of the Arctic Circle). The behaviour of gulls has been much studied by scientists, but, when Barbara and David Snow (1968) made a detailed study of the swallow-tailed gull, they had to invent a new set of names to describe the main behaviour patterns. It is not surprising that this species has been placed by taxonomists into a separate genus from other gull species—*Creagrus*. The entire repertoire of this species would take much space to describe, so only some of the most commonly seen displays and calls will be described here.

The alarm call used at the approach of people or potential predators is termed the "rattle-and-whistle" and is a gurgling scream normally made when the bird is turning its head from side to side. The call seems contagious and if one bird gives the call, many nearby birds will do likewise, some without seeing the cause for alarm. It is the loudest and most often heard call of this species. "Downward piping" is the next most used of the calls; it is used as a greeting between members of a pair. The call is a loud rapid "kweek, kweek, kweek" and is typically made with the head and neck curved forward to the ground.

A major advertising display of unmated males is the "upward jerk." In this movement, the neck starts by being stretched upward; from this position, the beak is jerked upward and backward half a dozen times; the movement is usually finished by bringing the head back so that the beak is pointing downward. This is sometimes followed by downward piping or by "foot watching." Foot watching is a common behaviour of the swallow-tailed gull and is thought to be an appeasement display. Sometimes this is exaggerated to the point where the bird looks back through its legs, perhaps indicating a greater degree of fear. It also appears to be a displacement activity, one that is done when the bird is not sure what to do, like biting nails for humans.

Part of the courtship behaviour involves the male regurgitating to the female. In the early stages, he does not usually let her have the regurgitated morsel, but when the female is ready to lay, the male will often give his mate a substantial feed. Males and females also engage in much mutual preening, especially around the head and neck. As a preliminary to mating, there is often a head-tossing display accompanied by plaintive "kewing."

Each pair attempts to breed every nine to ten months or so. Outside the breeding period, they migrate to the seas off Ecuador and Peru and during this time their plumage is much less distinctive (the dark head colour being almost entirely lost).

The young, once they lose their mottled grey down, become white and heavily spotted with dark brown. It is thought that it takes five years for a bird to reach maturity and start to breed; during this time, it lives an oceanic life in the eastern Pacific.

There are some 10,000 to 15,000 pairs of swallow-tailed gulls in the Galápagos Islands, and these virtually constitute the world population of the species, although a few breeding pairs have also been found on Isla Malpelo, off Colombia.

Lava Gull

The lava gull, *Larus fuliginosus*, is thought to be the rarest gull in the world, numbering only some 400 pairs. It is found only in the Galápagos. Though few in number, it is widely distributed around the coasts of the archipelago. The adult lava gull is dark grey all over with the head and upper neck almost black, forming a hood. Its white eye-ring contrasts sharply with the hood, as does its scarlet gape. The densest population is at Academy Bay, where there is always an abundance of fish and other waste in the harbour.

It is a highly territorial species and will attack anything that comes near to its nesting sites. The long, loud, laughing call of the lava gull is unmistakable and often helps to pinpoint this dusky coloured bird amongst the lava rocks. This call is used as a threat display to members of its own species and denotes territorial ownership. Sometimes, a pair will call together and this laughing duet is unforgettable.

Adult lava gull.

Noddy tern on nesting ledge, Tagus Cove, Isabela Island.

Lava gulls are solitary nesters, laying two heavily blotched eggs in a scrape near a lagoon, on a sandy beach, or rocky spit. The young have much brown in their plumage.

The lava gull is primarily a scavenger, though it will also catch small fish from the sea surface. Lava gulls will also take seabird eggs and newly hatched iguanas and turtles. They are unafraid of people and will often rest on the stern of yachts at anchor.

Brown Noddy

The brown noddy, *Anous stolidus*, is a dark brown tern-like bird with pointed wings and a long wedge-shaped tail. The whitish forehead and white eye-ring of the adult contrast sharply with the rest of the body. Brown noddies feed mainly on small fish and fry that are at the sea's surface. They can sometimes be seen in large flocks where schools of fish are being attacked from below by tuna or other game fish.

The brown noddy is also often seen feeding together with pelicans and other seabirds. When with a group of pelicans, these small dark birds flutter about frequently alighting on a pelican's head or back. From this vantage point, they wait for the bird to empty its pouch and then snatch up any scraps that drain out. This behaviour is a remarkable example of how one species can take advantage of another's actions without, seemingly, interfering.

The brown noddy nests in small colonies on sea cliffs and overhangs. The courtship involves much vigorous head-nodding, and low guttural growls. A single egg is laid on bare rock, occasionally with some twigs or seaweed as nest material. Brown noddies are widespread in the Galápagos and are found in most tropical and subtropical seas, though rarely far from land.

Other Gulls and Terns

Both Franklin's gull, *Larus pipixcan*, and the royal tern, *Thalasseus maximus*, are regular visitors to the islands in small numbers during the northern winter. Franklin's gull breeds in the interior United States and the Canadian prairies. In both of these places, it feeds mainly on flying insects and by scavenging. It is a common gull on the prairies. The sooty tern, *Sterna fuscata*, is resident in the Galápagos but only breeds on Darwin Island, where it has a large colony, and is rarely seen by visitors. It has black upperparts and white underparts.

Seabird Ecology

The Galápagos Islands harbour a diverse assemblage of seabirds. The seabirds are well enough known for it to be possible to look at and compare the various ways in which they use their environments and therefore coexist with little apparent competition. The nineteen species of seabirds in the islands use the resources of the sea and the space on land in different ways and so are able to occur together. Food is an important factor in determining tropical seabird numbers, so species that occur in the same areas have, through the course of evolution, arrived at different ways of obtaining their food. The main ways in which species may differ in this respect are by feeding in different places, at different times, using different methods, or catching different prey.

   Ten of the fifteen Galápagos species that have been studied in detail have suffered periodic breeding failures which are probably related to a shortage of food, indicating the importance of food in determining the life strategies of these birds. Consequently, competition between species for food would be expected to be an important factor in the ecology of the seabirds. Dr. Michael Harris (1977) and others have collected data over many years on the feeding and breeding ecology of Galápagos seabirds and these data are summarised in Table 12. From the table, it can be seen that the various species do have feeding strategies that vary in such a way as to avoid competition. The table shows that squid and flying fish form an important part of many species' diets, as do crustaceans and other fish. Most of the range of food that is available is taken by one or other species of seabird. On the whole, the size of prey taken is related to the size of the bird except that the lava gull catches small fish from tide pools and the brown pelican filters small fish with its pouch as well as taking larger fish.

   This is how Dr. Harris (1977) describes the ways in which different birds can take the same prey:

Red-footed boobies caught flying fish in the air, great frigatebirds picked them from the surface, swallow-tailed gulls caught them just below the surface, masked boobies caught them some distance below, and waved albatrosses took them while swimming on the surface. Similarly, brown noddies hovered to take the smallest fish, storm petrels made a quick pounce, and Audubon's shearwater pursued them underwater.

The various species are adapted to catch their fish in different ways, and the bills of these species reflect their feeding methods.

Only the swallow-tailed gull, the waved albatross, and the Galápagos storm petrel obtain most of their food at night. It is perhaps surprising that more species do not do so, as flying fish and squid are more abundant near the surface at night. Audubon's shearwater is diurnal in the Galápagos but largely nocturnal elsewhere. It is thought that other species may feed more at night than has been recorded, but, of course, this is difficult to observe.

In Galápagos waters most species have well-defined feeding areas. Eight species feed within a kilometre or so of shore, seven are pelagic, and four feed between the islands. The flightless cormorant is the closest feeder, requiring shallow rocky reefs to find its food. It rarely ventures more than 100 m from shore. The inshore feeders tend to breed in many small, well-dispersed, colonies which are close to the feeding areas, whereas the pelagic feeders have fewer, much larger and more separated colonies.

It seems that Galápagos seabird populations remain close to the ecological carrying capacity. This may explain why few migrant species overwinter in the islands as there would rarely be enough food to maintain extra populations of birds. Only the northern phalarope occurs in large numbers and this species takes smaller food than any of the resident species. Twenty-seven other species have been recorded at various times, showing that there is little problem for these migrants to get to the islands. Birds from a range of geographical origins reside and breed in the Galápagos. Twelve species are from tropical or subtropical waters, while four or five are more typical of cooler waters, such as are found in Humboldt Current off Peru.

The three species of booby make rewarding subjects for a study in evolutionary ecology (Nelson 1978). They are evolutionarily closely related and are similar in many respects; therefore, it is interesting to see what the differences are between them that allow for peaceful coexistence. All three species use more or less the same technique to catch their fish and the sizes caught overlap considerably. It seems that, in the course of evolution, they have adapted primarily to feed in different areas. The red-foot feeds mainly outside the archipelago, whereas the blue-foot's feeding habits are coastal. The masked booby feeds offshore but mainly within the archipelago. These basic differences in feeding strategy have led to complementary variations in behaviour and other aspects of their ecology. The blue-foot's feeding area is limited to a maximum of 1,350 km of coastline where the water is shallow

Table 12. Ecology of Galápagos Seabirds[a]

Species	Where observed at sea[b]	Main feeding methods[c]	Food brought to young[d]	Number of colonies	Nesting sites	Nesting season[c]	Age of first breeding	Eggs per clutch	Breeding interval (year)
Galápagos penguin	Inshore	Pursuit-diving	Medium-sized, mid-water and reef fish	Many	Coastal caves, crevices	Variable	?	2	<1
Waved albatross	Pelagic	Surface-seizing	Squid, flying and other fish, crustacea	1	Near coastal cliffs	April to June	4	1	1
Audubon's shearwater	Inshore	Surface-seizing, pursuit-diving	Planktonic larval fish, minute crustacea, minute cephalopoda	29+	Cliff holes, burrows	Variable	?	1	<1
Dark-rumped (Hawaiian) petrel	Pelagic	?	Medium squid and fish	5	Highland burrows	June to August	3 to 4	1	1
Madeiran storm petrel	Pelagic	Dipping	Fish 30–50 mm long, very small cephalopoda	15	Rock crevices, cliffs	Variable	?	1	1
Galápagos storm petrel	Pelagic/between islands	Dipping	Small fish, few cephalopoda, and crustacea	3	Rock crevices, cliffs	May to June	?	1	1
Elliot's storm petrel	Inshore	Pattering	Very small fish and crustacea	?	Unknown	April to Sept.	?	?	?
Red-billed tropicbird	Pelagic	Deep-plunging	Flying and other fish to 200 mm	30	Cliff holes	Variable	5	1	<1
Brown pelican	Inshore	Surface-plunging	Fish from 40 to 350 mm	Many	Coastal trees and shrubs	Variable	?	2–3	<1
Blue-footed booby	Inshore	Deep-plunging	Medium fish, maximum 250 mm	35+	Coastal open areas	Variable	3	2–3	<1
Masked booby	Between islands	Deep-plunging	Medium fish, sometimes squid	23	Coastal open areas	Variable	3	2	1
Red-footed booby	Pelagic	Deep-plunging	Medium fish, sometimes squid	5	Trees and shrubs	Variable	?	1	>1
Flightless cormorant	Inshore	Pursuit-diving, bottom-feeding	Bottom-living fish, eels, octopuses	112+	Coastal shoreline rocks	Variable	2	3	<1
Great frigatebird	Pelagic	Dipping, cleptoparasitism	Flying and other fish, sometimes squid	12	Coastal trees and shrubs	Variable	5+	1	1–2
Magnificent frigatebird	Inshore/between islands	Dipping, cleptoparasitism	Fish, including reef species, offal	12	Coastal trees and shrubs	Variable	?	1	>1
Swallow-tailed gull	Between islands	Surface-plunging	Flying and other fish, squid to 200 mm	55+	Coastal cliffs and rocks	Variable	4	1	<1
Lava gull	Coastal	Scavenging	Mostly scavenges, few small fish	Solitary nester	Coastal areas	Variable	?	2	?
Brown noddy	Inshore	Dipping	Small fish, usually 15–20 mm long	Many	Coastal cliffs	Variable	?	1	<1
Sooty tern	Pelagic	Dipping	No data, elsewhere fish and squid to 80 mm	1	Unknown	Variable	?	?	?

[a]Ecological details are based on the work of Nelson (1977, 1979), Boersma (1976), de Vries, Gordillo and Harris, and an anonymous manuscript at the CDRS.

[b]*Inshore* refers to birds feeding within one and a half kilometres of the coast, *between islands* to species feeding among the islands without being inshore, *pelagic* to birds feeding well away from the islands.

[c]Feeding methods are defined as follows: *dipping* is picking food from the surface of the sea without landing and without using the feet; *pattering* is similar, except that the feet are used; *surface-plunging* and *deep-plunging* are where the bird dives into the water from a height and is either incompletely or completely immersed; birds swimming on the surface can either seize food directly (*surface-seizing*) or dive and chase it (*pursuit-diving*). *Cleptoparasitism* is the chasing of other species to make them regurgitate or drop any food they are carrying.

[d]Small fish and squid are up to 50 mm long, medium 50 to 150 mm, large above 150 mm.

[c]*Variable* means either the species' breeding season varies from one year to another at the same place or that it varies from place to place in the archipelago, or both.

? = data not available.

and rich, while the red-foot has thousands of square kilometres of open ocean as its feeding domain, but the food is much more sparsely distributed and harder to get. Though the blue-foot is more commonly seen, it is actually less abundant than the other two species. The more easily available but more limited food of the blue-foot versus the harder to get but virtually unlimited food of the red-foot has led to the two species having markedly different breeding strategies. The blue-foot leads a "fast" life, raising as many as three young in two-thirds of the time needed by the red-foot to raise one. Though data are not available, the red-foot would be expected to be longer-lived than the blue-foot to compensate. The masked booby is in most respects intermediate between the red-footed and blue-footed boobies.

The behaviour of these species at the colony shows a range of variations related to the type of nesting area. The blue-foot has the most typically open and flat nesting area and has been able to incorporate more dramatic actions into its postures and displays than have its congeners. The masked booby nests principally on steeper slopes and cliff tops, and the red-foot nests in trees. In both the latter species' nesting habitats, life is more precariously balanced and, as a result, display behaviour can not be as active.

Coastal Birds and Migrants

The 1,350 km of coastline in the Galápagos Islands, comprising beaches, rocky shores, mangrove lagoons, and tidal salinas, provide magnificent habitats for herons, flamingos, ducks, stilts, oystercatchers, and some migrant species. The first part of this chapter discusses the resident shore birds, while the second covers some of the common migrant species.

Resident Shore Birds

Herons and Egrets

Five species of the heron family live in the Galápagos, and one other is a regular migrant. Herons and egrets are carnivorous birds, feeding primarily on small fish and crabs, but are also found inland where they will feed on rats, lizards, insects, young birds and young iguanas. Most herons feed by patiently remaining motionless until their prey comes within reach, at which point they stab quickly with their beaks. They are expert "sit and wait" predators.

Great Blue Heron

The great blue heron, *Ardea herodias*, by far the largest of the Galápagos herons, stands 1.4 m high and is mainly grey with some black and white markings on the head, neck and breast. This species occurs throughout North and Central America and should not be confused with the closely related white-necked heron found on the adjacent South American mainland. The great blue heron breeds on all the main islands either in isolated pairs or in small colonies. They favour mangroves or solitary rocks on which to build their large nests.

Though its diet consists mainly of fish caught along the shoreline, the great blue heron will take lizards, young marine iguanas and turtle hatchlings.

Great blue heron.

Great egret.

Certain pairs seem idiosyncratic in their habits. A pair at Punta Espinoza, Fernandina, spent much time during the marine iguana emergence period stalking the nesting beaches in search of newly hatched iguanas. Two birds on Bartolomé could regularly be seen waiting for turtle hatchlings to emerge. As soon as a hatchling disturbed the sand's surface, the heron's beak would stab into the sand and pull out the little turtle. It would then take it to the water's edge to wash it before swallowing. In Academy Bay, these herons have been so tame that they will enter houses and restaurants to look for food.

Great blue herons are usually silent but when disturbed will often take flight uttering a raucous "kraak." Their flight is slow and steady, with the head drawn back into the shoulders.

Great (American) Egret

This large white bird is not as common as the great blue heron but the great egret, *Casmerodius (Ardea) alba*, is regularly seen around the coasts and occasionally inland. Its habits are not well known but are thought to be similar to those of the great blue heron, though it will take smaller food including insects. Sylvia Harcourt tells of an individual that came over to South Plazas Island every day during the land iguana hatching season and was probably one of the main predators on iguana hatchlings and lava

Great blue heron with turtle hatchling prey.   Lava heron in hunting poise.

lizards during that time. This occurred for at least two consecutive years. They have also been recorded as taking young rats on Santa Cruz Island.

Cattle Egret

White but much smaller than the great egret, the cattle egret, *Bubulcus ibis*, is now a resident species. It frequents the highlands where it is often found with cattle or tortoises. It nests in mangroves such as are found at Tortuga Bay, Santa Cruz. Until the late 1800s, this species was known only in western Africa, but since then it has spread and is now virtually worldwide. It is a species associated with human activity, feeding on insects and other invertebrates disturbed by cattle and other large animals.

Lava Heron

The hunched shape of this small dark heron is a characteristic sight along the coasts of all the islands. Though well camouflaged against lava, the lava heron, *Butorides (Ardeola)sundevalli*, is the most frequently seen of the Galápagos herons and the only endemic one. It is found on most types of shore where it catches small fish in tide-pools and tidal creeks. It also stealthily hunts small crabs and lizards among the rocks. In mangroves, it perches amongst the stilt-roots and catches small fry by diving like a kingfisher. I have also seen it picking flies off the carcasses of sea lions. Young birds of this species are brownish with much dark streaking. Lava herons usually nest under rocks or in mangrove thickets where up to three eggs are laid in a twig nest. Most nesting is from September to March (Kushlan 1983).

Striated Heron

This species and the lava heron may be just different varieties of the same species, though the relationship between them is still not clear. Although

Yellow-crowned night herons, James Bay, Santiago Island.

widespread, it is not common. The two species (varieties?) are differentiated by the striated heron having a pale neck and breast and a black cap. The striated heron, *Butorides (Ardeola) striatus,* is also found throughout most of coastal tropical South America.

Yellow-crowned Night Heron

This medium-sized heron is, as its name suggests, mainly active at night when it catches beetles, locusts, other insects, crabs, scorpions and centipedes. It has a distinctive yellow crown and large yellow-orange eyes that give it a permanently surprised expression. On one occasion, I saw an individual spear a Sally Lightfoot crab so forcibly that the crab was impaled around the base of the heron's bill and the bird had great trouble freeing its bill. If a bird can be embarrassed, this one was; the already large eyes became seemingly larger as it struggled in front of a group of visitors!

In Academy Bay, the yellow-crowned night heron, *Nyctanassa violacea,* can often be found at night near street lamps where it catches a wide variety of insects and other arthropods which are attracted to the light. It is common and widespread in the islands, though by day individuals are usually found in the shade of shrubs or rocks. Like the other herons, this species is usually quiet, but it is occasionally heard making a ventriloquial whooping sound.

Feeding flamingo, Rábida Island.   Flamingos mating.

Greater Flamingo

A small group of flamingos feeding quietly and moving gracefully through a brackish lagoon is a most peaceful sight (Plate 51). Some five hundred of these attractive pink birds are found in salty lagoons around the archipelago. The rich mud of these lagoons is the habitat of water-boatmen (*Trichocorixa reticulata*) and a shrimp (*Artemia salina*). These two species, as well as minute crabs, are found in the "organic ooze" which forms the main food of flamingos in the Galápagos. The greater flamingo, *Phoenicopterus ruber*, feeds in an unusual way with its head upside down. Its neck is almost as long as its legs, and it can bring its head down to its toes where it sucks in water from the front and pumps it out through the side. The water and mud pass through sieve-like plates in the bill which filter out the small animals that make up its diet. Moving their head from side to side, and sometimes "puddling" with their feet to stir up the bottom, the flamingos wend their way haphazardly about the lagoons. Their method of feeding is akin to that of the great whales which filter shrimps out of the water with their baleen.

Flamingos are spectacular in flight, with their long necks outstretched and their legs trailing behind. To take off, they begin by running along the surface of the water, flapping their large pink and black wings. If the water is deep, they will often swim with their legs tucked up and their graceful necks give them the appearance of pink swans.

White-cheeked pintail duck.

In the Galápagos, the flamingos usually breed during the coastal hot season. They are social breeders and will not nest on their own. The court-ship is not well known, but before and during the breeding season flocks of birds will stand up to their full height and parade ballet-like with fluffed-up feathers. The nests are built from mud into small sand castle-like structures on which a single large egg is laid. Both sexes help to build the nest and to incubate the egg for about a month. Flamingos are nervous creatures and are likely to desert their nests if they are disturbed. It is important that visitors avoid making unnecessary noises or movements that might disturb the birds. The chicks are fully covered with down when they hatch and are able to walk about almost immediately. The parents feed their young for a few weeks, as, when they hatch, their bills are straight and do not take on the adult curved shape until some three weeks of age. Within a few days, the chicks leave the nest area and form crèches (a "daycare"), which are guarded by adults. Though all the chicks from a colony stay in a group, there is mutual parent-chick recognition and chicks are only fed by their own parents. They are not able to fly until about three and one half months old but are able to feed on their own well before that. If there is not enough food available for both adults and young in the breeding lagoon, the adults will usually leave the pale grey young behind to look after themselves. It is thought that flamingos do not breed until five years of age and that they live for about fifteen years.

The small population in the Galápagos is a vulnerable one, so care must be taken that these birds are disturbed as little as possible, especially during the breeding season when their lagoons should be protected.

White-cheeked (Bahama) Pintail Duck

Small groups of white-cheeked, ruddy-beaked ducks are found in most lagoons and ponds, from the shorelines to the highlands. These

MONICA J. JACKSON

Oystercatcher with eggs.   Feeding black-necked stilts.

"puddle-ducks" feed on aquatic creatures and vegetation by dabbing at the surface or by up-ending and probing the mud in shallow water. Little is known about the ecology of these birds even though they are frequently seen. These ducks take off vertically from the surface of the water. The most often heard sound is like that made by a baby's squeezy bath toy, and is probably involved in courtship. The white-cheeked pintail duck, *Anas bahamensis*, prefers to breed in dense vegetation where it may lay up to ten pale brown eggs.

The blue-winged teal has also been recorded from the islands, its blue wing patch clearly separates it from the pintail which has a green wing patch.

Wading Birds—Charadriformes

This large and successful order of birds is represented by six families in the Galápagos and also includes the gulls which were discussed in the last chapter. Many waders are long-distance migrants that overwinter or pass through the islands in varying numbers.

American Oystercatcher

A small population of some 200 pairs of this large black and white shore bird, *Haematopus palliatus*, is found in the Galápagos. Its stout red bill and orange-yellow eyes make it unmistakable (Plate 52). It is found mainly along rocky shores and beaches where it searches for intertidal creatures, mainly crabs and molluscs. Its loud call is often used in flight and is a repetitive "kleep." When displaying in the air, the wingbeats are exaggerated and the flight is erratic. On land, the display involves much mutual bowing and calling. The nest is merely a scrape amongst the rocks just above the high-tide line, in which two speckled eggs are usually laid. When the young hatch, they are ready to leave the nest and move about with their parents as they roam the shores. Adults are usually seen in pairs.

Semi-palmated plover.   Ruddy turnstone.

Black-necked (Common) Stilt

This graceful black and white bird, *Himantopus himantopus*, is a commonly seen resident lagoon bird. It is tall and slim with long thin red legs and has a thin straight black bill with which it probes the mud for food. It is a noisy bird, especially when it takes flight.

Migrant Species

The migrant species found in the Galápagos are those that breed in North America during the summer, as far north as the Arctic, and spend the northern winter months in the tropical eastern Pacific or around South America. Some species are brief visitors on their way further south, while others pass the whole winter in the islands. Most migrants are found near the coast, but a few species regularly venture inland to freshwater ponds in the highlands. The Galápagos Islands are important wintering grounds for only six migrant species, though more bird species have been recorded as migrants than breed in the islands.

Semi-palmated (Ringed) Plover

This small plump shore bird, *Charadrius semipalmatus*, is a common migrant and is seen regularly in small numbers, especially from August to April. It is brown above with a white forehead and collar and yellow legs. Like many plovers, it has a habit of running a few steps at a time and then standing quite still for a few moments before moving on.

Ruddy Turnstone

The ruddy turnstone, *Arenaria interpres*, is a robust, orange-legged shore bird. It has a russet to grey-coloured back and curious black face and breast

Wandering tattler.

markings. It is a handsome bird, especially in flight when the striking black and white wing pattern is seen. It is a common species, found on most types of shore between August and March. It has gained its name from its frequent habit of turning over stones in its search for small, intertidal marine life.

Wandering Tattler

The most commonly seen of the migrant shore birds is the wandering tattler, *Heteroscelus incanus*. It is often identified by its lack of obvious markings and by its bobbing walk. It has grey-brown upper parts, grey breast and a white belly. Its musical call is striking. It breeds by mountain streams above the timber line in north-western America.

Sanderling

This attractive pale or white sandpiper, *Crocethia alba*, is commonly seen on sandy beaches (Plate 54). It is a small bird that runs back and forth along the waters' edge, its legs moving like those of a clockwork toy. It is usually found in groups.

Whimbrel

The long down-curved bill and long legs of this large wading bird make it unmistakable. Whimbrels, *Numenius phaeopus*, are usually found on rocky shores or in lagoons in all months, but numbers are low from May to July when most have gone to the Arctic to breed. Sometimes large groups can be seen in the highlands of Santa Cruz and San Cristóbal islands. Its call consists of half a dozen rapid whistles—a common sound around Galápagos lagoons.

Whimbrel.

Northern phalarope in non-breeding plumage.

Northern (Red-necked) Phalarope

Between August and April, flocks of these pale grey birds, *Lobipes lobatus*, are frequently seen at sea between the islands. Some are also found on salty lagoons. When feeding, they often spin like tops, creating a vortex in the water, which brings plankton to the surface. Phalaropes are unusual because it is the female that is more colourful in the breeding season. In its boreal breeding areas, the female has a red neck patch and she courts the male rather than vice versa. She may also have more than one mate. The more energetic female defends the territory, while the drabber male defends the nest, incubates the eggs and takes care of the young. I often see these birds on the Strait of Juan de Fuca near my home in Canada.

Land Birds

Few species of land birds inhabit the Galápagos, and three-quarters of these are endemic. Unlike the seabirds, most of which are excellent long-distance fliers, land birds from the tropics have little cause to make long flights. Twenty-two of the twenty-nine resident species are endemic and only fourteen successful colonisations could account for the present land bird fauna. Though relatives of all the Galápagos species may be found on the nearby mainland, only a freak of fate would bring them out a thousand kilometres from land. This must have happened, however, at least fourteen times in the past.

The colonisation of the Galápagos by land birds is difficult to explain. The only agency likely to help them there would be strong winds. These are virtually unrecorded in the tropical eastern Pacific and we can only suppose that rare and abnormal storms have taken place in the lifetime of the Galápagos. Chance must have played an important part in the colonisation by land birds.

With few exceptions, the land birds a are singularly dull-coloured lot. As if to make up for this lack of exciting colour, their "tameness" is unsurpassed. With attitudes to man that seem to range from indifference, through curiosity and fearlessness, to outright impudence, the Galápagos land birds are a pleasure to watch and study.

Everyone who has visited these islands has been struck by this phenomenal lack of fear of humans as the following quotations show:

> Turtle-doves were so tame, that they would often alight upon our hats and arms, so as that we could take them alive: they not fearing man, until such time as some of our company did fire at them, whereby they were rendered more shy. (Darwin 1845)

> One day . . . a mocking-thrush alighted on the edge of a pitcher, made of the shell of a tortoise, which I held in my hand, and began very quietly to sip the water; it allowed me to lift it from the ground whilst seated on the vessel. (Darwin 1845)

> Even before I reached the top of the sandy beach I was greeted by the first land birds of Indefatigable—three mockingbirds which ran rapidly down towards me—one singing as his feet flew over the sand. They stopped a yard away and looked me over.... All the native birds in sight, instead of being warned and alarmed at our presence, came straight to the nearest bushes or actually hovered about our heads in mid-air, striving to make us out.... If the tameness of the Galápagos birds in general was astonishing, the fearlessness of the little flycatcher was unbelievable. He alighted three feet from me, and when I drew back to focus my Graflex camera, the mirror was suddenly obscured, and looking up I saw the bird clinging to the lens, pecking at the brass fittings. (Beebe 1924)

Man has been discontinuously present in the islands for over four centuries and despite his abuse of their trust, the birds are still naively indifferent to him. Mockingbirds still greet us at the landing beaches and I have often shared my breakfast table with finches. I have had a flycatcher take hair from my head for its nest. On Española Island, a mockingbird landed first on my head and then proceeded to investigate my camera on its tripod. I was totally unprepared to take its photograph!

Scientists and authors alike have puzzled over such tameness. Charles Darwin (1845) came close to the answer when he wrote:

> It would appear that the birds of this archipelago, not having as yet learnt that man is a more dangerous animal than the tortoise or the Amblyrhynchus, disregard him, in the same manner as in England shy birds, such as magpies, disregard the cows and horses in our fields.

Some of the species or their ancestors have been in the islands longer than others. From the range of differentiation between Galápagos species and their mainland relatives, we can infer that some of them are descended from chance immigrants which reached the islands a long time ago, whilst others are of more recent origin. Some species, such as the cuckoo and moorhen are near-identical with their mainland relatives. Others have diverged slightly, producing endemic subspecies or races (yellow warbler, short-eared and barn owls, vermilion flycatcher), while yet others (Galápagos hawk, Galápagos rail, Galápagos dove, and Galápagos flycatcher) have formed distinct species. The mockingbirds belong to an endemic genus with different species on different islands. Darwin's finches, one of the classic examples of adaptive radiation, form a subgroup of the finch family found only in the Galápagos and Cocos islands. Evolutionary divergence gives only an indication of time since arriving in the islands, as different species may diverge at different rates depending upon ecological opportunity. These inferences are backed up, however, by the fact that the dark-billed cuckoo, the least divergent species, is also the shyest. David Steadman, of the Smithsonian Institution, has studied small bird fossils on various islands and his results support the conclusion that certain species, including the cuckoo and yellow warbler, are more recent arrivals.

The land birds as a group include two of the most impressive examples of evolutionary change in the Galápagos: the mockingbirds and Darwin's finches. After being told about the inter-island variability of the giant tortoises, Darwin (1845) wrote:

> My attention was first thoroughly aroused, by comparing together the numerous specimens of the mocking thrushes. . . . I never dreamed that islands, about fifty or sixty miles apart, and most of them in sight of each other, formed of precisely the same rocks, placed under a quite similar climate, rising to a nearly equal height, would have been differently tenanted.

The curious, dull-coloured, dumpy looking Darwin's finches have attracted more attention from evolutionary scientists than perhaps any other group of birds. When Darwin had his collections of finches identified by John Gould at the British Museum as all belonging to one family, he was led to write:

> The remaining land-birds form a most singular group of finches related to each other in the structure of their beaks, short tails, form of body, and plumage. Seeing this gradation and diversity of structure in one small, intimately related group of birds, one might really fancy that from an original paucity of birds in this archipelago, one species had been taken and modified for different ends. (Darwin 1845)

One hundred and fifty years later, this unusual group of birds remain the focus of much scientific research.

The distributions of species of Galápagos land birds are shown in Table 13.

Galápagos Hawk

No other bird of prey can be as fearless as the Galápagos hawk (*Buteo galapagoensis*). Where they occur, these birds will come and investigate visitors, often approaching within a few yards. In 1845, Charles Darwin Wrote: "A gun is here almost superfluous; for with the muzzle I pushed a hawk out of the branch of a tree." The juveniles especially are the most curious. Walking along the rim of Alcedo Volcano, I have been shadowed by young hawks for over three kilometres at a time (Plate 57).

The adult Galápagos hawk is almost uniformly dark brown (Plate 56), with the female being somewhat larger than the male. The young birds are lighter brown and heavily mottled. The nests are usually made in trees and can become quite large as they are reused with new twigs added at each breeding attempt. Up to three young may be raised at a time. The Galápagos hawk has an unusual mating system, termed cooperative polyandry (Faaborg et al. 1980). As many as four males may mate with a single female and all will aid the female in caring for the eggs and young.

Table 13. Distribution and Landbird Species

	Isabela	Santa Cruz	Fernandina	Santiago	San Cristóbal	Floreana	Marchena	Española	Pinta	Baltra	Sante Fe	Pinzón	Genovesa	Rábida	N. Seymour	Wolf	Darwin	Daphne Major	Plaza Sur
Galápagos hawk	+	+	+	+	X	X	+	+	+		+	+		+					
Barn owl	+	+	+	+	+	?													
Short-eared owl	+	+	+	+	+	+	+	+	+		+	+	+	?			+		
Galápagos rail	+	+	+	+		+			+										
Paint-billed crake		+				+													
Common gallinule	+	+	?		+	+													
Galápagos dove	u	u	+	+	u	u	?	+	+	?	+	?	+	+	+	?	?	+	
Dark-billed cuckoo	+	+	+	+	+	+						+							
Vermilion flycatcher	+	+	+	+	+	+	+		+		X	+		X					
Galápagos flycatcher	+	+	+	+	+	+	+	+	+	+	+	+		+	+				?
Galápagos martin	+	+	+	+	+	+		?		?	?	?		+			+		
Galápagos mockingbird	+	+	+	+			+		+	+	+		+	+	+	+	+		?
Hood mockingbird								+											
Chatham mockingbird					+														
Charles mockingbird						★													
Yellow warbler	+	+	+	+	+	+	+	+	+	+	+	+	+	+	+	?	?		?
Large ground finch	+	+	?	+	X	X	+		+	+	X	+	+	?	+	+	+	o	?
Medium ground finch	+	+	+	+	+	+	+	X	+	+	+	+		+	+			+	+
Small ground finch	+	+	+	+	+	+	+	+	+	+	+	+		+				o	+
Sharp-billed ground finch	X	X	+	+	X	X		+			+				+	+			
Cactus ground finch	+	+		+	+	+	+		+	+	+	X		+	+			+	+
Large cactus ground finch								+					+			+	+		
Large tree finch	+	+	+	+	?	+	+		+	?	?	?		+					
Medium tree finch						+													
Small tree finch	+	+	+	+	+	+			+	+	+	+		+					
Woodpecker finch	+	+	+	+	+	?			?		?	+		?					
Mangrove finch	+		+																
Vegetarian finch	+	+	+	+	+	+	+		+			?		+					
Warbler finch	+	+	+	+	+	+	+	+	+	+	+	+	+	+	+	+			?

Notes:

+   present as a breeding species on this island.
x   probably extinct as a breeding species.
u   uncommon on this land.
?   status uncertain on this land.
★   found on the satellite islets of Floreana.
o   rare breeding.
Source: Harris (1974) and Grant (1984b).

A young Galápagos hawk.

These birds have no native natural enemies (excepting other hawks) and thus need to fear no one. Their own prey includes a wide range of Galápagos animals including lizards, young iguanas, native and introduced rats, doves, mockingbirds, centipedes, grasshoppers, and various young seabirds. The females tend to take larger prey than the males (de Vries 1976). Their food spectrum varies from island to island, but on every island they are also major scavengers. They will feed on virtually any dead animal. I have seen them at the carcasses of sea lions, marine iguanas, seabirds and even fish (Plate 56). They seem to be particularly fond of goat meat. On many islands where hunters are trying to eradicate goats, hawks will follow the hunters until they have made a kill. After the kill, the hawks appear surprisingly rapidly. On one occasion, within five minutes of a goat being killed, thirteen birds arrived and sat within 5 m of myself and the carcass. It is not unusual for more than twenty birds to arrive at a kill and as many as forty hawks have been observed at a goat kill on Santiago.

The eyesight of these birds is phenomenal. I have seen a hawk take flight and fly directly for about 100 m to pounce on an unwary lava lizard. Mockingbirds will mob hawks in much the same way as small birds do elsewhere. On one occasion, I was delighted to see one vent its anger by jumping on a sitting hawk's head.

Barn owl.   Short-eared owl, Genovesa Island.

Owls

Two owl species, the short-eared owl and the barn owl, are found in the Galápagos. Both are cosmopolitan, but the Galápagos populations form endemic subspecies that are considerably smaller and darker than their continental relatives (de Groot 1983a). Compared to most owls, both of these silent fliers are relatively fearless. De Groot estimates that 8,500 pairs of barn owls and 9,000 pairs of short-eared owls are in the Galápagos.

Galápagos Barn Owl

The ghostly pale Galápagos barn owl (*Tyto punctissima*) is not often seen but is endemic to Santa Cruz, Isabela, Santiago, San Cristóbal and Fernandina islands. The Galápagos species is distinctly smaller and darker than the common barn owl (*T. alba*). It is wholly nocturnal and feeds mainly on small rodents and insects. The barn owl is generally found in drier and more sparsely vegetated areas than the short-eared. It nests mainly in cavities of rock outcrops, holes in trees and abandoned buildings, whereas the short-eared owl nests more under trees and shrubs. The barn owl is more fully nocturnal than the short-eared, leaving the roost around dusk and returning around dawn. Nesting occurs at all times of year, though it is more concentrated during the warm/wet season.

Short-eared Owl

Though it is no more abundant, the short-eared owl (*Asio flammeus*), which has a mottled dark brown plumage, is seen more often than the barn owl. It is markedly diurnal in its hunting habits and is frequently seen on Santa Cruz and Genovesa islands. It catches fewer insects and rodents than the barn owl but many more birds. When this species and the hawk occur on the same island, the owl becomes more crepuscular. On Santa Cruz, this owl is mainly active from 4 to 10 p.m., and from 5 to 10 a.m. (de Groot 1983). Where all three predators occur together, the short-eared owl is much rarer than the others. Many short-eared owls visit seabird colonies where they take nestlings. On Genovesa, one can almost always find one or two at the storm petrel colonies. Here the owls reach into the shallow nest cavities to prey on the birds. Both species of owl hunt primarily from a perch or from the air, but the short-eared is also known to hunt "on foot." This species is found on almost every major island except Wolf.

Galápagos Rail

Smaller than some of the finches, this tiny, endemic rail (*Lateralus spilonotus*) scurries about the damp highlands where it searches for insects and other arthropods amongst the soil and leaf litter (Franklin et al. 1979). Found above 500 m, it is secretive and not often stumbled upon even though it is common. It is remarkably tame. Only 15 cm long, it is all dark except for some chestnut markings on its upper parts and white spots on its wings. Like most small rails, it is loath to fly and behaves more like a small rodent than a bird. This rail is the only Galápagos land bird species that is known to breed during the cool/dry season and not during the warm/wet season.

Paint-billed Crake (Rail)

Slightly larger than the Galápagos rail, this species (*Neocrex erythrops*) is easily distinguished by its red legs and yellow-and-red bill. It has all dark plumage with no markings. It is a poor flier and is usually only seen when disturbed from cover. Common in northern parts of South America, it has only been recorded from the Galápagos since 1953 and breeds in an around the farmlands of Santa Cruz and Floreana, though it may occur elsewhere.

Common Gallinule (Moorhen)

This sooty bird with a yellow-tipped, bright red, bill is unmistakable. The moorhen (*Gallinula chloropus*) is one of the most widely distributed birds of the world, but, in the Galápagos, it is found only in a few areas of brackish water and some inland ponds on most of the larger islands. It is timid and uncommon and therefore not often seen by visitors.

Galápagos rail (left) and paint-billed crake.

Common gallinule.

When swimming, its head moves back and forth in a characteristic way, and it often flicks its tail showing the white patch under its rump. It feeds on plants and aquatic invertebrates.

Galápagos Dove

The Galápagos dove (*Zenaida galapagoensis*) is an attractive bird (Plate 58). The upper parts are mainly a reddish brown with some black and white on the wings. The neck and breast are tinged with pink and the feet are bright red. The eye is surrounded by a spectacular bright blue ring. Below and behind the eye is a small black-bordered creamy stripe. To complete this magnificent plumage, both sides of the neck have an iridescent bronze-green patch. The juvenile plumage is much duller.

This beautiful bird is found in the drier zones on most of the main islands and is abundant where introduced predators, especially cats, are rare. In the past, large numbers of these fearless birds were killed as a source of food for sailors, and many visitors have remarked on how easy these birds were to kill. This no longer occurs, as they are protected. As recently as 1965, Roger Tory Peterson (1967) reports that ten men on Santiago Island ate a total of 9,000 doves in three months. The doves have lost much of their tameness since the times when they were recorded as settling on the shoulders and head gear of buccaneers.

Though all populations in the archipelago belong to the same endemic species, the population on Darwin and Wolf islands are considerably larger

Dark-billed cuckoo.

and are classed as a separate subspecies. The nearest mainland relative is the spot-eared dove (*Zenaida auriculata*), which is common in the highlands of Ecuador.

The Galápagos dove has a more curved bill than most pigeons. The work of the Thalia and Peter Grant (1979) shows that it feeds principally on seeds picked from the ground, mainly from the *Opuntia* cactus. When available, the seeds of the abundant shrub, *Croton scouleri*, are eaten, and, at least on Genovesa, the doves' breeding is timed to coincide with the availability of these seeds. They will also take caterpillars (when abundant) and *Opuntia* flowers. Cactus pulp forms part of their diet and is probably their major source of water.

Active nests are found in all months, but the peak of breeding starts in the middle of the warm/wet season. They nest under rocks and will also use disused mockingbird nests. Usually , two eggs are laid. Courtship involves both display flights, in which wing beats are slower and exaggerated, and a curious bowing ceremony. In the bowing ceremony, the birds dip forward until the breast almost touches the ground and proceed to walk about each other. The males also make a deep, quiet cooing call when displaying. When threatened near the nest, these doves will try to lead the intruder away by feigning injury.

Dark-billed Cuckoo

This attractive bird (*Coccyzus melacoryphus*) is often glimpsed but rarely observed for long. It is secretive and shy of humans, probably because its relatively recent arrival from mainland South America. Unlike the European cuckoo, it is not parasitic, but it has the long tail which is so characteristic of the family. It is common on most of the larger central islands and is wide-spread in South America. Its upper parts are brown with the nape and crown grey. Underneath, it is rusty yellow. It has black "ear" patches and the tail feathers have white tips. Its low chuckling voice is often heard. It is mainly an insect eater.

The cuckoo starts breeding with the onset of the rainy season. It lays four or five eggs which hatch at different times after a short incubation period. The chicks grow rapidly, and are able to move about in the vegetation before they are capable of flight (Ervin 1989).

Smooth-billed Ani

The smooth-billed ani (*Crotophaga ani*) is a recently introduced species. It is common in the highland farm zone of Santa Cruz. It is an all black bird with a long tail. Its call is a whining whistle. It forages, usually in small groups, for insects which it finds in the foliage of bushes or on the open ground. Anis are often seen feeding around cattle—their spanish name *"garrapatero"* means "tick-eater." It is likely that anis were introduced by farmers to help alleviate tick problems on their cattle. Rosenburg et al. (1990) estimate about 4,800 anis on Santa Cruz and about 100 on Isabela. The diet of anis, grasshoppers, caterpillars and spiders, overlaps with native bird species. They also may disperse the seeds of introduced plants.

Vermilion Flycatcher

Amongst the drab browns, greys and greens of the Galápagos, nothing could be brighter than this flycatcher (Plate 60). The male vermillion flycatcher (*Pyrocephalus rubinus*) has a brilliant red crown and underparts that are set against black upper parts, tail and eye stripe. The female is dull by comparison but is bright yellow underneath and brown above with pale throat and chin (Plate 61). The young are like the female, but immature males become pink underneath before developing adult colours.

In the Galápagos, it is mainly a bird of the highlands, though it does occur at the coast on some islands such as Marchena. It is also found from the southwestern United States to Argentina in a wide range of habitats. It is the only bird you are likely to see both in the Galápagos and in Quito. Steadman (1988) regards the Galápagos populations as being distinct from the mainland species in several ways and classifies them as a separate species, *Pyrocephalus nanus*. The Galápagos individuals have shorter wings and tails, are lighter coloured, less vividly red, and sing a different song. He also suggests that the San Cristóbal population comprises yet another species, *Pyrocephalus dubius*.

It feeds in characteristic flycatcher fashion, mainly on insects. It will also forage on the ground and chase insects in the air. In the highlands of Santa Cruz, they are attracted to areas where people are walking, as a feast of insects is often stirred up by the moving feet. I have often seen them land on people and also use the top of a tortoises carapace as a perch.

The display flight of the male is beautiful to watch. He flies above his territory and proceeds to dip and rise in large swoops all the while singing

Galápagos flycatcher.

Galápagos martin.

and bill-snapping. The nest is made from mosses, lichens and liverworts and usually placed high in a tree. Breeding is during the warm/wet season when insects are most abundant.

Galápagos (Large-billed) Flycatcher

This endemic species (*Myiarchus magnirostris*) is larger than the vermilion flycatcher and has a broader bill. Its plumage is similar the that of the female vermilion flycatcher but its chin, throat and breast are grey and only the belly is sulphur-yellow. It is widespread on all the main islands where its habits are similar to those of the vermilion flycatcher. It is more confined to the arid lowlands than the vermilion flycatcher. The Galápagos flycatcher is inquisitive and fearless and often comes to investigate groups of visitors.

The Galápagos and vermilion flycatchers belong to the tyrant flycatcher family which occurs throughout the Americas. Though only two species are found in the Galápagos, over 150 are recorded from mainland Ecuador. Birdwatchers are fortunate in the Galápagos to have two clearly distinguishable species, as tyrant flycatchers are notoriously difficult to identify.

Galápagos Martin

The endemic Galápagos martin (*Progne modesta*) is the only resident member of the swallow family. Three other species have been recorded as

Galápagos mockingbird, Genovesa Island.

Nesting mockingbird, Santa Fé Island.

transients. The male is glossy black, while the female is a dark brown. Fledglings are brown and white, becoming dark brown, and are fed in mid-air by their parents after leaving the nest. They nest in small holes in cliffs, such as those found around Tagus Cove, which they line with grass and feathers. The Galápagos martin is very closely related to the southern martin, *Progne concolor*, and may, in fact, be part of the same species.

Though nowhere very common, Galápagos martins are found throughout the islands, especially near cliffs and ridges where they catch insects, carried by updrafts. They are particularly fond of caldera and crater rims and may usually be seen hawking above Sugar Loaf on Santiago Island and Daphne Major. The Galápagos martin cannot be mistaken for any other resident Galápagos bird because of its sharp-pointed wings and flight pattern. It alternates glides with brief periods of wing-flapping.

Mockingbirds

One of the first birds to greet you at almost every landing area will be the tame and inquisitive mockingbird. Though the population of each island is somewhat different from that of its neighbours, all are easily recognised as the only thrush-sized, long-tailed, grey and brown streaked land bird. Its call is strident and is a characteristic sound of the Arid zone.

Traditionally, the mockingbirds of the Galápagos are classed as four species in the genus *Nesomimus*. These are distinct from, but closely related

MONICA J. JACKSON

Hood mockingbirds scavenging on a beach. Right-hand bird is in a submissive posture.

to, the long-tailed mockingbird (*Mimus longicaudatus*) on the Ecuadorean mainland. The four commonly recognised species and six subspecies do not have overlapping ranges. One species, the Hood mockingbird (*N. macdonaldi*) (Plate 59), is endemic to Española and Gardner-near-Española; another, the Chatham mockingbird (*N. melanotis*), is on San Cristóbal; and a third, the Charles mockingbird (*N. trifasciatus*) is only on Champion and Gardner-near-Floreana. Historically, this third species also occurred on the main island of Floreana, but for unknown reasons, it has become extinct since Darwin's time (perhaps because of cat or rat predation). The total population of this species is estimated at between 250 and 300 individuals. The fourth species, the Galápagos mockingbird (*N. parvulus*), occurs as seven subspecies on the remaining major islands except for Pinzón, which lacks a mockingbird.

Though omnivorous, the mockingbirds are distinctly predatory when compared to mainland relatives. They will eat young finches, lava lizards, insects, centipedes, carrion, seabirds' eggs, and also the remains of feeds given by hawks and seabirds to their young. Their curved bill is somewhat larger than that of their mainland relatives and they will often run along the ground with their wings spread out for balance rather than fly. The Española species is particularly aggressive and predatory, having a larger bill than the other species. It is so fearless of humans that it has become the bane of scientists working on the island. It will steal any food that is not carefully guarded or stored. It also likes liquids.

The social structure of these birds is unusual and interesting, particularly on Genovesa and Española (Curry and Grant 1990). These birds often form cooperative breeding groups consisting of a breeding male and female plus the offspring of previous broods. These assist their parents in territory maintenance and raising the next brood. Outside the breeding season, large communal territories are formed, of two to twenty-four individuals on Genovesa and as many as forty on Española, with all members helping to defend and forage in the territory. Many groups contain more than one breeding female. At the contested borders of territories, confrontations can be exciting to watch. Members of each territorial group will line up opposite each other on either side of the imaginary line defending the border. Amidst much squawking and tail-flicking, birds will rush at their opposite numbers, occasionally fighting.

Unlike the North American mockingbird (*Mimus polyglottus*) these mockingbirds are not mimics though they make a variety of calls.

Yellow Warbler

This all-yellow warbler is familiar to many North Americans as it ranges from Alaska and Canada south to Peru. The male is usually brighter than the female and has chestnut-brown markings on the crown and breast. The immature is much greyer (often olive-yellow) and can be confused with the warbler finch which has no yellow in its plumage.

It occurs on most islands from shore to mountain top where it is ever active searching for insects with its probing bill. It seems never to stay still for more than a second. Though it finds most of its food by searching vegetation, it will hunt insects on the ground and also by flycatcher-like hawking.

Second only to the vermilion flycatcher in brightness and colour, the yellow warbler has the sweetest song of Galápagos birds. It nests during the warm/wet season in the canopy of trees and shrubs where it constructs an attractive nest of mosses, lichens and other vegetation.

Darwin's Finches

The undistinguished appearance of Darwin's finches belies their importance in the history of evolutionary theory. There are few textbooks of biology that fail to make some reference to these sparrow-like birds. As was mentioned earlier, thirteen species occur in the Galápagos and a fourteenth occurs on Cocos Island, (Costa Rica) some 650 km to the north-east in the Panama basin. Together, they form a unique subtribe, the Geospizini. The diversity of beak structure and feeding habits within this group is remarkable. The individual species feed in a variety of ways with each specialised in a particular way. Some eat seeds, some eat insects, some remove ticks from

Yellow warbler.

Finch nestlings and nest.

tortoises, some eat leaves, some eat flowers, some drink blood from seabirds, and there are two species that use twigs or cactus spines to extract insect larvae from holes in the dead branches of trees. Together, they fill the roles of seven different families of South American mainland birds.

These differences in ecology are reflected in the morphology of the various species, and especially in the shape of the beak. The range of beak shapes from that of the large ground finch to that of the warbler finch is phenomenal considering their relatively recent evolution from a common ancestor. The identification and feeding habits of the various species are summarised in Fig. 13.

Naturally enough, several researchers have sought close relatives for the Galápagos finch assemblage. No clear closest relative has emerged but there are several continental and Caribbean species that show resemblances to Darwin's finches. Those that have been proposed, such as the blue-black grassquit (*Volatinia* (*Geospiza*?) *jacarina*) and the St. Lucia black finch (*Melanospiza richardsoni*) are the subject of controversy. Biochemical work is in progress to clarify the relationships of the Galápagos finches.

All the Darwin's finches are about sparrow-sized (there is considerable variation between species) with mottled grey, brown, black or olivaceous plumage. Their wings are short and rounded as are their tails. The tail is often held slightly cocked giving them a wren-like appearance. Because of their superficially similar looks, they are often hard to identify. Do not despair, but heed Michael Harris's (1974) caution: "It is only a very wise man or a fool who thinks he is able to identify all the finches which he sees."

With most species, mature males are virtually all black (Plate 53), while females and immatures are a drab, mottled, grey-brown (Plate 55). The males of vegetarian and tree finches never become completely black, retaining only a black head, neck and upper breast. Warbler, mangrove, and woodpecker finches never have any black plumage and are mainly an olive

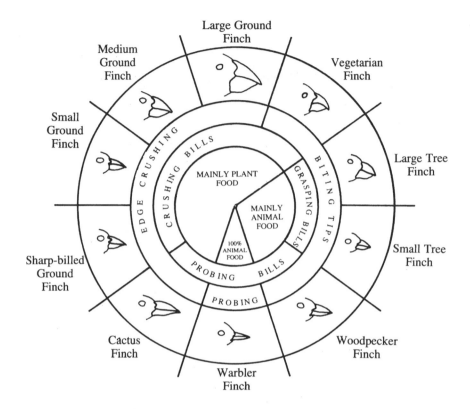

Figure 13: Feeding methods and identification of some Galápagos finches. (Based on Bowman 1961; Courtesy of University of California Press.)

colour. Bill colour is of little use in identifying Darwin's finches, as most species have a black bill during the breeding season and a yellowish one at other times.

The name "Darwin's finches" was not used by Darwin, nor by John Gould (1841) who first classified them. It was coined by P.R. Lowe in 1936 and later popularised by David Lack (1947; 1953), who made the first major ecological and evolutionary studies of these unique birds during his 1938 and 1939 visits. Our present understanding of their evolutionary history is in large part based upon his work and that of Robert Bowman and Peter Grant. Biologists differ in their opinions as to what factors were involved in the evolutionary process, as much of the evidence is equivocal. However, all agree that this group evolved from a common ancestor because they are all more similar to each other than to other species in Central or South America. Peter Grant (1981) has recently reviewed the evidence and hypotheses relating to the

Woodpecker finch using tool.   Male ground finch.

ecological aspects of the evolution of Darwin's finches. Interested readers should look to this for a more detailed discussion than is possible here. Figure 8 provides an overview of their evolutionary relationships. A hypothetical model of speciation for the Galápagos finches is also discussed in Chapter 3 (Fig. 9).

It has been difficult to distinguish between the effects that geographical and ecological isolation may have had on the evolution of these species. The consensus is that the colonisation and isolation of populations on previously vacant islands, new environmental conditions, ecological isolation and competition have all played key roles. Much recent research and controversy has focussed on the role of competition in the evolution of these finches. The importance of having a number of isolated islands for differentiation is indicated by the fact that Cocos Island has only one species, while the Galápagos have thirteen. A key difference between the evolution of Darwin's finches and that of other Galápagos vertebrates, such as tortoises, lava lizards, and mockingbirds, is that the various descendant species are now found together in various combinations even though they may have originally diverged in isolation.

Some feeding methods of the Darwin's finches deserve special mention. On Wolf Island, the population of sharp-billed ground finches has taken up a habit that has led to them being named "vampire finches" (Bowman and Billeb 1965). They frequently hop onto the backs or tails of masked and red-footed boobies and proceed to peck at the skin round the base of the feathers until they have drawn blood upon which they feed. The boobies do not seem to be overly disturbed by this, but they occasionally swipe at the tiresome finch. It is thought that this behaviour may have evolved from the finches eating parasitic flies which occur on these boobies. On other islands, three finch species, the small, medium and sharp-billed ground finches, remove ticks and mites from giant tortoises, land iguanas, and marine iguanas. These, together with certain mockingbirds, will respond to the

Cactus finch, South Plaza Island.

ritualised soliciting posture of the first two reptile species by removing these parasites (see Chapter 5). The ground finches will also kick seabird eggs against rocks, and, when a crack appears, open it and eat the contents (Grant pers. comm.)

Undoubtedly the most unusual and striking feeding behaviour is shown by the woodpecker (also known as the tool-using) and mangrove finches. Both species feed mainly on insects, most of which are caught by searching vegetation in a woodpecker-like manner. They also eat some plant material. Frequently, though, an individual will discover a hidden insect larva or grub and will then search around for a suitable tool such as a cactus spine or slender twig. It then uses this to coax or to pry the grub out of its hole. Tool-using is uncommon in animals. They will also occasionally modify unsatisfactory tools and sometimes will retain a "good" tool and carry it from tree to tree.

Darwin's finches are not noted for the brilliance of their calls or songs; however, Robert Bowman (1979;1983) has discovered that these too vary from island to island and from habitat to habitat. Birds tend to develop song dialects that transmit best in their respective environments. Birds in brush or dense forest have songs differing in type from those that live in open environments. This effect of environment on the optimal song type has probably helped maintain interspecific barriers between closely related species.

Though the various finch species have beaks adapted to certain ranges of food types, most species are generalised feeders. During severe dry seasons, food availability is reduced, and at these times the dietary preferences of the various species diverge most. Natural selection will be most severe during these times, and it is then that specialisation on a food resource becomes of prime value. This has been clearly demonstrated on both Genovesa and Daphne Major by Peter Grant's team (Grant 1986, Grant and Grant 1989).

The finches usually begin their reproductive cycle after the first heavy

Large ground finch, Genovesa Island.   Sharp-billed ground finch, Genovesa Island.

rains of the wet season. The male establishes a territory, proclaimed by song and fighting, and builds one, or several, dome-shaped nests with a small round side entrance and he displays to females on or by the nest. After the female has chosen a mate, she will either select one of the male's nests or the pair will work together on yet another nest. The nest is made from twigs, grass, pieces of bark, lichen, feathers and other materials. Nests vary in size from about the size of a clenched fist (warbler finch) to the size of a small soccer ball (large ground finch). Nests are surprisingly similar in construction from one species to another, indicating the close relationship of the species.

The female is fed by the male before laying and during incubation. Two to five eggs are laid which are incubated for twelve days before hatching. Both parents feed the young for 10 to 14 days with soft seeds, greens, insect larvae and berries. A high standard of nest hygiene is maintained. The faecal sacs produced by the nestlings are taken out by the parents and disposed of at some distance from the nest. The male usually continues to feed the fledglings for about two weeks, while the female will often start another brood with another male if conditions are still favourable. Occasionally, males from previous breeding attempts are known to help in the raising of a second brood even though they are not the parents of the new nestlings.

Native Mammals

Only six species of mammals can be considered as native to the islands. The two weeks or so that it would take for a raft to drift out to the Galápagos from the mainland is too long for most mammals to survive. The tropical sun and lack of food and water for the 1,000 km journey has screened out most of the mammal order which has been so successful elsewhere. The two bat species certainly arrived by air, probably in the same way as the native land birds, while the rice rats must have rafted to the islands. The sea lion and fur seal arrived by swimming.

Oceanic islands are typically lacking in mammals and the Galápagos are no exception. The absence of large mammalian predators probably accounts for the fearlessness of the other native fauna toward humans. Some of the land birds, in particular the mockingbirds, some ground finches, and the rail are more terrestrial in their habits than most birds and seem to have fitted partly into the niches that would have been occupied by small mammals under continental conditions.

Two species of bat and two species of rice rat occur, and there are two species from the sea lion family in the islands.

Sea Lions and Fur Seals

Sea lions and fur seals both belong to the Otaridae, or eared seal family. Unlike true seals (Phocidae) the sea lions have small but visible ears and use their front flippers for swimming. They also have enough strength in their flippers to support the front part of their body in the characteristic sea lion pose. True seals use their hind flippers for propulsion and their front flippers seem almost useless on land.

Galápagos Sea Lion

No animal captivates the attention of visitors to the Galápagos as much as the sea lion. The largest animal in the islands, these creatures seem almost

Sea lions resting on beach, Española Island.

human in so many ways. They are inquisitive and playful, yet aggressive at times. They are attractive and endearing, but also lazy as they lie on the beaches soaking up the sun and replenishing their oxygen (Plate 62). Youngsters, and occasionally adults, will body surf when the waves are right. They always seem to be playing with something, whether with each other, marine iguanas, penguins, red crabs, or just a piece of seaweed. After seeing these animals in their natural environment, it is no surprise that their Californian cousin is the favourite of circuses and sea aquariums.

The Galápagos sea lion has its origins in the northern hemisphere. It is a subspecies (*wollebacki*) of the Californian sea lion (*Zalophus californianus*) from which it differs mainly in its smaller size. Despite being smaller than its Californian relatives, a full-grown male is a magnificent creature, weighing up to 250 kg. The males differ from the more graceful females (Plate 63) in being much larger, having a characteristic "bump" on the forehead, and having a massive, thick, neck. When wet, both sexes are dark brown, but when thoroughly dry, the fur is often a creamy brown.

Sea lions are common in the islands where there are sandy beaches and gentle rocky shores. It is estimated that there are about 50,000 individuals. Their food is mainly fish for which they will often make extended trips away from the colony. Little is known about their life at sea, but on land they form colonies at their hauling-out areas. Each colony, or harem, is composed of a dominant bull and from a few to thirty cows with their young. Though usually referred to as harems, sea lion colonies are not true harems because

STEPHEN HERRERO

Female sea lion suckling pup, Fernandina Island.

females are free to wander from one territory to another. The male's harem is really only a piece of land on which females prefer to lie. The dominant bull has a stretch of coastline that he jealously defends against all other adult males. He spends much of his day swimming from one border of his territory to the other. While patrolling his territory he frequently rears his head out of the water to utter a series of barks. These barks are also made underwater and indicate his territorial ownership.

Territories are frequently challenged and fights often ensue. On land and in the shallows, these start by posturing and barking in an attempt to test each other's courage. If one or other opponent is not scared off, they will start pushing each other and biting at the opponent's neck. The males' neck is thick and strong to protect vital organs, but blood is often drawn. Scars are common amongst male sea lions. Losers are chased well away from the territory. In the water, these chases are dramatic with much splashing and porpoising.

Because there are many males without harems, there is always an excess of bachelor males. Bachelor males are not tolerated near females and, when not trying to gain themselves a harem, these surplus males often congregate fairly peaceably in "bachelor colonies." Such colonies are usually in less favourable areas of coastline. One of these is found atop the cliffs of South Plaza Island. Territorial males cannot feed while defending a territory and when they become tired and weakened they will be ousted by a fresh bull. Territory tenure varies from a few days to as much as three months.

Bull sea lion, South Plaza Island.

Females give birth to a single pup which is suckled for one to three years. In any one colony, pupping occurs mainly at one time of year, but this varies by as much as three months from one part of the archipelago to another, being earlier on Fernandina than on Española. It is usually timed to coincide with the cool/dry season. Females become receptive or in "heat" about three weeks after giving birth and it is at this peak time that territories are most severely contested. Mating usually occurs in shallow water or on land where the male pins the female down for copulation. The females solicits the male's attention and, if not satisfied with the male from her colony, she will seek elsewhere. Sea lions, in common with many other pinnipeds, keep their breeding to an annual cycle but only have a nine-month gestation period. They get around this by a strategy called "delayed implantation." The fertilised egg only divides a few times before it stops developing. The wall of the uterus then does not accept the embryo until two months later (implantation is delayed) when development resumes normally. Sea lions can raise a pup each year and it is common to see two different sized pups suckling from one female.

Before giving birth, the female moves a short distance from the colony. The precocious pup is born head first and quite quickly. I was once privileged to watch one of these births on North Seymour. For the first few moments we thought that the pup was still-born but suddenly, when the head and shoulders were almost out and the flies were settling, the little pup gave a great shake, opened its eyes and gave a bleat. It quickly found itself on

Young sea lions playing in a dinghy.

Sea lion showing wet and dry fur.

the sand where it continued to bleat. The afterbirth follows after about an hour. It is much prized by scavengers, and once the mother and pup have moved away, hawks, mockingbirds, and frigatebirds will arrive to feed on it. The mother stays with the pup for the first four or five days of its life when the two get to know each other intimately by sound and smell. The newborn pup receives little or no help in finding its mother's teats but once found, the young one suckles the very rich milk and starts to grow rapidly. After about a week, the female resumes fishing. About a month later, the pups lose their first "puppy" fur and gain a dark coat which lasts about another five months.

After the first month, the pups usually congregate in "nurseries" while the parents are away. Often a single adult female watches over the fold. The young ones are not allowed to play in deep water and are restricted to the shallow pools. Sea lions are too fearful of sharks to allow the young out of the safety of their care. The territorial bull seems paternalistic, shepherding pups and juveniles within a safe distance of the beach. If a shark should come near, he will call loudly to send his "family" to safety on land. I have seen bulls sally out to chase fair-sized sharks away. The pups begin to fish for themselves after about five months, gradually becoming independent of their mothers' milk (Bonner 1984).

Female sea lions become sexually mature at about five years and may live to about twenty. Males may become mature a little earlier but do not hold territories until they are older. Their lifespan is also less. Recently, a virus disease, called "sea lion pox," has been affecting populations of Galápagos sea lions. The virus is thought to be transmitted by mosquitoes to open wounds. It causes lumps and paralysis and the animal dies of starvation. During my stay in the islands, the Española Island populations were severely hit by the disease and we regularly saw their carcasses. There is evidence that some degree of resistance has developed within the species.

Despite their tameness and curiosity, sea lions, especially males, can be unpredictably aggressive to humans. I have known a few people to receive nasty bites for not respecting their privacy. Be warned!

Fur seal, James Bay, Santiago Island.

Galápagos Fur Seal

Galápagos fur seals are less often seen than the sea lions, even though their total populations are similar. This is because fur seals prefer rockier, steeper, more rugged shores with plenty of shade. The Galápagos fur seal (*Arctocephalus galapagoensis*) is closely related to the southern fur seal (*A. australis*) which is distributed in cool waters from Brazil around to southern Peru and some Antarctic islands. It is less tolerant of heat than the sea lion and thus prefers cooler waters and shade. Despite their confusing name, fur seals are really a type of sea lion.

Like the sea lion, the Galápagos fur seal is smaller than its nearest relatives. Visitors often find them difficult to distinguish from sea lions, but there are many minor differences that aid identification. They are smaller in overall size and the head is broader and shorter. The nose is almost pointed. The head resembles that of a bear; hence, their generic name; *Arcto* = bear, –*cephalus* = head. Their ears stick out more and the front flippers are relatively larger (they are better climbers). The eyes are also bigger giving them a sad expression. Their voices are different from those of the sea lions, being hoarse and more guttural, but they are less often used. The major difference is in their coat. This is much thicker and denser in the fur seal, consisting of two layers: an outer one of long hairs and an inner one of short dense fur. This coat is a magnificent insulator, enabling their relatives to live in near-freezing water, but it is somewhat of a liability in the Galápagos

Visitor swimming with a fur seal, James Bay, Santiago Island.

because of the risk of overheating. Their coat was much prized by furriers, and during the 1800s tens of thousands were taken. They were hunted almost to extinction. Benjamin Morrell reported that he took some 5,000 skins aboard his ship in only two months. Now protected from hunting, they are making a remarkable comeback, and grace many Galápagos shores. Good places to see them are at the fur seal grottos at James Bay, Santiago, and in Darwin Bay, Genovesa.

Fur seals eat fish and squid, leaving the colony at night to hunt. Fritz Trillmich (1984b) has spent several years studying the behaviour of these animals and has discovered that they have a lunar periodicity to their hunting trips. Many more fur seals remain ashore during the full moon than during the new moon. This may be because they are more visible to sharks when the moon is bright and also because their prey tends to move deeper during full moons. Shark attacks on animals of all ages are a regular phenomenon.

The social behaviour and breeding of fur seals is similar to that of sea lions. On Fernandina, the breeding season extends from August to November, with a peak of births in the first week of October (Bonner 1984). Breeding bulls establish large territories on shore that they defend against intruders. During territory tenure, which may last up to fifty-one days, bulls do not feed, but may enter the water at mid-day to cool off. This is in contrast to the sea lion that defends his territory primarily from the water.

Female fur seals give birth soon after coming ashore and remain with their pups for about a week before leaving to feed again. This time corresponds to the beginning of oestrus ("heat"). Females are mated at this time, mostly on land. Pups will suckle for two to three years. They moult into the yearling coat after about six months and after a year begin to feed independently, though still relying on their mothers' milk. Though all females mate right after giving birth, only about 15 per cent give birth the following year if they are still suckling a pup. Of those without dependent young, about 70 per cent give birth. If a yearling sibling is still suckling, the newborn pup almost always dies in the first month, despite being defended by its mother; if the older sibling is a two-year-old, the newborn pup's chances of survival are about 50 per cent. This means that a female can, at best only raise one pup every two years.

Rice Rats

Only two species (possibly three) now remain of what once was a remarkable assemblage of seven rice rat species: *Oryzomys bauri* of Santa Fé, and *Nesoryzomys narboroughii* of Fernandina. The five other species have become extinct since human colonisation of the islands. It seems that rice rats cannot coexist with black(ship) rats (*Rattus rattus*). The black rat is established on many islands, and, where it occurs, no endemic rodents survive. It is not known why these endemic rats became extinct, but it seems likely that competition and possibly a viral disease transmitted by black rats were important factors. It appears that rice rat species on the Galápagos originated form two separate colonisation events. *Nesoryzomys* on Fernandina has diverged sufficiently from mainland *Oryzomys* to be classed as a different genus. The native rats of the Galápagos hold the world record for sea crossings by terrestrial mammals (Thornton 1971).

On Santa Fé, *O. bauri* is mainly vegetarian, eating seeds and vegetation and is common in the arid scrub of that island. It is a fearless creature, coming out to feed at dusk and during the night. Scientists working on Santa Fé must protect their food carefully from this adventurous species. Breeding is restricted to the warm/wet season when four young may be raised. Clark (1984) points out that the San Cristóbal rice rat (*O. galapagoensis*) and the Santa Fé species may have been populations of the same species, but this cannot be determined as the former "species" is now extinct. The existence of a second species, *Nesoryzomys fernandinae*, has recently been discovered on Fernandina (Clark 1984, Adsersen 1987); however, not much is known about this species as it has only been found in owl pellets.

A third genus of rat is known to have lived in the Galápagos. *Megaoryzomys curiori* was a very large rat which has only been found as subfossil remains that are more than 100,000 years old. It is now extinct.

Bats

Two species are known from the islands: the possibly endemic *Lasiurus brachyotis*, and the widespread hoary bat *Lasiurus cinereus* and their life cycles are poorly known. *Lasiurus cinereus* is the most widespread bat from North America and is a well-known migrant. These bats are insect eaters and roost singly or in small numbers in trees. Mangroves appear to be favoured daytime roosts, as are other woody shrubs. Though few visitors will have the opportunity to see either of these bats, the best chance will be in Academy Bay near street lights.

A recent study by Gary McCracken has shown that *L. brachyotis* is locally abundant on Santa Cruz and San Cristóbal. It is found in both the highlands and the lowlands and may make seasonal migrations between these two areas. *L. cinereus* is found on Santa Cruz, San Cristóbal, Isabela, Santiago, and Floreana. The two species have different "calls" and are easily distinguished with a bat detector. *L. brachyotis* seems to forage close to the ground, while *L. cinereus* forages higher (above 8 m).

The hoary bat is attractively coloured. Its fur is mainly light brown with heavily frosted white tips and a buff throat. As well as being a widespread American species, it is also the only species found in the Hawaiian Islands. *L. brachyotis* is thought to be most closely related to the red bat (*L. borealis*) of the South American mainland (Clark 1984).

Dolphins and Whales

During the nineteenth century, the Galápagos Islands were a centre of whaling activity in the Pacific. Many whales were taken, but fortunately this has stopped. Whales are seen occasionally as they pass through the archipelago, but dolphins are regularly seen as they spend much time in and around the islands.

The dolphins, porpoises, and whales together form the cetaceans, which are an order of totally aquatic mammals. Unlike sharks and other fish, but like other mammals, they are warm-blooded and breathe air. The young develop within the body of the mother and are suckled until they become independent. Most land mammals, the seals, and sea lions are clothed with hair or fur, but the cetaceans have little or virtually no hair. Most cetaceans have a fatty layer of blubber which serves as an energy reserve for migrations and may sometimes serve to insulate their bodies against the cold of the water. It is this blubber that originally made whales valuable economically as it can be rendered down to make fine "whale-oil."

The cetaceans are divided into two major groups according to whether they have baleen or teeth. The baleen whales comprise most of the larger whales including the blue, finback, sei, humpback, Bryde's, and minke

Humpback whale seen near Baltra Island.

whales, which are seen in Galápagos waters. These whales are all plankton feeders, sieving out shrimps, sardines and other small marine creatures from the water using their baleen plates. These plates are large, heavily fringed, triangular pieces of "whalebone" through which water is pushed and in which plankton creatures are caught. This feeding method is somewhat similar to that of the flamingo. Though very large, most whales are difficult to identify at sea without experience and a comprehensive handbook. The world's largest animal, the blue whale, is occasionally reported from Galápagos waters.

Perhaps the most easily distinguished of the whales seen in the Galápagos is the humpback (*Megaptera novaeangliae*). This species has a characteristic angled back (hence its name), and is also prone to "spy-hopping" and "breaching." When spy-hopping, the whale raises its head vertically out of the water and twists around, seemingly to have a good look around. I have seen these whales breaching in the Galápagos, north of Isabela, and it was a tremendous sight. The huge creature succeeded in flinging its entire 30 tonne body out of the water to drop down with a resounding smack and an enormous splash. This behaviour is thought to have some territorial significance.

The toothed whales are more diverse and include the large sperm whale (or cachalot) (*Physeter macrocephalus*), the orca (or killer whale) (*Orcinus orca*), the false killer whales (*Pseudorca crassidens*), the short-finned pilot whale (*Globicephala macrorhynchus*) and several dolphins. All the above are

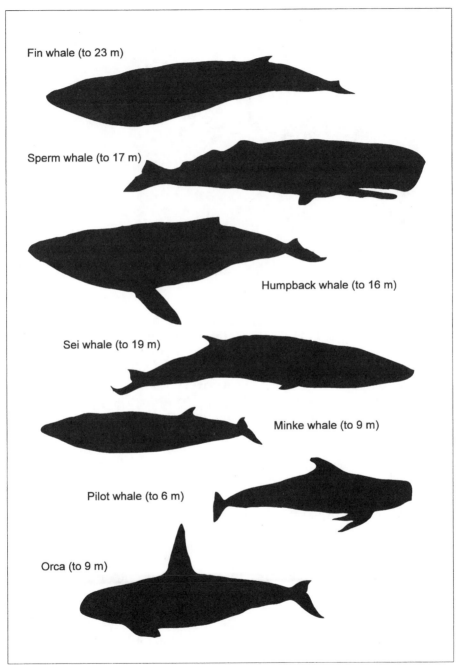

Fin whale (to 23 m)

Sperm whale (to 17 m)

Humpback whale (to 16 m)

Sei whale (to 19 m)

Minke whale (to 9 m)

Pilot whale (to 6 m)

Orca (to 9 m)

Figure 14: Some whales seen in the Galápagos.

Bottle-nosed dolphin.

recorded quite regularly in Galápagos waters. The common names "dolphin" and "porpoise" are confusing as they are frequently used interchange-
ably by different people. "Dolphin" is usually used to refer to the long-snouted
or beaked species, while "porpoise" is used for the blunt-nosed ones. Two
species of dolphin are frequently seen while touring the islands. These
are the bottle-nosed dolphin (*Tursiops truncatus*) and the common
(white-bellied) dolphin (*Delphinus delphis*). The bottle-nosed dolphin is
the one most likely to be seen swimming in front of boats, riding the bow
wave. By day or by night, from two to a dozen or more of these graceful
creatures may come to the bow and spend as much as half an hour "piloting"
the boat. This is especially spectacular on dark nights when the bioluminescence outlines their bodies and makes them glow as they race through the
water. As they swim close to the boat you may hear their high-pitched
squeaking.

The common dolphin is less likely to come to your ship, but, when seen,
it is often in schools of over one hundred individuals. It is smaller and has
more white on its underparts than the bottle-nosed dolphin.

The orca is often seen in small groups. These whales are easily distinguished by their black and white colouration, their large size (to 9 m), and the
enormous back fin of the male (1.8 m high). The orca is a ferocious predator
and will eat sea lions, fur seals, penguins, dolphins, and other large animals.
Orcas, dolphins, and other cetaceans are thought to be highly intelligent and
are known to use a type of sonar to echolocate their prey and to communi-
cate. Very little is known about their life in the open sea.

The presence of sperm whales around the Galápagos Islands was one of the most important factors in the exploitation and degradation of the islands (Whitehead 1985). During the nineteenth century whalers from many countries came to the "Galápagos Grounds" in search of sperm whales and their oil (spermaceti). Hunting was so intense that by the middle of the century, the Galápagos were termed "dry cruising" (not enough whales) and the whalers went there no more. One of the prime regions for whaling was the area west of Isabela where the Cromwell current upwells. This is still one of the best areas for seeing whales, though I have seen them in most parts of the archipelago.

Hal Whitehead and his colleagues have been studying the Galápagos' sperm whales for several years since 1985 to learn more about their social behaviour. Unlike the whalers before him he used acoustic and photographic research techniques to listen to and identify the whales. He estimates that there are approximately two hundred sperm whales in the area at any time which are part of a larger population of 2,600 to 5,300 individuals. The whales often swim in groups of 20 to 25 individuals and may form a several kilometre long rank moving at 2.5 to 3.0 knots for 24 hours or more as they hunt for squid. They also form slow moving "social" clusters. These whales may dive to over 400 m and begin echolocating (with clicks) at depths of 150 to 300 m. When feeding they will dive for about 40 minutes followed by ten minutes at the surface. In April of 1985, Whitehead reported an interesting "skirmish" with what is probably the only non-human predator of the sperm whales—a group of orcas. For two hours and 45 minutes, orcas attacked a huddled group of sperm whales, without apparently inflicting any serious injury. After the attack, the sperm whales fled silently, in a compact group for at least five and one half hours at 10 km/hr.

Terrestrial Invertebrates 10

> I took great pains in collecting the insects [of the Galápagos], but, excepting
> Tierra del Fuego, I never saw in this respect so poor a country. . . . the insects,
> for a tropical region, are of very small size and dull colours. (Darwin 1845)

The Galápagos have relatively few species of terrestrial invertebrates, albeit far too many for all to be individually mentioned in this book. This poverty of species is partly because of the archipelago's isolation, small size and the problems of colonisation, and partly because most of the land area is dry and inhospitable. The greatest diversity of invertebrates is found in the humid zones of the higher islands.

Stewart Peck (in press) reports that there are some 1,995 species of terrestrial (and freshwater) invertebrates in the Galápagos, of which 1,061 (53%) are endemic. This may seem like a large number of species, but it pales in comparison to the numbers which would be found in a comparable area of mainland Ecuador. There have been 1.8 million species of animals and plants described by scientists, and, of these, 55 per cent are insects!

In contrast to vertebrate species, relatively little research has been done on the invertebrates. Many new species await discovery and description. Despite the paucity of species, and the lack of thorough study, there is a fair body of knowledge about some species. The presence of only a few common species makes looking at invertebrates a much less daunting prospect for the non-specialist. The terrestrial invertebrates that the visitor is likely to see belong to the molluscs (snails) and arthropods (spiders, scorpions, ticks, mites, centipedes, and insects). Many of these will be described or discussed in the following pages.

Most of the species found in the Galápagos have their origins in the dry coastal parts of South and Central America. The main methods of dispersal to the islands are likely to have been rafting and transport as aerial plankton. As with other groups of plants and animals, some species have a world-wide distribution and some are endemic.

Of the larger moths, which are a well-studied group, about 30 per cent are endemic species and a further 18 per cent are endemic subspecies. These proportions correspond well with those found with the plants (40–50% total endemics). This should not surprise us, as many insects are closely tied to their plant hosts.

The taxonomic disharmony that was found to occur with the plants and the vertebrates also holds true for the invertebrates. This is yet further evidence that the islands have never been connected to the South American continent. This disharmony again arises from the problems of dispersal to and establishment on the islands. For example, weevils, a group of typically plant eating beetles, are represented by remarkably few species. Colonisation by rafting or aerial transport would not favour species with narrow tolerances of light, humidity, or temperature, to reach the archipelago. The low diversity of invertebrate types is undoubtedly a result of the isolation of the islands and their relatively small sizes. The relatively smaller size of insects in the Galápagos may be related to the short growing season. Most insects are closely tied to their host-plants and must complete their life cycles while the plants are rapidly growing. The rainy seasons in the Galápagos are both short and unpredictable. It seems reasonable to suppose that smaller individuals are at a selective advantage. Most Galápagos habitats are well-lit and open. In these conditions, it is probably advantageous for insects to be dull-coloured and cryptic to avoid predation by foraging birds and lizards.

Many Galápagos insects have reduced flying abilities when compared to mainland relatives. For smaller organisms, whose flying power is usually not stronger than the wind, it may be disadvantageous, once settled on an island, to be a regular flyer as the chances of being carried out to sea are greater. Thus, many insects that do not need to fly as a regular part of their life-cycle may be expected to have reduced wings or to have lost them altogether. This has been found to be the case for numerous beetle species, certain grasshoppers, and some cockroaches. This loss of dispersal ability is analogous to that which has occurred with birds, such as the flightless cormorant, and certain plants, such as members of the genus *Scalesia*.

Since I wrote the first edition, a great deal of work has been done on the Galápagos invertebrates by Stewart Peck of Carleton University (see Bibliography). As a result of this work, I have had to revise many of the species counts (insects: 1,000 to 1,600; beetles: 200 to 411) and to completely change some statements. In the first edition of this book, I stated that "cryptozoic insects are virtually absent." Cryptozoic arthropods are those that live hidden lives in spaces at or beneath the earth's surface. Peck (1990) reports fifty-six eyeless and reduced-eyed species alone. This example illustrates the constantly changing (or evolving!) nature of scientific information in the

Table 14: Notable "Species Swarms"

Group	Number of species or subspecies
Vertebrates	
Darwin's finches	13
Giant tortoises	11 subspecies
Invertebrates	
Bulimulus (*Naesiotes*) (land snails)	65
Insects	
Dagbertia (mirid bugs)	9
Philotis (issid plant bugs)	16
Nesodyne (delphacid plant hoppers)	7
Euxesta (otitid flies)	8
Nocticanace (canaceid flies)	8
Beetles	
Pterostichus (carabids)	11
Physorinus (elaterids)	7
Stomion (tenebrionids)	9
Ammophorus (tenebrionids)	12
Pedoneces (tenebrionids)	16
Plantomorus (weevils)	6
Pseudopentarthrum (weevils)	6
Plants	
Scalesia (composites)	20
Opuntia (cactus)	14

These species or subspecies groups are each thought to have arisen from a single ancestral colonisation.
Source: Peck (1990).

Galápagos. Species numbers in this book represent "current" knowledge and are most certainly not the "last word."

The formation of species swarms, groups of species each of which has evolved on different islands or habitats from a single ancestral species, has occurred for some invertebrate species in much the same way as with the giant tortoises, Darwin's finches and *Scalesia* plants (see Table 14). Flightless grasshoppers, of the endemic genus *Halmenus*, have formed four species in the archipelago. Three of the most similar species occur on four of the central islands and the fourth, and most distinct, occurs on Wenman. Two endemic species of the ant *Camponotus* occur together on most islands; however, the population of each species on the various islands are distinctly different from one another. Seven beetle genera have differentiated into six species or more. Recent research has shown that the marine pond-skater, *Halobates robustus*, has markedly different characteristics on the various islands. There are over sixty endemic species of land snails in the genus *Bulimulus*; some are endemic to single islands, while others are endemic to certain zones of a group of islands. These small snails are probably the most dramatic example of archipelago speciation to be found in the Galápagos, but more examples are likely to be found when the invertebrate fauna is better known.

It is unfortunate, scientifically at least, that many invertebrates are small enough to be easily and unwittingly carried from one island to another by humans. This human-caused inter-island transport can destroy the genetic integrity of island populations, thus reducing their value for research. Some introduced invertebrates, such as fire ants, can cause havoc with natural invertebrate populations in just the same way as goats and dogs destroy native reptiles. Night-flying insects, especially moths, are attracted to the riding and cabin lights of boats where they may roost and be carried to another island.

Land Snails—Molluscs

There are many species of small land snails in the Galápagos, but these are mainly inconspicuous. Most species hide on the undersides of leaves or in cracks and crevices where they are less likely to be found by predators and where humidity is higher. Snails are found throughout the archipelago in various zones where they eat vegetation. Snails can only be active when humidity is relatively high, so many Galápagos species aestivate (a kind of hibernation) during the cool/dry season. They do so by attaching themselves to the substrate in a sheltered spot with a thick mucus layer and then secreting further mucus membranes or shell-like material to create a hermetic seal. They can thus survive long periods of drought in a state of suspended animation. These species were probably brought to the islands in this state attached to rafts or on bird's legs.

Snails are preyed upon by many Galápagos animals including ants, ground beetles, tiger beetles, and mockingbirds. The latter often leave piles of empty shells in spots where they break them open.

The speciation of snails in the genus *Bulimulus* is still poorly understood. The variations in shell type from island to island and between zones is dramatic, there being over sixty species. On Santa Cruz alone, there are twenty-four species and the distribution of these species follows a zonation pattern with altitude that parallels the zonation of plants (Coppois 1984).

Arthropods

The arthropods are the most varied animal phylum. In this group are included insects, spiders, ticks, centipedes and many marine creatures such as crayfish, crabs and barnacles. All these groups share the characteristics of a fairly hard external skeleton and jointed limbs and other organs. The insects are the most abundant and best known of the invertebrates, accounting for about three-quarters of all known animal species. Arthropods are an important group, despite their small size. One of their more than a million species can be found feeding on just about every type of plant or animal.

Insects and other arthropods are marvels of nature's design and are really worth a closer look. Even though many of them are "creepy crawlies" most of them are totally harmless. It is impossible to do justice to arthropods as a group in this book as the diversity of function and adaptation is so wide. Because of lack of space and ecological knowledge, only a few of the more prominent and interesting species and groups are discussed.

An unusual group of arthropods are those with little or no vision. Stewart Peck reports fifty-six species of arthropods which are either eyeless or have reduced eyes. These are animals which live in soil litter, caves and ground water.

Insects

The Galápagos insect fauna is both poor in variety and in numbers. Nevertheless, there are about 1,600 species of insect in the Galápagos. Unlike mainland Ecuador, where insects are a conspicuous component of forest life, most Galápagos insects must be searched for and few are attractive. The problems of dispersal and suitable habitat have prevented some orders of insects from becoming established. These include stick insects (Phasmida), mayflies (Ephemeroptera),stoneflies (Plecoptera) and caddisflies (Trichoptera). The arid, almost desert-like, climate of much of the archipelago's land area provides an inhospitable environment for most insect species. It is therefore not surprising that most Galápagos insects are nocturnal to avoid the desiccating sun and spend the daylight hours hidden in dark humid places. This in part explains why most are hard to find and why few are colourful.

Insects, like other arthropods, have hard external skeletons made of chitin. This means that, to be able to grow, insects must moult their entire "skin." Most insect species pass through many moults before reaching adult size and maturity. Many spend more time as immatures than they do as adults. Some of the more highly evolved insect groups have dramatically different adult and immature stages. It is hard to believe that a maggot and

Male carpenter bee.   Female carpenter bee.

a fly, a caterpillar and a butterfly, a grub and a beetle, each belong to the same species, but this is the way of life for the flies, beetles, butterflies, moths, ants, wasps, and bees. It is these groups that have "inherited the earth." Beetles alone account for over a third of the world's known animal species. It was this fact that prompted the eminent British scientist, T.S. Huxley, to suggest that the creator must have had "an inordinate fondness for beetles."

Though poor in species number, the Galápagos insect fauna is often abundant, especially during the warm/wet season. Insects have adapted in many ways to the harsh Galápagos environment.

In this brief overview of the insect class (based in part on notes by Yael Lubin), only a few species from some of the major orders have been mentioned. In addition to these are some dragonflies (Odonata), cockroaches (Blattaria), earwigs (Dermaptera), termites (Isoptera), fleas (Siphonaptera), bird lice (Mallophaga), sucking lice (Anoplura), and booklice (Psocoptera). A more detailed account of the insect life of the Galápagos may be found in Norman Hickin's (1979) *Animal Life of the Galápagos*.

Beetles—Coleoptera

Some 411 beetle species from 238 genera and 59 families are found in the Galápagos (Peck, in press). Most of these are small and inconspicuous. The beetle species are 24% native, 67% endemic and 9% introduced. Two hundred and fifty seven successful colonizations are thought to be responsible for 335 native and endemic species (Peck and Peck 1990). This may seem like many colonizations, but, averaged over 3 million years, this would only be one every 11,700 years! Some of the more noticeable species are:

Stenodontes molarius—A large beetle with long antennae and powerful jaws. The larva of this species bores in wood and causes damage to trees. The grubs of longhorn beetles are an important food source for the tool-using woodpecker finch.

Calosoma spp.—These ground beetles are shiny green-black with long legs. They are fast runners and active predators. There are three species in the Galápagos, two of which are flightless.

Trox suberosus—One of the scarab family. Its larvae live in the eggs of reptiles, especially the green sea turtle, causing considerable mortality in the nests. Other members of this family breed in dung, in particular that of giant tortoises.

Gersteckeria sp.—A cactus eating weevil about 0.6 cm long. It is dark brown with a long, curved "snout" and some creamy spots. The adults and young feed on cactus pads.

Cincindela spp.—Two species of tiger beetle are known. These fast running predators have similar habits to the Calosoma beetles.

Ants, Bees and Wasps—Hymenoptera

There are about twenty native ant species, a few wasps and only one bee in the Galápagos. Some of these are:

Carpenter ants; *Camponotus spp.*—These yellow-brown ants bore galleries in wood for their nests.

Little fire ant; *Wasmannia auropunctata*—This species is a recent introduction and a serious pest. Only 2 mm long, it has a vicious bite and sometimes is so abundant that farmers have to leave their fruit and coffee unpicked. It also preys on and out-competes other native ant species. Great care should be taken not to transport this species to islands where it does not occur. It is presently found on Santa Cruz, Isabela, Santiago, San Cristóbal and Floreana. It is easily transported on fresh fruit and vegetables.

Carpenter bee; *Xylocopa darwini*—This is a solitary bee which makes its nest in wood. The black females are often seen visiting flowers where they collect nectar and pollen. They are one of the most important insect pollinators for Galápagos flowering plants. The males are yellow-brown, smaller, and much less abundant. Males set up territories in which they make figure-of-eight flights to court females.

Butterflies and Moths—Lepidoptera

Eight species of butterfly and many species of moth are known from the Galápagos. This is a low diversity, but quite a few species are commonly seen. Butterflies by day and moths by night are important pollinators of flowers. Because of the hot dry nature of the daytime environment, a high proportion of Galápagos flowers are white, indicating the advantages of night-time pollination.

Galápagos sulphur butterfly on a
morning glory flower.

Queen butterfly.

The larvae, or caterpillars, of butterflies and moths are vegetarian and can be found feeding on most Galápagos plant species. Many caterpillars are highly host-specific and can only survive on one type of plant, while others are fairly catholic. Like most other insects, they are most frequently seen during the warm/wet season when humidities are higher and there is more vegetation available. Sometimes caterpillars of some species become so abundant locally that they completely defoliate their host plants. This occurs with different species of plants and caterpillars in different parts of the archipelago at different times and shows that the Galápagos environment is an unpredictable one with few regulatory controls for insect populations. Caterpillars and adult lepidopterans are an important food source for many birds, even seed-eating finches feed their young on small caterpillars.

Many butterflies and moths from the Galápagos are significantly smaller than their mainland relatives. The Galápagos fritillary, *Agraulis vanillae galapagensis*, is almost a third smaller as is the hawkmoth, *Hyles lineata florilega*. This reduction of size is probably related to the problems of food supply and dispersal mentioned earlier.

Butterflies have clubbed antennae and usually fold their wings vertically. Moths usually fold their wings horizontally and over each other.

Butterflies

Galápagos sulphur butterfly; *Phoebis sennae marcellina*—This is the only yellow butterfly in the islands. It is a small subspecies of a species that occurs throughout the western hemisphere. It is common and wide-spread in the islands.

Galápagos silver fritillary; *Agraulis vanillae galapagensis*—This medium-sized (5 cm) black and orange butterfly, with silver spots on the underside, is commonly seen from the coast to the highlands.

Green hawkmoth.

Painted ladies; *Vanessa spp.*—Two species, *V. carye* and V. *virginensis,* are locally abundant. Both are red, orange and black above, like the fritillary, but with pastel-coloured underwings.

Monarch butterfly; *Danaus plexippus*—This is the largest Galápagos butterfly (10 cm across wings). It is the same species as the well-known migrating Monarch of North America. The wings are brownish-red with black veins and wing tips. There are white spots on the wingtips and trailing edges.

Queen butterfly; *Danaus gilippus*—Similar to the Monarch, but smaller and less heavily marked with black on the wings. This species is found on Isabela. The bright colours of this and the above species indicate the distastefulness of these species to birds. Once tasted, twice shy.

Leptodes parrhasioides; Galápagos blue butterfly—This beautiful little blue butterfly is endemic to the islands and common within them. It is alert and does not allow close approach. It has a fast fluttering flight as it moves about the vegetation.

Large-tailed skipper; *Urbanus dorantes*—This little brown butterfly has large blunt "tails" to its hind wings and a few yellowish spots on the fore wings. It is common in the highlands of the larger islands, especially in open areas.

Moths

Green hawkmoth; *Eumorpha labruscae*—This species is common and wide-ranging. Though the larvae feed on a vine in the humid and transition zones, the adults are often found in the arid zone and have been caught at the lights of boats well out to sea. Hawkmoths, especially this species, are rapid fliers. The adults feed on the nectar of flowers and have a very long tongue or proboscis. The proboscis of this species is almost twice as long as the insect's body. When feeding they look much like hummingbirds or small bats.

Hawkmoth; *Hyles lineata florilega*—this Galápagos subspecies of an almost cosmopolitan species is widespread and common in the islands. It often comes to lights on boats and is easily recognised by the striking black and white lines on its wings. Its larvae are green with black and yellow stripes and a long curved yellow-red "tail." It is usually found on Portulaca.

Hawkmoth; *Manduca rustica calapagensis*—This mottled grey-brown species is common at lights. Its larvae are green to purplish with yellow speckling and oblique white stripes edged with purple. The tail horn is yellow-green. The larva feeds predominantly on *Cordia* and *Clerodendrum*, which it frequently defoliates.

Footmen moths; *Utethesia spp.*—These white, day-flying moths are attractively black and red spotted with red underwings that are displayed when disturbed. Four species occur in the Galápagos, two of which are quite common at most elevations up to the humid zone.

Noctuid moth; *Ascalapha odorata*—this is the largest moth in the Galápagos with a wingspan of up to 15 cm. Its colouration is nondescript dark brown and it is found on many islands. It is usually seen around dusk.

Atteva sp.—this small and brightly coloured moth is occasionally abundant on *Scalesia* plants in the Arid zone.

True Bugs—Hemiptera

Some eighty species of true bugs are found in the Galápagos. These insects have piercing and sucking mouth parts and more or less hard forewings that are folded over the body. Most species feed on plant sap, but quite a few are predators of other insects. Shield bugs (Pentatomidae) are quite common in the Arid and Transition zones. These are broad, flat insects, triangular in shape and green or dark-coloured. Pentatomids can produce a strong smelling juice that apparently repels potential predators such as lizards or birds.

Some scale insects (Coccidae) are found in the islands. These feed on plant sap and appear like small scales on a leaf. Because of a high intake of sap, these insects secrete a sugary liquid like honeydew which is much liked by ants. I have seen ants regularly visiting these insects on *Parkinsonia* leaves. The ants appear to protect the scale insects in return for their "drinks."

Perhaps the most unusual Galápagos insect is the ocean skater, *Halobates robustus*. These insects live on the surface of the sea, usually in calm water and lagoons, where they skate about in search of prey. They are in the same family as the familiar pond skaters or water striders of the temperate zone. They are supported by surface tension forces in the water. Their long legs are water repellent and ensure that this aquatic insect never gets wet.

Common yellow scorpion with young
on its back.

True Flies—Diptera

Few of the 100 or so Galápagos flies are notable, but this order includes some tiresome creatures. These include a mosquito, *Aedes taeniorhynchus*, a horsefly, *Tabanus vittiger*, a biting midge, *Forcipomyia fuliginosa*, and the biting housefly, *Stomoxys calcitrans*.

Praying Mantis—Mantodea

One species, *Galapagia solitaria*, is found in the Galápagos. Pale brown, it blends well with the dry vegetation of the arid lowlands. It preys on other insects.

Grasshoppers, Locusts, Katydids and Crickets—Orthoptera

Twenty-one species of this order are found in the Galápagos. Amongst the short-horned grasshoppers (Acrididae) is the brightest and most conspicuous Galápagos insect—the painted locust, *Schistocerca melanocera* (Plate 64). This species is black, red, green, and yellow and is abundant in the lowlands. These are popular prey for the lava lizards. Two other genera of grasshoppers, *Sphingonotus* and *Halmenus*, are also found, but these are smaller and well camouflaged. Species from these genera have diversified somewhat within the archipelago.

Katydids, or long-horned grasshoppers (Tettigoniidae), occur in the islands. They are most active at night when their shrill, loud, song can be heard during the warm/wet season. Like most other members of this order, they are vegetarian. There are also crickets (Gryllidae) in the Galápagos.

Scorpions

Two species of scorpion are found in the Galápagos. These are the endemic scorpion, *Centruroides exsul*, and the common yellow scorpion, *Hadruroides lunatus.* The former is uniformly reddish-brown to dark brown with slender pincers, while the latter is yellow with stockier pincers. Both species are predators of insects and other arthropods, which they hunt at night. They sense their prey largely by vibrations in the air and ground. They are in turn often eaten by lava lizards; the scorpion's sting seems to have little effect on reptiles. During the day they hide under rocks and vegetation.

The courtship of scorpions is usually only observable in captivity, but it is a magnificent *pas-de-deux.* The male will lock pincers with the female and then deposit a spermatophore (packet of sperm) on the ground. He then "dances" with the female until he able to manoeuvre her onto the spermatophore. Frequently, the male is eaten by the female after mating; he is much smaller. Young scorpions develop within the mother's body. At birth, the tiny white young clamber onto the mother's back where they remain for a week or two until they are able to look after themselves.

Hadruroides lunatus is found on most of the major islands except for Española, Genovesa, Marchena, and Pinta, while *Centruroides exsul* is found only on Santa Cruz, San Cristóbal, Pinta, Española, and Floreana. Both live in the Arid zones of these islands. The stings of these scorpions can be painful but are usually not serious.

Spiders

There are over fifty species of spider in the Galápagos. Many of these are widely distributed; few are endemic. Galápagos spiders fall into two main groups: hunting spiders and orb web spiders. The former do not weave webs but actively chase their prey over the ground or on walls and ceilings. The latter group usually make a new web each day and wait either on the web, or near it, for their prey to become entangled in the sticky silken fibres. Spiders do not usually chew their prey but inject digestive juices into their hapless victims and allow the digestive processes to occur in the victim's body. They then suck out the resulting liquid, leaving empty exoskeletal husks.

Two of the most frequently encountered hunting spiders are the giant crab spider (*Heteropoda venatoria*) and the smaller *Selenops sp.* Both these species live in houses and other buildings where they chase around at night after insects. Despite their formidable size, both these species are beneficial to us as they prey on many tiresome insects. Heteropoda females can often be seen carrying their whitish egg sacs under the body. Female spiders are usually larger than the males and mate only once. They can store sperm and lay several batches of eggs. Males often mate with many females.

A relative of the black widow, the endemic *Lathrodectes apicalis* is common and is found in rock crevices and under fallen tree trunks. It spins a small web in front of its "burrow." Its abdomen is black with one yellow and three red stripes. Beware of this species as its venom may be dangerous.

Centipede, Punta Pitt, San Cristóbal Island.

Spider, *Argiope argentata*, with "X".

Orb web spiders build large, typical, "spider webs" between vegetation and other objects to trap flying insects in their sticky threads. An often seen species in the Arid zone is the silver argiope, *Argiope argentata*. Its back is silver and black and it characteristically sits in the middle of its web in a *X*-posture. The web itself often has an *X*-shaped design of white silk in the centre. Another species, *Neoscona cookoni*, makes a very large web which is often strung across paths. It sits on its web at night, but usually hides by day in the vegetation nearby. These webs can be so abundant at times that it is impossible to walk more than a few metres without encountering one.

The most beautiful Galápagos spider is the star spider, *Gasteracantha servillei*. This species has a hard, shell-like and spiny abdomen that dwarfs the rest of the body. This dramatically sculptured abdomen is bright yellow and black. They are found commonly in mangroves and other shore vegetation near lagoons and are also found up to the humid zone.

The young of many web-spinning spiders secrete a long thread of silk that enables them to be carried long distances from their birthplace. This is probably the manner in which these species reached the islands. The use of these "parachutes" enables them to colonise islands effectively and is probably why there are few endemics.

Ticks and Mites

Ticks and mites are found on many Galápagos animals (89 species and subspecies have been reported; Schatz 1991). Giant tortoises and other larger reptiles harbour several tick species (*Ambyloma spp.*), which can form an important part of the diet of finches and mockingbirds. These birds remove the ticks from the reptile's skin and elicit a special cleaning posture from them. A close look at a lava lizard will reveal that it has numerous small red mites. Only one species of tick will transfer itself to humans and it is not known to transmit any diseases.

Centipedes—Chilopoda

There are thirteen centipede species in the Galápagos, of which eight are native (Shear and Peck, in press). One, the endemic *Scolopendra galapagensis*, may grow as large as 30 cm. This species is common in the Arid zone of most islands where it preys by night on insects, lizards, and even small birds. It has a dark brown body and reddish legs. During the day, the centipedes usually hide in crevices and under rocks and fallen trees. They are eaten by the Galápagos hawk, night herons and some mockingbirds. Centipedes kill their prey with a venom that is injected through the tips of their poison claws. The bite can be very painful to humans. This has given them the honour of being the most feared Galápagos creature.

Intertidal and Marine Life

Beneath the Galápagos waves, there is another fascinating, hardly explored, world that awaits the visitor. Humans are strangers in the underwater world and can only see it from the surface with mask and snorkel, or for short periods with scuba equipment. What little we can see of life in the sea is so different from our experiences on shore and so beautiful that we cannot fail to be enchanted yet again.

Many of the animals that we see on land depend on the sea for all or part of their livelihood. Seabirds must fish, as did most of the human residents before tourism, and marine iguanas dive to graze the algae. Sea lions too leave the shores to catch their food. From the flies that feed on sea lion carcasses to the hawks that eat marine iguanas and the owls that take storm petrels, the webs of life on land and in the sea are inextricably intertwined. This is why so much of Galápagos wildlife is concentrated along the coasts, even though these seem the most inhospitable of the islands' environments.

For more detailed information and help with identification, I recommend Godfrey Merlen's *A Field Guide to the Fishes of Galápagos* (excellent drawings) and Pierre Constant's *Marine Life of the Galápagos* (excellent photographs). Both Paul Humann's *Galápagos: A Terrestrial and Marine Phenomenon* and James Cribb's *Subtidal Galápagos: Exploring the Waters of Darwin's Islands* have beautiful photographs of Galápagos marine life. Paul Humann's *Reef Life Identification—Galápagos* should be a great help to anyone studing the marine life of these islands.

As is the case on land, many of the species found are invertebrates. There are over 1,900 species of marine invertebrates reported from the Galápagos of which about 18 per cent are endemic (James 1991 and Peck in press). One of the most important events of the past decade was the declaration of the "Galápagos Marine Resources Reserve" in 1986. It is hoped that this will give some measure of protection to about 70,000 square kilometres of Galápagos waters. The reserve and marine conservation issues are discussed in more detail in Chapter 12.

Within the marine environment of the Galápagos Islands is a wide variety of habitats (rocky shore, sandy beaches, mangrove lagoons and coral reefs) which harbour an unusual variety of marine organisms. These organisms come from temperate, subtropical and tropical waters (Wellington 1984). Of almost 1,300 marine species from a variety of groups, about 28 per cent are endemic to the islands and about 53 per cent are from the Panamic region. The remaining 19 per cent are either temperate, cosmopolitan or Atlantic in their affinities. This strange mixture of species is largely due to the unusual oceanographic conditions surrounding the islands.

Between the tides is yet another fascinating environment. Organisms here must adapt to spending part of their time submerged and part above water, as well as resist the incessant action of waves. Only a few of the intertidal creatures, like the marine iguana and Sally lightfoot crab, will be familiar to most visitors, but if you take a close look at life on the tidal rocks and in the tide pools, you will discover an ecosystem every bit as complex as that on land.

One major difference between life on land and life in the sea is that water is a much more hospitable medium than air. Relatively few animals have colonised the air, but in the sea many plants and animals are free-floating (planktonic). Many more active animals, such as fish, can swim about in open water in search of food. On land we usually associate plants with a sedentary life and animals with an active one, but in the sea many animals lead a sedentary life, filtering out small organisms from the water or entangling them with tentacles. These filter feeders include creatures from very diverse groups: barnacles, sponges, anemones, fan worms, corals and others.

Intertidal Life

The Galápagos Islands have over 1,350 km of shoreline, more than the coastline of mainland Ecuador. Though the intertidal zone is but a strip around all the islands, the total area has been estimated as about 40 km^2 or two thirds the size of Española Island.

Because of the gravitational attraction of the moon on the earth's waters, most coastal areas of the world experience nearly two tidal cycles a day, which vary in amplitude with the time of the lunar month. In the Galápagos, tidal ranges are not great, ranging up to 2.6 m at new and full moons, with a mean of about 1.8 m. There are many different types of intertidal habitat including rocky shores, sandy beaches, mangrove lagoons and mud flats, each with its own characteristic flora and fauna. Rocky shores are the best known and most diverse intertidal habitats in the Galápagos. These vary in character from one place to another, mainly as a result of differing slopes and exposure to wave action.

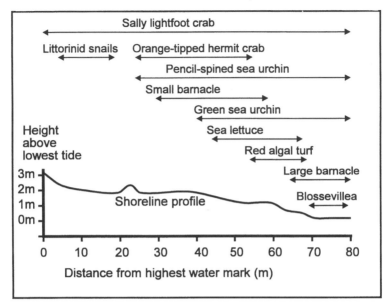

Figure 15: Zonation of intertidal organisms. (Based on Meatyard et al. 1982.)

One of the most characteristic features of intertidal areas is their zonation. Different life forms occur at different levels of the intertidal range because they are variously adapted to the amount of exposure to the hot sun and drying air (see Fig. 15). Creatures that live at the top of the tidal range may be out of water for most of the time, while those at the bottom are only briefly exposed. Once uncovered, the temperature of the black lava rocks may soar quickly to 40 or 50°C. These high temperatures are certainly why the upper intertidal zones of the Galápagos are almost barren. Even in the lower zones, few organisms are found on the upper surfaces of rocks. Most of the interesting intertidal life is to be found in the cracks and crevices and under rocks.

Most of the creatures that live in the intertidal zones are invertebrates and there are many hundreds of species. In this brief chapter, only a few of the most common and notable species are discussed.

Seaweeds—Algae

The algae or seaweeds are a primitive group of plants, most of which are small. Those that occur on land are mostly microscopic, but in the sea some grow to great sizes. The giant kelps of the Pacific United States and Canada may grow to 30 m, but these giants are not found in tropical waters. In the intertidal areas of the Galápagos, few grow more than a few centimetres high, mainly because they are heavily grazed by marine iguanas, crabs and

The results of some beach combing!

fish. The most noticeable alga in the middle and lower zones is the bright green sea lettuce, *Ulva lobata*, which is a favourite food of the marine iguanas. Less noticeable because of their reddish-brown colour, but actually more abundant, are genera such as *Centroceras*, *Gelidium*, and *Spermothamnion*, which make up a "red algal turf" in the lower zones. At the lower end of the intertidal zone, we encounter the large brown alga, *Blossevillea galapagoensis*, which is avoided as food by marine iguanas and crabs, as well as species of *Sargassum* and *Ahnfeltia*.

Vertebrates

Marine iguanas are the most conspicuous intertidal vertebrate. They can be seen feeding on algae in the lower tidal zones whenever the tide is out during the day. Numerous birds spend time in the intertidal areas feeding on crabs, molluscs and other invertebrates. These include the herons, oystercatchers, turnstones, semi-palmated plovers, finches, yellow warblers, and others. Lava lizards too, come down when the tide is out and can be seen catching flies and other insects.

The major aquatic class of vertebrates, the fish, is well represented in the intertidal zone. When the tide is in, many fish species graze on the algae and feed on the intertidal invertebrates. There are a few small fish that remain in tide pools, the most unusual of which is the endemic four-eyed blenny, *Dialomus fuscus*. This small fish spends much of the time out of the water

Green sea urchin; note the tube feet.   Pencil-spined sea urchin.

hopping about the wet rocks in its search for small shore crabs and insects (McCosker and Rosenblatt 1984). It is able to respire aerially for as much as two hours at a time. Like a chameleon, it is able to change its skin colour. It gets its name because each eye is divided vertically into two facets at 110 degrees to each other. This is thought to enable the fish to see well both in and out of the water. Some small moray eels also lurk amongst the rocks.

Sponges—Porifera

There are several relatives of the natural ancestor of the bathroom sponge that can be found under rocks in the intertidal zone. These amorphous, variously coloured blobs are really animals that filter out minute plants and animals from the water. A cubic centimetre of sponge can actively filter two litres of water daily. Intertidal forms include *Haliclona, Tethys* and *Cliona* species.

Sea Anemones

Sea anemones are related to the corals, hydroids and jellyfish and are sedentary predators. These "animal-flowers" have numerous stinging tentacles that they use to immobilise and kill their prey, which includes small fish and invertebrates.

Echinoderms—Starfishes, Sea Urchins and Relatives

This diverse group of animals is exclusively marine and is characterised by having a radial symmetry based on five or more arms.

Starfishes, brittle stars and sunstars are a familiar group. Most species are predatory, eating molluscs and the like. Starfishes, when preying on a clam, will evert their stomach into their prey through a small gap and retrieve it

Part of a pencil-spined sea urchin shell.

once digestion is complete. Starfish are often brightly coloured and can regrow their limbs, if lost. Two species of sunstar, *Heliaster spp.*, are common in intertidal areas. These look like many-armed "starfish."

Sea cucumbers (Holothurians) are soft bodied relatives of the starfish which live on the sea bed and feed on debris and small creatures that they take in with the help of tentacles around the mouth. Just as starfish can eject their stomach to start the external digestion of a mollusc, so sea cucumbers can eject and abandon their lower intestine and other entrails when disturbed. Like the lizard's tail, these regrow.

Sea urchins are common in the Galápagos. One species, *Eucidaris thouarsii*, the pencil-spined urchin, is covered with thick pencil-like spines that disintegrate only slowly and often cover beaches. This species feeds on corals and other organisms. The endemic green sea urchin, *Lytechinus semituberculatus*, is also common (Plate 67). The tests, or shells, of these species tend to retain their short spines better than most and are frequently washed up on beaches. Like sea cucumbers and starfish, the sea urchins move about slowly with many small "tube-feet." Sand dollars and sea biscuits are also echinoderms.

Molluscs

The molluscs are a diverse phylum of animals including the octopuses, squid, sea slugs, and all "sea shells." Molluscs are soft-bodied animals, most of which have some type of shell. The shells that we find tossed up on the beaches, and that we associate so closely with the seaside, are the discarded "homes" left after their inhabitants have died. The variety is tremendous, even in the Galápagos, where many species are endemic.

Chitons are a primitive type of mollusc whose carapace consists usually of eight angled plates which overlap like shingles to form an effective armour. Chitons are common in the intertidal zone. One species, *Chiton goodallii*, is large, growing to 10 cm. They feed by rasping off microscopic algae from the rocks.

Bivalves, or pelecypods, are a familiar and abundant group that includes the clams, cockles, mussels, oysters, and scallops. Most species filter feed on microscopic plant life. They have a muscular "foot" which they use to move around. Some can "swim" by ejecting a forceful jet of water.

The gastropods are the largest group of molluscs and include limpets, sea slugs, cowries, cones, whelks, and many other types. A great variety are found in the Galápagos and the interested reader should consult one of the guides or handbooks listed in the bibliography for this chapter.

Cephalopods—Squid, Octopus and Nautilus

Octopuses are frequently found lurking in tide pools. They are predatory and can change their colour from almost black to white. Shells of the related paper nautiluses are sometimes washed up on beaches. Squids are common offshore and form a major part of the diet of many seabirds.

Crustaceans—Crabs, Barnacles and Shrimps

Crabs are among the most active of the intertidal organisms and barnacles the least so, yet they are closely related. Both share the characteristics of jointed limbs and tough external skeleton. Barnacles, though sedentary in the adult stage, have six pairs of feathery limbs which they extrude when covered by water and catch small organisms for food. Across the middle of the intertidal zone is usually a wide band of small white rock barnacles, *Tetraclita sp.* These are resistant to drying and endure a considerable portion of the day out of the water when they are closed up. In the lowest intertidal and subtidal zones is the large acorn barnacle, *Megabalanus galapaganus*, which grown 5 cm or more high. When dead and washed ashore, the "shells" are white and pink.

There are over a hundred crab species in the Galápagos but one stands out from the rest. The Sally lightfoot, or red lava crab, *Grapsus grapsus*, is so abundant and so brightly coloured with red above and blue below that no visitor could miss them (Plate 65). Their name comes from their habit of skipping across short stretches of water. The young of this species are black and even faster runners than the adults. The large pincers on this crab can give a nasty pinch but the spoon-shaped tips are adapted to grazing on algae and scavenging. This bright denizen of the lava rocks follows the tides in and out, day and night, picking up tiny fragments of algae and detritus. Sally lightfoots are very alert to moving objects and are not easily approached. However, if you remain still they will walk over you, as if you were a marine iguana. When disturbed, they often eject one or two squirts of water rather like a water pistol. They fall prey to herons, moray eels, and occasionally hawkfish.

BARRY TAYLOR

Sally lightfoot crab.   Ghost crab.

Ghost crabs, *Ocypode*, are common on beaches where they dig burrows in the sand and prey on other beach creatures. I have seen them taking turtle hatchlings into their burrows. They also leave characteristic traces of "sand-balls" on the beach which are pellets of sand that they have sorted through for micro-organisms. Their eyes are unusual in that they can be raised vertically on their eyestalks or lowered into grooves of their carapace.

Fiddler crabs, too, live in sandy areas. These small crabs gain their name from the huge pincer that the males have. When courting, the males wave these huge "flags" rather like a violinist bowing his instrument.

Hermit crabs are another interesting group. They have a soft abdomen which they protect by living in abandoned gastropod shells (Plate 66). As they increase in size, they discard small shells for large ones. They may switch "house" some four or five times before reaching adult size. The small black hermit crab, *Calcinus explorator*, with orange stripes on its pincers and legs is very abundant in tide pool areas. One species, the semi-terrestrial hermit crab, *Coenobita compressus*, is common in mangrove-fringed sandy areas. It spends much of the day in the shade of vegetation and scavenges at night. It grows quite large and inhabits shells 5 cm or more across.

Marine Life

The marine life of the Galápagos is exceptionally rich for the tropics. The combination of cool upwelling waters in some parts and warm tropical waters in others allows for an astounding diversity of marine creatures. Sharks, turtles, sea lions, fish and invertebrates abound. Some 306 species of fish are found in Galápagos waters of which nearly a quarter are endemic forms (Wellington pers. comm.). There are only a few small, and not very diverse, coral reefs, but the vesicular and creviced nature of the lava rock provides abundant shelter near the shores, and the open water is nutrient rich and swarming with life from the upwelling currents. Occasionally, with

Male fiddler crab, Genovesa Island.

the El Niño flow, the cool waters are displaced by warm waters and the ecology of the Galápagos marine ecosystem is drastically changed. Most Galápagos waters are still unexplored and new species continue to be discovered. Few visitors get a chance to scuba dive, but almost every visitor has the opportunity to don a mask and snorkel and peer down into the rich and varied shallows.

Much of the fearlessness that we find above water continues beneath the waves. You can get close to many fish, as spear-gun hunting has been forbidden. Turtles are easily approached and sea lions will approach you. I have had my fins and regulator tubes pulled by inquisitive sea lions on many occasions. Marine iguanas too can be watched feeding underwater at close range. In the rest of this section, some members of the more typically marine groups are discussed.

An unusual marine collecting expedition took place in 1986. Scientists from the Harbour Branch Oceanographic Institution/SeaPharm Project spent seven weeks cruising the islands, searching for new drugs from marine organisms. Nearly 1,200 organisms were collected from depths of up to 800 m using the four-man Johnson Sea-Link I submersible. Preliminary results indicate that as many as 15 per cent of these species may have anticancer, antiviral, antimicrobial or immunomodulatory activity.

Fishes

The Galápagos Islands have an interesting mix of tropical and temperate types of fish. Water temperatures are known to fluctuate from a cool 15°C to a warm 29°C, depending on time of year and site, thus providing a range of temperature regimes. Fish are divided into two main groups: the cartilaginous fishes, which include the sharks and rays, and the bony fishes, which include all of what we normally think of as fishes.

PAUL HUMANN

Yellow-tailed surgeonfish swimming by endemic black (*Antipathes*) coral.

Sharks and Rays

Several shark species are found in the Galápagos waters. These range from the giant, but harmless, whale shark (up to 20 m) to the small Port Jackson shark. Though dangerous species do occur, they do not seem to be aggressive. I have made several scuba dives in the vicinity of sharks and have had no problems nor have I heard of anyone else having trouble. Care should be taken, of course, not to tempt fate by swimming with open wounds or grazes.

Most sharks bear their young alive, but some are born in egg cases or "mermaid's purses." Some common sharks include white-tipped and black-finned reef sharks, Galápagos shark, Port Jackson shark, tiger shark, and the well-known hammerhead shark.

Small rays such as the spotted eagle (leopard) ray and mustard (golden) rays are common especially in sheltered bays. Larger eagle rays and manta rays are seen in open water. Sting rays are common at some beaches. The manta ray is a huge fish, reaching 6 m across and weighing up to 450 kg. It is a plankton feeder. I have seen these rays and eagle rays leaping out of the water on numerous occasions. By Rábida, I once saw a single ray leap a metre out of the water six times in succession, each time making a resounding "thwack."

Large rays and sharks, as well as turtles, dolphins and whales, are frequently accompanied by remoras. These fish attach themselves to any large marine animal and are carried about. They are a type of cleaner fish as they remove parasites from their hosts and scavenge during feeding events.

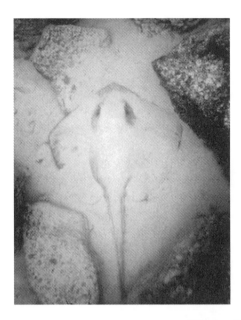

Sting ray

Bony Fishes

The shore fishes of the Galápagos are fairly well known, there being 309 species from ninety-one families recorded. About fifty-one species (17%) are endemic while about 60 per cent have their origins in the tropical eastern Pacific. About 8 per cent are pantropical and 15 per cent are from the Indo-Pacific region (McCosker and Rosenblatt 1984). Many are difficult to identify as they can change shape and colour with age and sex. Some can change colour in a few seconds with mood, while some of the wrasses can even change sex as a normal part of their life cycle.

Several kinds of fish are commercially exploited or caught for local consumption. These include trout grouper (Span. bacalao) (*Mycteroperca olfax*); mullet (Span. lisa) (*Mugil spp.*), and various tuna and bonitos (*Thunnus spp.*, *Euthynnus spp.* and *Sarda sp.*). Bacalao is a favourite local food fish and is also dried for shipping to the mainland. There is also a rare golden-coloured phase of these species called "the king of bacalao" by locals. Thread herring (*Opisthonema sp.*) and anchovies (*Anchoa sp.*) are caught as bait fish.

A few commonly seen fishes are described below and in the illustrations (see Fig. 16). The descriptions are based on notes made by Sir Peter Scott (1974).

Five-spotted anthias (Creole fish); *Paranthias colonus*—A small grey fish with up to five white spots on the side. Males have reddish-tinged edges to the fins. They are found in large schools as they search for planktonic food.

Hieroglyphic hawkfish; *Cirrhitus rivulatis*—A medium-sized, grouper-like fish. Its basic colour is blue-black with brownish bands subdivided by paler bluish lines. This fish hides amongst lava rocks and crevices and is shy. It has been found with marine iguana remains in its stomach.

White-banded (king) angelfish; *Holocanthus passer*—This beautiful fish is often seen near rocks and by boats at anchor. Its colour is blue-black with a vertical white stripe, orange-yellow tail and orange shoulder. Its forehead has some iridescent blue spots.

Blue-eyed damselfish; *Stegastes arcifrons*—A small black fish with yellow tail, blue eye-rings, and yellow lips. This and the similar white-tailed damselfish (*S. lleucorus beebei*) are both territorial and aggressive, despite their small size. The latter species has yellow above the eye and a whitish tail band. Both species maintain algal "gardens" which they vigorously defend. I have seen them chase off much larger fish as well as picking up and removing sea urchins.

Eastern Pacific Sergeant major; *Abudefduf troschelli*—A small grey fish with five vertical dark bars. Sometimes the bars are interspersed with yellow. It is known locally as "roncador" and is common in warm seas worldwide.

Moorish idol; *Zanclus cornutus*—A conspicuous white and yellow fish with vertical dark bands and a long white streamer from the dorsal fin. It is uncommon but dramatic to see.

Yellow-tailed surgeonfish; *Prionurus laticlavius*—A grey fish with a yellow tail and two vertical black bands on the head divided by a whitish band. These fish occur in schools. They have three scalpel-like plates on each side of the tail from which their name is derived.

Blue parrotfish; *Scarus ghobban*—The male is primarily light greenish blue with the edge of each scale outlined in pink. There is much pink in the tail fin and in the inner halves of the dorsal and anal fins. The tail has prominent streamers. The female is different, being greenish bronze with five or six irregular blue vertical bands. There are also three other parrot fish that may be commonly seen. Some parrotfishes sleep in mucous cocoons.

Large-banded blenny; *Ophioblennius steindachneri*—A long, dusty brown, large blenny with three paler vertical bands on the front half of the fish. It has small protuberances in front of its eyes and is rather shy as it squirms about the rocks.

Yellow-bellied triggerfish; *Sufflamen verres*—A blackish fish with an extensive area of dull yellow on the lower posterior of both flanks. They move

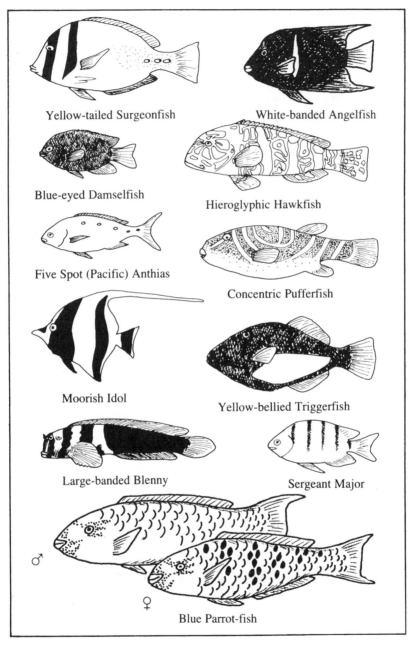

Yellow-tailed Surgeonfish

White-banded Angelfish

Blue-eyed Damselfish

Hieroglyphic Hawkfish

Five Spot (Pacific) Anthias

Concentric Pufferfish

Moorish Idol

Yellow-bellied Triggerfish

Large-banded Blenny

Sergeant Major

♂

♀

Blue Parrot-fish

Figure 16: Some Galápagos fishes. (Based on drawings by Sir Peter Scott.)

with a characteristic waving of the dorsal fins. Like surgeonfishes, triggerfishes can make sounds by rubbing together spines on their fins. The teeth are strong and chisel-like and are used to open mollusc shells.

Concentric pufferfish; *Sphoeroides annulatus*—Dark above with concentric white lines and pale below, this fish often accompanies boats. These and other pufferfish can expand themselves by sucking in air or water when disturbed. Pufferfishes are highly toxic; Godfrey Merlen notes that dead pufferfishes have been seen surrounded by thousands of dead flies.

Dusky chub; *Girella fremenvillei*—A dark grey fish with a white spot on each nostril below the eye. They have a wide head, thick lips and are often found in schools.

Jewel moray eel; *Muraena lentiginosa*—This and fifteen other species of moray are voracious predators that lurk amongst the rocks in wait for their prey, which is mainly other fish. They are known to have bitten people who have tempted them.

Amberjack (Palometa); *Seriola dorsalis*—This large tuna family fish, with a diagonal dark eye-stripe, occurs in large schools, which often surround divers. I have been circled by such schools for as much as half an hour at a time.

Red-lipped batfish; *Ogcocephalus darwini*—This indigenous shore fish is truly bizarre in appearance (Plate 69). The upper surface is studded with spines and is flattened. The pectoral fins are large and situated on arm-like extensions. The pelvic and anal fins are smaller and resemble limbs. The fish has a long "snout" with whitish protuberances in the angle made with the mouth. This is used as a "bait" to catch prey. Its diet includes small fish, small molluscs, clams and worms. It lives on sandy bottoms in deep and shallow water.

Flying fish; Exocoetidae—Flying fish are common in Galápagos waters and are an important prey for many seabirds as they spend much time near the surface. These fish readily take to the air, gliding on their long wing-like pectoral fins, to escape predators. They may cover 30 m or more in a single glide.

Harlequin wrasse (vieja); *Bodianus eclancheri*—A wonderfully coloured fish with variable splotches of black, white, orange and yellow. This species changes sex from female to male without any obvious difference in appearance.

PAUL HUMANN

Slipper lobster foraging underwater.

Lobsters

Three species of crayfish, or "spiny lobster" in the islands, are known. All three species are regularly caught at night by divers equipped with flashlights. They are the blue lobster, *Panulirus gracilis*, the red lobster, *P. penicillatus*, and the slipper lobster, *Scyllarides astori*.

Corals

Reef-forming corals are not abundant in the Galápagos, but a few decent sized "heads" may be seen at Devil's Crown (Onslow Island), Floreana. Patches of reef coral are found scattered throughout the archipelago and substantial coral reef development occurs on the south side of Bartolomé, the eastern side of Wolf, and at the southern tip of Darwin (Wellington 1984). The coral animals that make reefs live with a symbiotic alga that produces food for the animals in return for protection. Corals grow out in layers and can be aged as with tree-rings. Recent studies are using them to trace previous climatic changes and El Niño events by looking at the rates of growth of corals in different years. Black corals were previously abundant, but have been decimated by divers collecting for the jewellery market. One species, the endemic yellow-black coral, *Antipathes galapagensis*, is still quite common as it rarely grows large enough to be commercial.

Red spiny and slipper lobsters.

Molluscs

Squid are common in Galápagos waters, coming to the surface at night where they can be seen racing away in the phosphorescence from ships' bows. They are an important food supply for many seabirds.

The largest bivalve is a beautiful scallop, *Lyropecten magnificens*, which occurs in deep water around the west coast of Isabela. Its red shell halves, 20 cm across, are fringed by a red mantle with blue spots. One of the largest gastropods is the brightly coloured horse conch, *Fasciolaria princeps*, with a blue-spotted scarlet foot. It reaches 25 cm in length and feeds on gastropods such as *Muricanthus sp.*

Starfishes and Sea Urchins

There are many starfish in the Galápagos. Some of these are large, and the giant sea star, *Luidia superba*, is the world's largest species with a radius of over 40 cm. Many of those that occur in deeper water are red-coloured but appear dark without extra lighting. This is because red light is lost first when penetrating water and only blue wavelengths reach the depths. One of the more common species is the gulf star, *Oreaster occidentalis* (Plate 68).

Both the intertidal sea urchin species mentioned in the previous section occur in deeper water and several others occur with them. One of these, *Diadema mexicana*, has long, sharp black spines that can give a painful reaction if touched. I have encountered its spines on occasion while looking for lobsters and have regretted the meeting. Another common species is *Centrostrephanus coronatus* which is brown with lightly banded spines.

Conservation in the Islands

12

Oceanic islands are "fragile." They are extremely vulnerable to many forms of human-related pressures, especially introduced species (Loope et al. 1988). The Galápagos Islands have managed to escape much destruction because of their isolation and recent discovery, but these islands are in danger of losing the very qualities that make them so special. The islands are at risk both because of past ravages and also because of modern economic and social pressures.

Though the first protective legislation for the Galápagos was enacted in 1934 and supplemented in 1936, it was not until the late 1950s that positive action was taken to control what was happening to the native flora and fauna. In 1955, the International Union for the Conservation of Nature organised a fact-finding mission to the Galápagos. Two years later, in 1957, UNESCO (in cooperation with the International Council for Bird Preservation, New York Zoological Society, Time Incorporated, and the Government of Ecuador) sent another expedition under the leadership of the Irenaus Eibl-Eibesfeldt and Robert Bowman to study the conservation situation and to choose a site for a research station.

In 1959, the centenary year of Darwin's publication of *The Origin of Species*, the Ecuadorean government declared all the islands, except areas already colonised, as a national park. In the same year, the Charles Darwin Foundation for the Galápagos Isles was founded, with its international headquarters in Brussels. Its primary objectives were to ensure the conservation of unique Galápagos ecosystems and promote the scientific studies necessary to fulfil its conservation functions. With the establishment of the Charles Darwin Research Station in 1960 (facilities were inaugurated in 1964), conservation work began. During the early years, conservation programs, such as eradication of introduced species and protection of native species, were carried out by C.D.R.S. personnel. Currently, most of the scientific work carried out in the Galápagos by resident scientists is directed toward conservation goals; the work of most visiting scientists is oriented towards pure research. In 1991, the Ecuadorean government extended the agreement that allows the Charles Darwin Foundation to operate the Charles Darwin Research Station for twenty-five more years.

In 1968, the National Park Service began work under the auspices of the Ecuadorean Forestry Service and the Ministry of Agriculture and Livestock. The Park Service and Research Station are based at Puerto Ayora, Academy Bay, Santa Cruz Island. Over the last two decades, they have been carrying out numerous conservation programs. Finance for the programs comes from various sources, mainly private donations, a variety of international organizations such as the Frankfurt Zoological Society, UNESCO, the World Wide Fund for Nature, and the Ecuadorean government. Funds are still urgently needed to restore the natural *status quo* of these special islands. Donations will be gratefully accepted by any of the above organisations whose addresses are listed in Appendix 4.

With the advent of organised tourism to the Galápagos in 1969, which now brings over 40,000 visitors to the islands each year, regulations were deemed necessary to ensure that visitors would not destroy the very wildlife they came to see. There are some strict rules, made by the National Park, which are stated at the front of the book. Tourists have so far done little damage to the islands and their wildlife, and I hope that this will remain the case. The rules are important; please observe them when you are in the islands. As a general rule, don't take anything from the islands that belongs there, take only photographs, and leave only your footprints. Do not disturb the wildlife.

In 1986, Ecuadorean President León Febres-Cordero proclaimed a decree establishing the Galápagos Marine Resources Reserve. This reserve includes the entire internal waters of the archipelago, as well as a surrounding zone fifteen nautical miles wide. The total area is in the order of 80,000 square kilometres. The successful implementation of this decree will depend on the cooperation of the various organizations involved as well as adequate funding. The archipelago and its surrounding waters have also been declared a whale sanctuary by the Ecuadorean government.

As a result of the work of David Steadman, it is possible for us to look at the conservation problems of the Galápagos with a geological perspective. Steadman has collected about half a million fossil bones of vertebrates from several sites in the archipelago. Many of these sites are lava tubes. Some of the bones are the result of animals falling in while many of them were brought to the caves by roosting barn owls. Steadman's fossil record shows that most if not all of the extinction or extirpation of native species in the islands occurred after the first arrival of humans in 1535 (Steadman 1986; Steadman et al. 1991). The record also suggests that the highest prehuman rate of extinction is probably hundreds of times less than the modern rate of

Feral cat, Tagus Cove, Isabela Island.

human-related extinction. Extinct or extirpated species have been found on several islands; barn owls on Floreana, giant rats on Santa Cruz, leaf-toed geckoes, land iguanas, and rice rats on Rábida, giant rats and two species of rice rat on Isabela. Some species such as the large ground finch of Floreana were recorded by early scientists and are now known to be extinct. The times of extinction of this species and that of the San Cristóbal and Santa Cruz rice rats coincide with the establishment of human colonies on these islands.

The problems that face the managers of the Galápagos National Park can be grouped into three areas: the control of non-native species, the restoration of native populations, and the management of current human impacts. The solutions to the problems of reviving native populations and eradicating exotic ones are complex and expensive. For example, it is no easy task to eradicate over 80,000 goats from Santiago. The Park Service and Research Station have made remarkable progress over the last two decades, especially considering the chronic shortage of funds.

Introduced Species and their Control

Once settlers came to the islands, they brought with them a full range of domestic animals and plants, some of which went wild and started feral populations. When the National Park was declared, it had a legacy of introduced animals and plants that were detrimental to the native creatures (see Fig. 17). Dogs, cats, pigs, goats, rats, guava plants, and the chinchona (quinine) tree are amongst the non-native species introduced by previous

Introduced guava, Sierra Negra Volcano, Isabela Island.

visitors, fishermen and colonists. Herbivores, such as goats, compete with native tortoises and iguanas, making food less available and destroying native vegetation. Predators, such as dogs and cats, kill native animals and have seriously depleted native populations. Introduced plants have spread and compete with native vegetation. The guava is easily distributed by feral cattle and the quinine tree is dispersed by wind.

Because of the relatively rapid introduction of alien species, the native species have had no time to adapt to these new threats. The effects have been devastating. Where introduced animals are a problem, the solutions are neither simple nor easy. Hunting is difficult due to the nature of the terrain and vegetation. Trapping is not very efficient and great care must be taken when using poisons to ensure that non-target species are not affected. Fencing is expensive and is only a short term solution. Biological controls, involving the introduction of a new predator, parasite or disease is risky and needs much research before implementation.

Dogs are a serious danger on many islands because they prey upon young tortoises and tortoise eggs as well as upon land and marine iguanas and penguins. In the late 1970s, wild dogs attacked a large colony of land iguanas on Santa Cruz. They killed over five hundred iguanas and left the bodies to rot. Similar attacks have occurred on Isabela also. A poisoning program was carried out on southern Isabela and this seems to have been successful in controlling the problem. Experiments are also being carried out to sterilise domestic dogs in the inhabited areas. This could prevent the reintroduction of dogs into the park.

Feral burros, James Bay, Santiago Island.

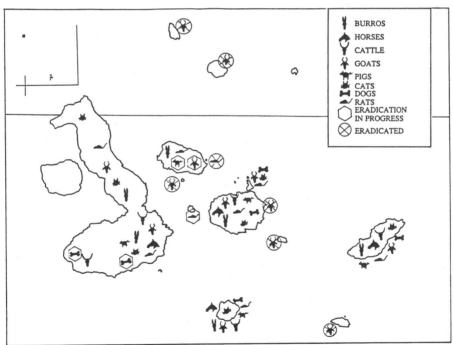

Figure 17: Introduced mammals and their distribution. (Based on Thornton 1971. Sheep and mice are also found in the Galápagos but are not recorded on this map.)

Feral goats, James Bay, Santiago Island.

Feral goats have seriously altered the natural vegetation on a number of islands. They have wiped out huge stands of native vegetation, leading to a lack of food for native species, as well as soil erosion. Their tough constitution and rapid reproductive rate has allowed the populations to thrive at the expense of other animals and the native vegetation. It is thought that the 38,000 goats killed on Pinta Island between 1971 and 1975 were the descendants of three goats introduced there only fourteen years earlier! Several plant species have become at least locally extinct because of the goats. As a result of intensive hunting programs by the Galápagos National Park Service, goats have now been removed from six of the smaller and medium-sized islands (see Fig. 17). However, goats are spreading northward on Isabela and must be controlled if the tortoise populations of Alcedo, Darwin and Wolf Volcanos are to be safe. Goat eradication is a high priority. The enormous population of 80,000 or more goats on Santiago has to be controlled, but first the large population of feral pigs on this island must be eliminated.

Pigs abound on some islands where they destroy vegetation, and dig up and destroy tortoise and turtle eggs, and prey upon young tortoises and ground-nesting birds. Wild pigs have been known to snatch the eggs of sea turtles literally as they are being laid! The pigs later use their keen sense of smell to find and destroy other turtle nests. Hatching success rates have dropped from eighty per cent to less than three per cent as a result. Pigs are a major problem for the tortoise populations on Santa Cruz and Santiago Islands. Bruce Coblentz (1987) estimates the population on Santiago to be between 2,000 and 3,000 individuals. Based on his studies of the pig population, Coblentz recommends that poisoning be used to control or eliminate the population.

A close associate of man, the black rat, occurs on many islands. It has probably led to the extinction of endemic rice rats on four islands; it kills and eats tortoise hatchlings and nesting dark-rumped petrels as well. For nearly a hundred years on the island of Pinzón, black rats have been killing every single giant tortoise hatchling, leaving an aging population of adults. The aggressive Norway rat was introduced in the late 1970s and is now present on at least two islands and rapidly expanding its range.

Little is known about the biology and detrimental effects of feral cats. Mike Konecny (1983) found that the most important food of the Galápagos cats is black rats, but they also eats native birds, insects, crabs and lizards.

Burros are found on the rugged parts of several islands. Lynn Fowler de Neira (1984) found that the 500 to 700 burros on Alcedo volcano were competing with adult tortoises for pasture and water, as well as trampling nests.

Wild cattle and horses are present on several islands, but their detrimental effects have not been fully assessed. On Isabela there are thousands of feral cattle, which trample native vegetation and promote the spread of grasslands.

Invertebrates too may be serious pests. The little fire ant, *Wasmannia auropunctata*, is present on five islands where it is a nuisance to people as well as having detrimental effects on the populations of other arthropods (Lubin 1984). Recently, a species of wasp *(Polistes)* has been introduced. It is aggressive and has been seen on many islands as well as out to sea. It is not known what its effects on native species will be, but we can be sure that it will compete with the native wasps and may eat caterpillars which are an important food source for young finches. A species of black fly, *Simulium bipunctatum* has recently been reported from San Cristóbal. This fly has a vicious bite and is possibly capable of transmitting parasitic diseases. Controlling this species will be hard as its larval stages live in the scant supplies of freshwater on the island.

Perhaps just as devastating as the threat of introduced animals is the introduction of exotic plants. Over 300 species of exotic plants are found in the Galápagos—100 of which were introduced in the last decade (Carrasco, 1992)! The most troublesome plant species are the guava tree (*Psidium guajava*), the quinine tree (*Chinchona succirubra*), the shrub *Lantana camara,* and elephant grass *(Pennisetum purpureum)* (Hamann 1984). The guava has formed extensive forests on Volcan Sierra Negra. *L. camara* has invaded the nesting areas of the dark-rumped petrel on Floreana and interferes with the passage of the birds into and out of their burrows. Since 1971, the National Park Service has been trying to eradicate guava and quinine trees. They have had only limited success due to the remarkable recovery ability of these plants: if cut to a stump, they frequently grow back as three or four stems! Recent experiments have been made using a combination of cutting down the trees and the selective application of herbicides. These appear to show some promise.

Figure 17 shows the distribution of the introduced mammal species, and shows that some have been successfully removed, while other programs are in progress. Notable successes to date have been the eradication of goats from six islands (Española, Santa Fé, Rábida, Marchena, South Plazas and Pinta), and of dogs on Isabela. Many exotic populations remain, however, and control programs need careful research and much money to carry out. Contributions are urgently required to fund these programs.

Only two of the main islands (Fernandina and Genovesa) are free from introduced organisms, but, through the continued good work of the National Park Service and the Charles Darwin Research Station personnel, it is hoped that this total will increase.

Restoring Native Populations

As well as introducing animals and plants, humans have killed large numbers of animals in the past and have cleared great areas of native vegetation for agriculture and ranching purposes. Tortoises, iguanas, fur seals, doves, and other birds have all been killed at one time or another for food or just for pleasure. Colonists in the agricultural zones of the main islands are known to have killed owls in considerable numbers (de Groot 1983a). The history of man's detrimental effects on the islands extends back to the 1600s, when buccaneers killed tortoises for food. Fur seals were exploited and nearly driven to extinction by North American and European hunters during the 1800s.

Since 1965, conservation personnel have been actively trying to boost the threatened populations of endangered species. Tortoise nests are protected and eggs and young are brought to Santa Cruz for captive raising, followed by repatriation once they are no longer thought to be susceptible to predation. Since the program began, over 1,400 young tortoises have been repatriated to their original islands (as of February 1993). At present, there are over 600 young tortoises in the rearing centre.

A remarkable success story is that of the Española Island tortoises. When captive raising programs began for this race, only two males and ten females survived on the island. These were brought to the Darwin Research Station to breed in captivity. Later, a third male was kindly returned to the islands by the San Diego Zoo. Since then, well over three hundred young tortoises have been returned. Some of these returned tortoises are now breeding back on their native island. Many tortoises have been returned to Pinzón Island in the same way and are also breeding.

Giant tortoise eggs being transferred to incubators at the Charles Darwin Research Station, Santa Cruz Island. Note the crosses that are used to keep the eggs the right way up.

Young giant tortoise at the Charles Darwin Research Station.

MONICA J. JACKSON

North Seymour land iguanas in the C.D.R.S. breeding program.

Since February of 1992, Lonesome George, the last individual from the Pinta Island subspecies, has been placed with two females from Wolf Volcano, Isabela, in the hope that offspring may be produced that might be used to repopulate Pinta Island.

Land iguanas were almost wiped out by the depredation of dogs on Isabela and Santa Cruz Islands and have been saved by a combination of captive breeding, repatriation, and the elimination of feral cats and dogs. In 1982, the first iguanas were returned to Isabela, and since then, over 250 young iguanas have been released at Cartago Bay, Isabela, and reintroduction is underway at Conway Bay, Santa Cruz.

On Baltra Island, land iguanas been absent since the World War II, probably because of habitat disturbance by goats. Fortunately, a scientist had transferred a few individuals to nearby Seymour a few years before. Some of these individuals have survived. Two have been brought to the Darwin Research Station where they have now bred successfully. One of these individuals is the largest known Galápagos land iguana, weighing 13 kg. In 1991, thirty-five five-year-old iguanas were repatriated to Baltra after over forty years of absence. This event was the result of cooperation between the Ecuadorean Armed Forces (which owns the island), the Charles Darwin Research Station, and the Galápagos National Park Service. More iguanas were repatriated in 1992, and further reintroductions should occur until the population is well established.

Beach garbage collected near Punta Nuñez, Santa Cruz Island.

Hood tortoises mating at the Charles Darwin Research Station.

The dark-rumped (Hawaiian) petrel is probably the only endangered bird species in the islands. This is as a result of predation by dogs, cats, pigs, and rats on the adults and young in their nesting burrows. This species is in even more danger in Hawaii, so predator control at the petrel colonies has become essential for these populations to survive. Before recent work began on Floreana, the breeding success of petrels was only thirty per cent (with 30% adult mortality). Reproduction is relatively slow at the best of times. A single egg is laid and the birds do not breed until six to eight years old. Now, as a result of the work of Felipe and Justine Cruz and the Galápagos National Park Service, the petrel colonies at Cerro Pajas on Floreana have eighty per cent breeding success and virtually no adult mortality. The main thrust of the work was to reduce predation by poisoning, hunting, and trapping rats and cats. Stephen Kneiss and Richard Podolski are attracting prospective breeders to specific sites where protection from predation can be provided. As a result of these projects, dark-rumped petrels are a much more common sight than they were when I first came to the islands in 1980. Since 1988, successful efforts have been made to protect the colonies on Santa Cruz also.

Though the dark-rumped petrel is the only endangered bird species, the flightless cormorants, penguins and flamingos all have such small populations that they are considered fragile. The 1986 census results suggest that the population of cormorants is between 800 and 1,000 adults, while the penguin population is between 2,400 and 4,400 adults (Rosenburg and Harcourt 1987). The breeding range of both these species is restricted to less than 400 kilometres of the coastlines of Isabela and Fernandina. The populations of these species seem safe at present, but their numbers should continue to be monitored.

Twelve species of Galápagos plants are considered to be in danger of extinction (Valdebenito 1992). On Santiago, efforts are being made to protect the threatened vegetation by using fenced enclosures. These enclosures help to protect small areas from the grazing of goats. Such stop-gap measures are needed until the goats can be eradicated.

Management of Human Impacts

Tourism in the Galápagos is not without its side effects. There are about eighty vessels operating in the islands, taking about 42,000 visitors around the archipelago in 1990. The islands are at the centre of a struggle between preservation and economic need. Nature tourism to the islands brings up to $100 million a year to Ecuador. We have to be careful that controlled educational nature tourism does not grow to become just tourism. Concerns still exist regarding the number of tourist boats operating in the Islands and the number of tourists visiting. There appears to be no clearly defined limit on either of these.

GALÁPAGOS VISITORS 1972-1995

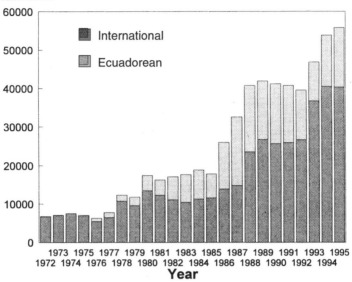

Figure 18: The growth of Galápagos tourism (after Carrasco 1992).

The boom in visitors (see Fig. 18) has attracted an uncontrolled influx of workers from other parts of Ecuador. The resident human population of the islands had doubled during the 1980s and was about 10,000 in 1990. All of this leads to the increase of problems such as sewage, resource overuse, crime, and other social problems. Population growth must be controlled and a sustainable economy developed. As the population grows, so does the demand for scarce resources. Residents need water, imported food, building materials and many other items. In 1988, the cargo ship MV *Iguana* struck a reef in Academy Bay and spilled its cargo and considerable quantities of oil into the bay. Many beaches around the islands are no longer clean.

Education is another very important function of the Park Service and Research Station. Tourist guides and park wardens are trained in park management and natural history. Ecuadorean students are trained in conservation and scientific methodology with the hope that they will later work in Galápagos conservation. Environmental education is carried out in the islands for local residents and their children, and on the mainland as well, to promote environmental awareness. The Charles Darwin Research Station has a library and resident scientific staff who are always willing to provide information. Since 1973, the Van Straelen Museum (named after the first president of the Charles Darwin Foundation) has served as an interesting and informative interpretative centre. It contains many exhibits and displays about the natural history of the islands and is well worth a visit.

The Galápagos National Park Service and the Charles Darwin Research Station are always short of funds to carry out their worthwhile programs. The ratio of tourists to park service personnel has increased from 221 in 1980 to 722 in 1990 (Carrasco 1992). The combined 1993 budgets for the Charles Darwin Research Station and the Galápagos National Park Service, with staffs of 65 and 58 persons respectively, is only US $1.3 million.

To help to set the Galápagos National Park on a firmer financial footing, an endowment fund has been set up so that the interest generated can be used to alleviate the continued funding problems. Companies, institutions and private individuals have made considerable donations to the fund; however, the $30 million target is still far from being reached. Donations are always gratefully accepted; see Appendix 4 for further details. The World Wide Fund for Nature was recently able to generate considerable funds for Galápagos conservation through a debt swap scheme.

Despite the ravages caused by humans to these islands' natural inhabitants, there is cause for optimism. With your support, and that of others, we can hope to return these very special islands to a more natural state and to keep them that way for the future. The Galápagos Islands have the potential to be an example to show us that we *can* save places!

Visiting the Islands

13

> In conclusion, it appears to me that nothing can be more improving to a young naturalist, than a journey in distant countries. (Darwin 1845)

For the people with varying budgets and varying interests, there are many ways to visit the Galápagos. These range from three to four days aboard a luxury liner, to two weeks aboard a comfortable yacht, to a week or so on small converted fishing boats. The more luxurious trips are advertised in major natural history magazines. Among the yachts are the *Andando*, the *Encantada*, the *Sulidae*, the *Cachalote*, the *Tigress*, the *Resting Cloud*, and the *Charles Darwin*. The large cruise ships are the *Santa Cruz*, the *Galápagos Explorer*, and the *Isabela II*. There are literally dozens of smaller (8–20 passenger) motor boats that operate out of Puerto Ayora, Santa Cruz, or Puerto Baquerizo Moreno, San Cristóbal. For further and more detailed information on touring the islands, I recommend Barry Boyce's *A Traveller's Guide to the Galápagos Islands.*

A week or more is recommended to be able to appreciate the splendour and diversity of these islands. My own preference is to travel on one of the comfortable yachts. These yachts have a wonderful ambience, excellent food, and first-class guides. The islands are reached by flying TAME airline from Quito or Guayaquil, Ecuador to Baltra Island or SAN/SAETA airline to San Cristóbal Island. From there people with organised tours usually board their ship or yacht. Those who wish to pick up a boat in Academy Bay must travel by bus and boat over to the island of Santa Cruz.

The National Park Service has created forty-eight visitor sites around the archipelago (Fig. 19). These are placed in areas with rich concentrations of wildlife or other interesting features. Through most of these areas, trails have been delimited by black and white stakes to keep visitor impact to a minimum (Plate 70). Please follow these trails with your guides and respect the park rules.

The *Cachalote*, one of the Galápagos touring yachts.

Gardner Bay, Española, one of Galápagos' beautiful beaches.

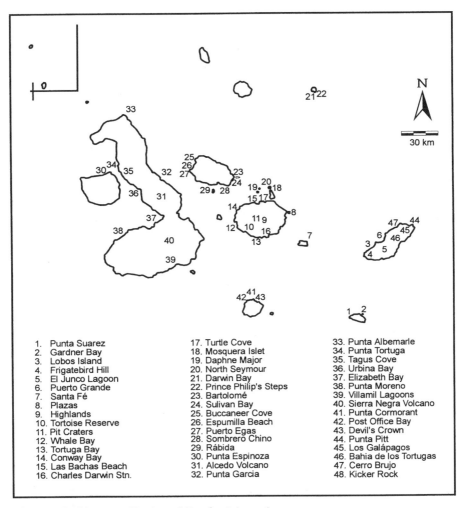

1. Punta Suarez	17. Turtle Cove	33. Punta Albemarle
2. Gardner Bay	18. Mosquera Islet	34. Punta Tortuga
3. Lobos Island	19. Daphne Major	35. Tagus Cove
4. Frigatebird Hill	20. North Seymour	36. Urbina Bay
5. El Junco Lagoon	21. Darwin Bay	37. Elizabeth Bay
6. Puerto Grande	22. Prince Philip's Steps	38. Punta Moreno
7. Santa Fé	23. Bartolomé	39. Villamil Lagoons
8. Plazas	24. Sulivan Bay	40. Sierra Negra Volcano
9. Highlands	25. Buccaneer Cove	41. Punta Cormorant
10. Tortoise Reserve	26. Espumilla Beach	42. Post Office Bay
11. Pit Craters	27. Puerto Egas	43. Devil's Crown
12. Whale Bay	28. Sombrero Chino	44. Punta Pitt
13. Tortuga Bay	29. Rábida	45. Los Galápagos
14. Conway Bay	30. Punta Espinoza	46. Bahia de los Tortugas
15. Las Bachas Beach	31. Alcedo Volcano	47. Cerro Brujo
16. Charles Darwin Stn.	32. Punta Garcia	48. Kicker Rock

Fig. 19. Galápagos National Park visitor sites.

Travel from island to island is by boat. The distances from one site to another vary from a few kilometres to over 150 km, and journey times vary from less than an hour to overnight. To visit each site, you will travel from ship to shore by small dinghy (locally called "panga") and land either on rocks or beaches. When landing on beaches your feet will get wet, so it is advisable to carry your shoes and a small towel ashore and to put on your shoes on the beach. Rocky landings are usually dry, so it is best to keep your shoes on, especially as the rocks may be sharp.

Tourist and sea lion, North Seymour Island.

Most visits take three to four hours of the morning or afternoon. This gives ample time to walk the trails at a leisurely pace and to study and photograph the fascinating plants and animals (Plates 71, 72). The sun is often intense, so it is recommended that you bring a good sun-screen cream and wear a hat. Some of the terrain is rough, owing to its volcanic nature, so it is a good idea to wear light walking boots or sturdy shoes. A spare pair is advisable as the first is likely to get wet. When going from ship to shore or back, it can be wet with spray, so it is always advisable to have your camera and other valuables well-protected in plastic bags or waterproof cases.

While you are on board ship, take advantage of the opportunities provided to scan for sea birds, whales and dolphins. Enjoy the beautiful scenery and take in the sunsets. If you can, look out for the "green flash." Frequently, as the sun sets or rises, a green glow is seen for an instant. This phenomenon is now understood to be the result of the effect of the atmosphere on various wavelengths (colours) of light. The dust in the atmosphere scatters the blue end of the spectrum more than the red end. This is what makes the sky above appear blue and the sun appear red when it is near the horizon (when the blue is "lost," red and orange are left. The atmosphere bends light as well as scattering it, but the red end of the spectrum is bent less than the blue. This means that when the sun sets, we lose the red first, then orange, yellow, green, blue and violet. Because the blue and violet are scattered, we see green as our last glimpse of the sun's light.

The author studying a young Galápagos hawk.

The yacht *Andando*.

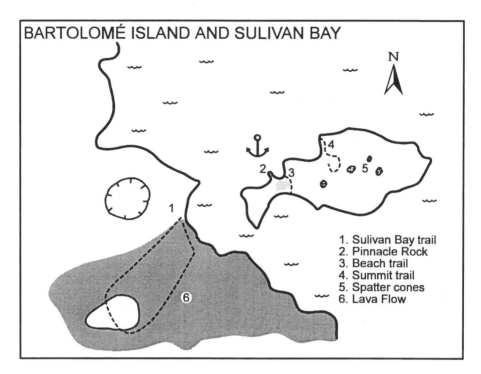

BARTOLOMÉ ISLAND AND SULIVAN BAY

1. Sulivan Bay trail
2. Pinnacle Rock
3. Beach trail
4. Summit trail
5. Spatter cones
6. Lava Flow

Notes About Some of the Visitor Sites

In the following section, many of the most often visited sites are described; sketch maps are provided for some of them. The sketch maps are based on Moore and Moore's booklet *Guide to the Visitor Sites of Parque Nacional Galápagos* (1980), produced by the Galápagos National Park Service.

Bartolomé Island

Dry landing, trail to summit (114 m), pioneer plants, *Tiquilia, Chamaesyce, Scalesia stewartii*, spatter cones, lava tubes, *Brachycereus*.

Wet landing, trail to south beach through mangroves and dune vegetation, turtles and sharks, herons, north beach, swimming and snorkelling. Pinnacle Rock, penguins often present.

Sulivan Bay (Santiago Island)

Dry landing, lava flow from turn of this century, still virtually uneroded, covers large area, pahoehoe or rope lava, hornitos, *Mollugo, Brachycereus*, lava colonisers.

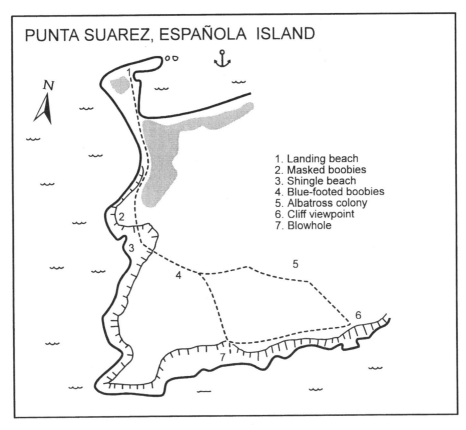

PUNTA SUAREZ, ESPAÑOLA ISLAND

N

1. Landing beach
2. Masked boobies
3. Shingle beach
4. Blue-footed boobies
5. Albatross colony
6. Cliff viewpoint
7. Blowhole

Española Island

Gardner Bay
Wet landing, long white sand beach, swimming, mockingbirds, sea lions.

Punta Suarez
Wet landing, sea lion colonies, colourful subspecies of marine iguana, Hood mockingbird, endemic lava lizard, large cactus finch, blue-footed booby colonies, masked booby colonies, swallow-tailed gulls, waved albatross colony, red-billed tropicbirds. oystercatchers, blowhole, low scrub vegetation.

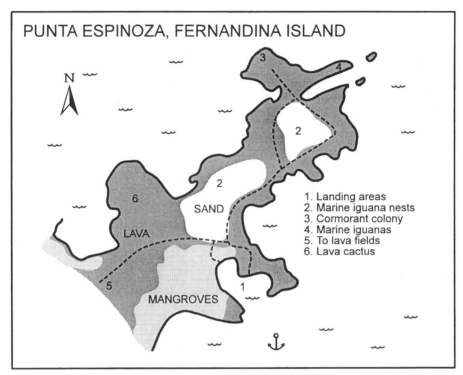

PUNTA ESPINOZA, FERNANDINA ISLAND

N

3
4
2
2
6
SAND
LAVA
5
MANGROVES
1

1. Landing areas
2. Marine iguana nests
3. Cormorant colony
4. Marine iguanas
5. To lava fields
6. Lava cactus

Fernandina Island

Punta Espinoza

Dry landing, marine iguanas, flightless cormorant, sea lions, penguins, Galápagos hawk, Brachycereus cactus, aa lava.

A visitor and marine iguanas, Punta Espinoza, Fernandina Island.

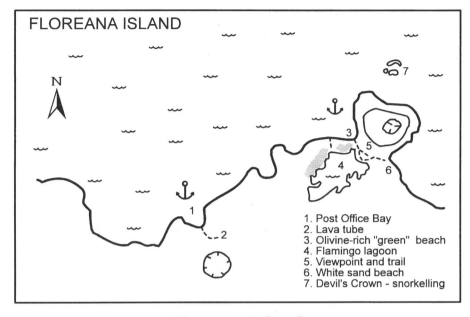

FLOREANA ISLAND

N

1. Post Office Bay
2. Lava tube
3. Olivine-rich "green" beach
4. Flamingo lagoon
5. Viewpoint and trail
6. White sand beach
7. Devil's Crown - snorkelling

Floreana Island

Devil's Crown
Dinghy ride around half-submerged crater, red-billed tropicbirds, herons, snorkelling in and around crater is excellent.

Post Office Bay
Wet landing, site of whalers' post office barrel and early settlement, lava tunnel.

Punta Cormorant
Wet landing on brown beach with greenish olivine crystals, flamingo lagoons, wading birds, *Lecocarpus pinnatifidus* and *Scalesia villosa*. Walk along lagoon, fine white sand beach, stingrays, turtles, sea grape and *Nolana* shrubs.

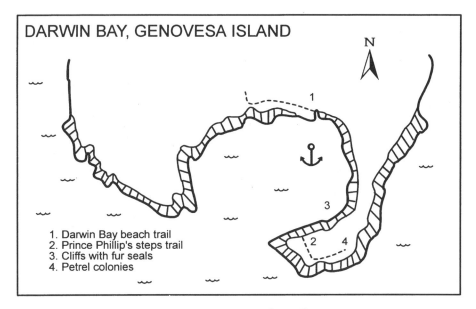

Genovesa Island

Darwin Bay

Wet landing, coral beach, swallow-tailed gulls, sea lions, red-footed booby, masked booby, large ground finch, large cactus finch, sharp-billed ground finch, no lizards, no snakes, small marine iguanas, great frigatebird, Galápagos dove.

Prince Phillip's Steps

Dry landing, cliff, fur seals, tropicbirds, storm petrels, great frigatebird, red-footed booby, masked booby, doves, finches.

Looking north from Alcedo Volcano, Isabela Island, at Darwin and Wolf Volcanoes.

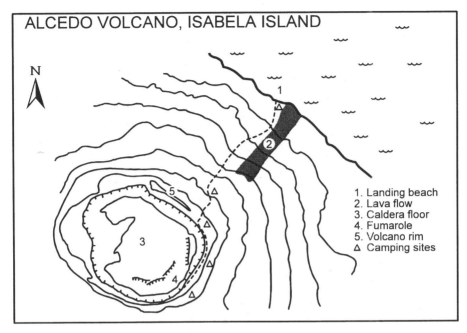

ALCEDO VOLCANO, ISABELA ISLAND

N

1. Landing beach
2. Lava flow
3. Caldera floor
4. Fumarole
5. Volcano rim
△ Camping sites

Isabela Island

Alcedo Volcano

Wet landing, long hike (overnight), giant tortoises, hawks, caldera views, fumarole, vegetation zones.

Elizabeth Bay

Dinghy ride, turtle lagoons, penguins, large mangroves, views of Sierra Negra Volcano.

Puerto Villamil

Dry landing, small town, long beach, trip to highlands and Sierra Negra Volcano. Lagoons with flamingos and wading birds.

Punta Garcia

Dinghy ride, flightless cormorants, pelicans, aa lava landscape.

Punta Moreno

Dry landing, lava fields, pioneer plants, occasionally flamingos in oasis-like green lagoons, flightless cormorant, marine iguana.

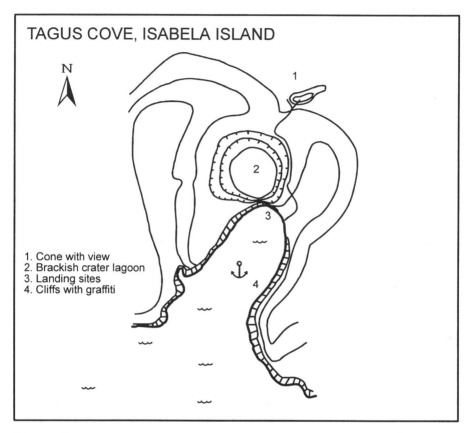

TAGUS COVE, ISABELA ISLAND

N

1. Cone with view
2. Brackish crater lagoon
3. Landing sites
4. Cliffs with graffiti

Tagus Cove

Dinghy ride along cliffs, Dry landing, tuff cone formations, ash deposits, salt lake crater, historical graffiti, view of Darwin Volcano, Arid zone vegetation, flightless cormorant, Galápagos penguins, finches.

Urbina Bay

Wet landing, uplifted corals from 1954, marine iguanas, flightless cormorant, dramatic landscape.

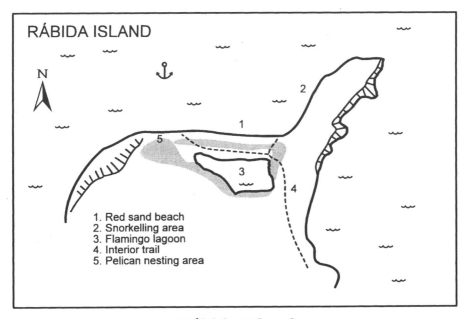

RÁBIDA ISLAND

N

1. Red sand beach
2. Snorkelling area
3. Flamingo lagoon
4. Interior trail
5. Pelican nesting area

Rábida Island

Wet landing, red sand beach, sea lions, flamingos and pelican colony, snorkelling.

A group of visitors taking a "panga" or dinghy ride.

San Cristóbal Island

Punta Pitt

Wet landing with sea lions, trail climbs up stream bed to plateau. *Nolana, Sesuvium,* red-footed, masked and blue-footed boobies.

Wreck Bay

Dry landing, capital of Galápagos province, Frigatebird Hill, trip to highlands, El Junco Lake.

Santa Cruz Island

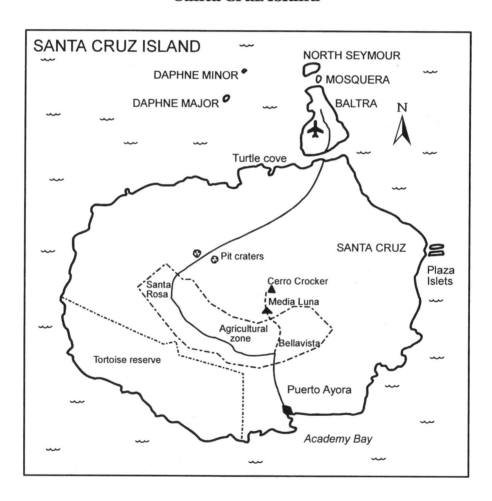

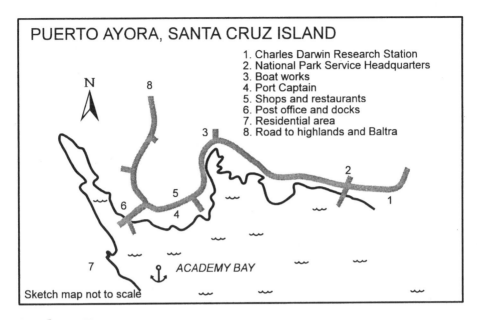

PUERTO AYORA, SANTA CRUZ ISLAND

1. Charles Darwin Research Station
2. National Park Service Headquarters
3. Boat works
4. Port Captain
5. Shops and restaurants
6. Post office and docks
7. Residential area
8. Road to highlands and Baltra

N

ACADEMY BAY

Sketch map not to scale

Academy Bay

Charles Darwin Research Station: Dry landing, Van Straelen Exhibition Hall, giant tortoise pens, tortoise raising house, Arid zone vegetation, many Darwin's finches.

Puerto Ayora: Shops, post office, refreshments, souvenirs.

Highlands

From Puerto Ayora, drive up through Transition zone vegetation, agricultural area in humid zone, Bellavista, Santa Rosa, Scalesia forest, pit craters. Tortoise Reserve/Caseta, Media Luna and Pampa vegetation, lava tubes, Darwin's finches, vermilion flycatcher, rain gear often required.

Turtle Cove

Dinghy ride, mangrove lagoons, turtles, pelicans, herons, rays, sharks.

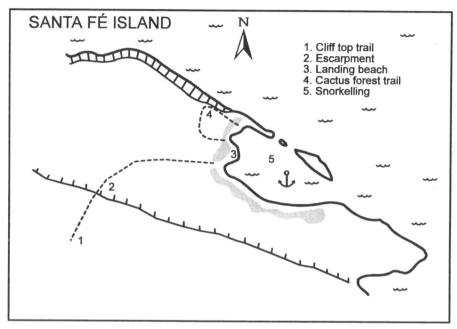

SANTA FÉ ISLAND   N

1. Cliff top trail
2. Escarpment
3. Landing beach
4. Cactus forest trail
5. Snorkelling

Santa Fé Island

Wet landing, sea lion beaches, cactus forest with giant *Opuntia*, Arid zone vegetation, walk to escarpment, *Scalesia helleri*, land iguanas.

The "saltmine" crater, James Bay, Santiago Island.

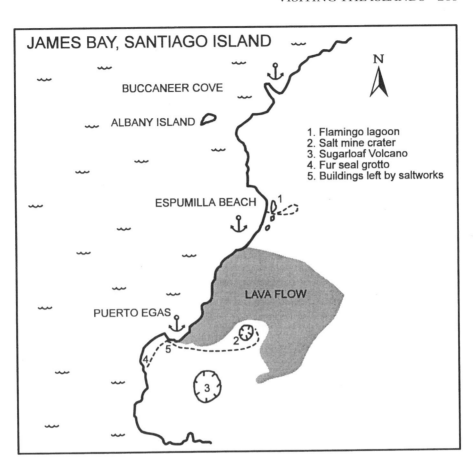

Santiago Island

Buccaneer Cove

Cruise along cliffs, interesting rock formations, area for protection of plants from goats.

James Bay

Espumilla Beach: Wet landing, flamingo lagoon, ducks, stilts, some waders, mangroves, turtle nesting beach, walk inland to Transition zone vegetation.

Puerto Egas: Wet landing, walk along coast to fur seal grotto, intertidal life, shore birds, marine iguanas, sea lions, snorkelling, swimming.

Walk to salt mine, Arid zone vegetation, Darwin's finches, hawks, feral goats.

Walk to spring and/or to Sugarloaf Volcano (395 m), goats, Galápagos hawks, Galápagos doves and finches at seepage, savannah vegetation as a result of goats, land iguanas extinct because of pigs and goats. Remains of building from saltworks.

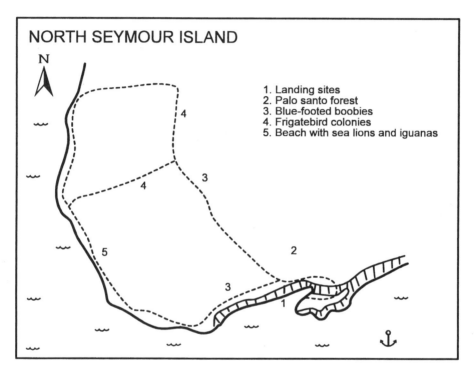

NORTH SEYMOUR ISLAND

N

1. Landing sites
2. Palo santo forest
3. Blue-footed boobies
4. Frigatebird colonies
5. Beach with sea lions and iguanas

Seymour Island (North Seymour)

Dry landing, uplifted island, loop trail, magnificent frigatebirds, blue-footed boobies, sea lions, marine iguanas, swallow-tailed gulls, snakes, endemic Palo santo, low shrubby-type *Opuntia*.

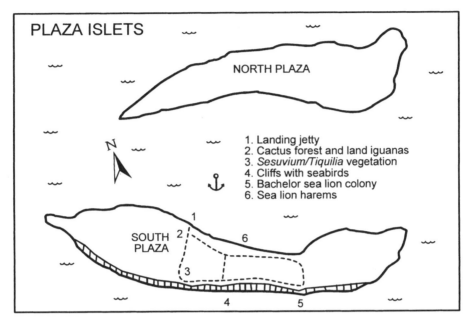

South Plaza Islet

Dry landing, uplifted island, sea lion colony, land iguanas and cactus forest, *Sesuvium-Portulaca* vegetation, cliffs with swallow-tailed gulls, red-billed tropicbirds, Audubon shearwaters, sea lion bachelor colony.

Selected Bibliography

Readers wanting to pursue further studies of Galápagos natural history may wish to consult the following books, articles and manuscripts. The list is by no means exhaustive, as a number of full bibliographies are already available. In particular, the bibliography provided by Ian Thornton in his *Darwin's Islands* is recommended for works prior to 1970. My intent in this bibliography is to concentrate on the more recent works.

The General Bibliography lists books that are of general interest or cover a wide range of topics. Following this come the chapter by chapter bibliographies, which list works that are directly relevant to the topic at hand. If a given work appears in the General Bibliography and is also listed under a specific chapter bibliography, the complete citation is usually not repeated. See, for example, Bowman 1966; Bowman et al. 1983; Darwin 1845; Darwin 1859; Perry 1984; and Thornton 1971.

General Bibliography

Amos, W.H.1980. *Wildlife of the Islands* (Wildlife Habitat Series). New York: H.N. Abrams.

Beebe, W. 1924. *Galápagos—World's End*. London and New York: C.P. Putnam.

Berrill, N.J. and M. Berrill. 1969. *The Life of Sea Islands*. New York: McGraw-Hill.

Black, J. 1973. *Galápagos, Archipiélago del Ecuador*. Quito, Ecuador: Imprenta Europa.

Bowman, R.I., ed. 1966. *The Galápagos*. Proceedings of the Symposia of the Galápagos International Scientific Project. Berkeley: University of California Press.

Bowman, R.I., M. Berson, and A.E. Leviton, eds. 1983. *Patterns of Evolution in Galápagos Organisms*. San Francisco: A.A.A.S., Pacific Division.

Boyce, B. 1990. *A Traveller's Guide to the Galápagos Islands*. San José, California: Galápagos Travel.

Brower, K. and E. Porter. 1968. *Galápagos: The Flow of Wildness*. San Francisco: Sierra Club.

Carlquist, S. 1965. *Island Life*. Garden City, N.Y.: Natural History Press.

Constant, P.R. 1983. *Guide de l'Archipel des Galápagos*. Lyons, France: Malmenaide.

Darwin, C. 1845. *The Voyage of the Beagle*. London: John Murray.

Darwin, C. 1859. *The Origin of Species*. London: John Murray.

Eibl-Eibesfeldt, I. 1961. *Galápagos—Noah's Ark of the Pacific*. New York: Doubleday.

Epler, D., A. White, and C. Gilbert. 1972. *Galápagos Guide*. Quito, Ecuador: Imprenta Europa.

Farb, N. 1989. *Galápagos*. New York: Rizzoli.

Harris, M.P. 1974. *A Field Guide to the Birds of the Galápagos*. London: Collins.

Hickin, N. 1979. *Animal Life of the Galápagos*. Quito, Ecuador: Libri Mundi.

Horwell, D. 1988. *Galápagos: The Enchanted Isles*. London: Dryad.

Humann, P. 1988. *Galápagos*. Santiago, Chile: Editorial Kactus.

Lewin, R. and S.A. Thompson. 1978. *Darwin's Forgotten World*. London: Bison.

Livingston, J. and L. Sinclair. 1966. *Darwin and the Galápagos*. Toronto: Canadian Broadcasting Corporation.

Maldonado-Robles, L. and C. Sarramon. 1982. *Galápagos Pacific*. Paris: Editions D.S.

Moore, T. 1980. *Islands Lost in Time*. New York: Viking.

Moorehead, A. 1971. *Darwin and the Beagle*. Harmondsworth, England: Penguin.

Nelson, B. 1968. *Galápagos: Islands of Birds*. London: Longmans, Green.

Perry, R. 1972. *The Galápagos Islands*. New York: Dodd, Mead.

Perry, R., ed. 1984. *Galápagos—Key Environments*. Oxford: Pergamon.

Rachiowiecki, R. 1989. *Ecuador & the Galápagos Islands—A Travel Survival Kit*, 2d ed. Berkeley: Lonely Planet.

Rogers, B.R. 1990. *Galápagos*. New York: Mallard.

Salwen, P. 1989. *Galápagos—The Lost Paradise*. New York: Mallard.

Steadman, D.W. and S. Zousmer. 1988. *Galápagos: Discovery on Darwin's Islands*. Washington, D.C.: Smithsonian Institution Press.

Stephenson, M. 1989. *The Galápagos Islands*. Seattle: The Mountaineers.

Thornton, I. 1971. *Darwin's Islands: A Natural History of the Galápagos*. Garden City, N.Y.: Natural History Press.

Vonnegut, K. 1985. *Galápagos, A Novel*. New York: Dell.

Chapter 1: Historical Background

Angermeyer, J. 1989. *My Father's Island*. New York: Viking.

Brower, K. and E. Porter. 1968. *Galápagos: The Flow of Wildness*. San Francisco: Sierra Club.

Darwin, C. 1845. *The Voyage of the Beagle*.

Darwin, C. 1859. *The Origin of Species*.

Galápagos National Park Service. 1979. An outline of historical events related to the development and conservation of the Galápagos. Mimeographed sheets prepared for the Galápagos naturalist guides' course. C.D.R.S. Library, Galápagos.

Geary, D. 1977. Violence in Eden. *Washington Post*, May 22.

Heyerdahl, T. 1963. Archaeology in the Galápagos Islands. *Occasional Papers of the California Academy of Sciences* 44:45–51.

Hickman, J. 1985. *The Enchanted Islands: The Galápagos Discovered*. Oswestry, U.K.: Anthony Nelson.

Latorre, O. 1990. *The Curse of the Giant Tortoise*. Quito, Ecuador: Latorre.

Morrell, B. 1832. *A Narrative of Four Voyages to the South Sea*. New York: Harper.

Perry, R. 1972. *The Galápagos Islands*. New York: Dodd, Mead.

Perry, R. 1984. The islands and their history. In: Perry 1984.

Porter, D. 1815. *Journal of a Cruise Made to the Pacific Ocean*, 2 vols. Philadelphia: Bradford and Inskeep.

Slevin, J.R. 1959. The Galápagos Islands: A history of their exploration. *Occasional Papers of the California Academy of Sciences* 25:1–150.

Sulloway, F.J. 1984. Darwin and the Galápagos. *Biological J. Linnaean Society* 21:29–59.

Townsend, C.H. 1925. The Galápagos tortoises in relation to the whaling industry. *Zoologica* 4(3):55–135.

Treherne, J.E. 1983. *The Galápagos Affair*. London: Jonathan Cape.

Vancouver, G. 1984. *A Voyage of Discovery to the North Pacific Ocean and Around the World*, ed. W. Kay Lamb. London: Hakluyt Society.

Wittmer, M. 1989. *Floreana*. Oswestry, U.K.: Anthony Nelson.

Woram, J.M. 1989. Galápagos island names. *Noticias de Galápagos* 48:22–32.

Chapter 2: Galápagos Environment

American Association of Petroleum Geologists. 1981. *Plate Tectonics Maps of the Circum-Pacific Region*. Tulsa, Oklahoma: American Association of Petroleum Geologists.

Alpert, L. 1963. Climate of the Galápagos Islands. *Occasional Papers of the California Academy of Sciences* 44:21–44.

Bailey, K. 1976. Potassium-argon ages from the Galápagos Islands. *Science* 192:465–66.

Chadwick, W.W. and K.A. Howard. 1991. The pattern of circumferential and radial eruptive fissures on the volcanoes of Fernandina and Isabela Islands, Galápagos. *Bull. Volcanol.* 53:259–75.

Chadwick, W.W., T. de Roy and A. Carrasco. 1991. The September 1988 intracaldera avalanche and eruption at Fernandina Volcano, Galápagos Islands. *Bull. Volcanol.* 53:276–86.

Christie, D.M. et al. 1992. Drowned islands downstream from the Galápagos hotspot imply extended speciation times. *Nature* 355:246–28.

Darwin, C. 1933. *Darwin's Diary of the Voyage of H.M.S. Beagle*, edited from the manuscript by N. Barlow. Cambridge: University Press.

Beebe, W. 1924. *Galápagos—World's End*. London and New York: C.P. Putnam.

Black, J. 1973. *Galápagos, Archipiélago del Ecuador*. Quito, Ecuador: Imprenta Europa.

Colinvaux, P.A. 1972. Climate and the Galápagos Islands. *Nature* 240:17–20.

Colinvaux, P.A. 1984. The Galápagos climate: Present and past. In: Perry 1984.

Cox, A. 1983. Ages of the Galápagos Islands. In: Bowman et al. 1983.

Francis, P. 1976. *Volcanoes.* Middlesex, England: Penguin.

Galápagos National Park Service. 1979. Notes on Galápagos geology. Mimeographed sheets prepared for the Galápagos naturalist guides' course. C.D.R.S. Library, Galápagos.

Geological Museum. 1972. *The Story of the Earth.* London: H.M.S.O. for Institute of Geological Sciences.

Geological Museum. 1974. *Volcanoes.* London: H.M.S.O. for Institute of Geological Sciences.

Hall, M.L. 1977. *El Volcanismo en el Ecuador.* Quito, Ecuador: Biblioteca Ecuador.

Hall, M.L. 1983. Origin of Española Island and the age of terrestrial life on the Galápagos Islands. *Science* 221:545–47.

Harris, M.P. 1974. *A Field Guide to the Birds of the Galápagos.* London: Collins.

Hickman, C.S. and J.H. Lipps. 1985. Geologic youth of Galápagos Islands confirmed by marine stratigraphy and paleontology. *Science* 227:1578–80.

Houvenhagel, G.T. 1984. Oceanographic setting of the Galápagos Islands. In: Perry 1984.

Instituto Geografico Militar. 1981. Mapa Fisica del Republica de Ecuador, 1:100 000. Quito, Ecuador: Instituto Geografico Militar.

Levenson, J. 1983. Pacific life struggles in a warming sea. *Discover* (October):29–32.

MacDonald, G. 1972. *Volcanoes.* Englewood Cliffs, N.J.: Prentice-Hall.

McBirney, A.R. 1988. Geological studies, 1984–1985. Charles Darwin Research Station *Annual Report* 5:23–24.

McBirney, A.R. and H. Williams. 1969. Geology and petrology of the Galápagos Islands. *Geological Society of America Memoirs*, 118.

Nordlie, B.E. 1973. Morphology and structure of western Galápagos volcanoes and a model for their origin. *Geological Society of America Bulletin* 84:2931–56.

Palmer, C.E. and R.L. Pyle. 1966. The climatological setting of the Galápagos. In: Bowman 1966.

Robinson, G. and E.M. del Pino, eds. 1985. *El Niño in the Galápagos Islands—The 1982–1983 Event.* Quito, Ecuador: Charles Darwin Foundation.

Simkin, T. 1984a. Geology of Galápagos. *Biological J. Linnaean Society* 21:61–75.

Simkin, T. 1984b. Geology of Galápagos Islands. In: Perry 1984.

Simkin, T. and K.A. Howard. 1970. Caldera collapse in the Galápagos Islands, 1968. *Science* 169:429–37.

Simpson, B.B. 1974. Glacial migrations of plants: Island biogeographical evidence. *Science* 185:698–700.

Smith, R.L. 1983. Peru coastal currents during El Niño: 1976 and 1982. *Science* 221:1397–99.

Williams, H. 1966. Geology of the Galápagos Islands. In: Bowman 1966.

Wooster, W.S. and J.W. Hedgpeth. 1966. The oceanographic setting of the Galápagos. In: Bowman 1966.

Chapter 3: Colonisation, Evolution and Ecology

Abbott, I.J., L.K. Abbott, and P.R. Grant. 1977. Comparative ecology of Galápagos ground finches. *Ecological Monographs* 47:151–86.

Attenborough, D. 1979. *Life on Earth*. London: Collins.

Boag, P.T. and P.R. Grant. 1981. Intense natural selection in a population of Darwin's finches (Geospizinae) in the Galápagos. *Science* 214:82–85.

Carlquist, S.J. 1965. *Island Life*. Garden City, N.Y.: Natural History Press.

Carlquist, S.J. 1966a. The biota of long-distance dispersal. I. Principals of dispersal and evolution. *Quarterly Review of Biology* 41(3):247–70.

Carlquist, S.J. 1966b. The biota of long-distance dispersal. II. Loss of dispersibility in Pacific Compositae. *Evolution* 20(1):30–48.

Carlquist, S.J. 1970. *Hawaii: A Natural History*. New York: Natural History Press.

Carlquist, S.J. 1974. *Island Biology*. New York: Columbia University Press.

Carlquist, S.J. 1981. Chance dispersal. *American Scientist* 69:509–16.

Colinvaux, P.A. and E.K. Schofield. 1976a. Historical ecology in the Galápagos Islands. I. A Holocene pollen record from El Junco Lake, Isla San Cristobal. *J. Ecology* 64:989–1012.

Colinvaux, P.A. and E.K. Schofield. 1976b. Historical ecology in the Galápagos Islands. II. A Holocene spore record from El Junco Lake, Isla San Cristobal. *J. Ecology* 64:1013–28.

Colinvaux, P.A. 1980. *Why Big Fierce Animals are Rare*. London: Allen and Unwin.

Connor, E.F. and D. Simberloff. 1978. Species number and compositional similarity of the Galápagos flora and avifauna. *Ecological Monographs* 48:219–48.

Cox, C.B. and P.D. Moore. 1980. *Biogeography: An Ecological and Evolutionary Approach*, 3d ed. Oxford: Blackwell Scientific Publ.

Darwin, C. 1845. *The Voyage of the Beagle*.

Darwin, C. 1859. *The Origin of Species*.

Darwin, C. and A.R. Wallace. 1859. On the tendency of species to form varieties, and on the perpetuation of varieties and species by natural selection. *J. Proc. Linnaean Society (Zoology)* 3:45–62.

Dawson, W.R., G.A. Bartholomew, and A.F. Bennet. 1977. A reappraisal of the aquatic specialisations of the Galápagos marine iguana. *Evolution* 31:891–97.

Einarsson, E. 1967. The colonisation of Surtsey, the new volcanic island, by vascular plants. *Aquilo Series Botanica* 6:172–82.

Elton, C.S. 1927. *Animal Ecology*. New York: MacMillan.

Fridriksson, S. 1975. *Surtsey*. New York: J. Wiley.

Fritts, T.H. 1984. Evolutionary divergence of giant tortoises in Galápagos. *Biological J. Linnaean Society* 21:165–76.

Gorman, M.L. 1979. *Island Ecology*. London: Chapman and Hall.

Grant, B.R. and P.R. Grant. 1983. Fission and fusion in a population of Darwin's finches. *Oikos* 41(3):530–47.

Grant, P.R. 1981. Speciation and adaptive radiation of Darwin's finches. *American Scientist* 69:653–63.

Grant, P.R. 1984a. Recent research on the evolution of land birds on the Galápagos. *Biological J. Linnaean Society* 21:113–36.

Grant, P.R. and P.T. Boag. 1980. Rainfall on the Galápagos, Ecuador, and the demography of Darwin's finches. *Auk* 97(2):227–44.

Grant, P.R. and B.R. Grant. 1980. Annual variation in finch numbers foraging and food supply on Isla Daphne Major, Galápagos, Ecuador. *Oecologia* 46(1):55–62.

Grant, P.R., J.N.M. Smith, B.R. Grant, I.J. Abbott, and L.K. Abbott. 1975. Finch numbers, owl predation, and plant dispersal on Isla Daphne Major, Galápagos. *Oecologia* 19:239–57.

Hamann, O. 1981. Plant communities of the Galápagos. *Dansk Botanisk Arkiv* 36(2):1–163.

Itow, S. 1975. Rain shadow effects on vegetation distribution in the Galápagos Islands. *XIII Pacific Science Congress Abstracts*, 100.

James, M.J. 1984. A new look at evolution in the Galápagos: Evidence from the late Cenozoic marine molluscan fauna. *Biological J. Linnaean Society* 21:77–95.

Johnson, M.P. and P.H. Raven. 1973. Species number and endemism: The Galápagos archipelago revisited. *Science* 179:893–95.

Krebs, C.J. 1978. *Ecology: The Experimental Analysis of Distribution and Abundance*, 2d ed. New York: Harper and Row.

Lack, D. 1947. *Darwin's Finches*. London: Cambridge University Press.

Lyell, Sir. C.I.L. 1830–33. *Principles of Geology*, 3 vols. London: J. Murray.

MacArthur, R.H. and E.O. Wilson. 1967. *The Theory of Island Biogeography*. Princeton: Princeton University Press.

Odum, E.P. 1971. *Fundamentals of Ecology*, 3d ed. Philadelphia: N.B. Saunders.

Patton, J.L. 1984. Genetical processes in the Galápagos. *Biological J. Linnaean Society* 21:97–111.

Porter, D.M. 1976. Geography and dispersal of Galápagos Islands vascular plants. *Nature* 264:745–46.

Porter, D.M. 1979. Endemism and evolution in Galápagos Islands vascular plants. In: *Plants and Islands*, ed. D. Bramwell. New York: Academic Press.

Porter, D.M. 1984a. Relationships of the Galápagos flora. *Biological J. Linnaean Society* 21:243–51.

Porter, D.M. 1984b. Endemism and evolution in terrestrial plants. In: Perry 1984.

Price, T.D. and S.J. Millington. 1982. Birds on Daphne Major. *Noticias de Galápagos* 35:25–27.

Reeder, G.W. and S.E. Reichert. 1975. Vegetation change along an altitudinal gradient, Santa Cruz Island, Galápagos. *Biotropica* 7(3):162–75.

Rick, C.M. 1966. Some plant-animal relations on the Galápagos Islands. In: Bowman 1966.

Rick, C.M. and R.I. Bowman. 1961. Galápagos tomatoes and tortoises. *Evolution* 15:407–17.

Thornton, I. 1971. *Darwin's Islands*.

Van der Werff, H. 1979. Conservation and vegetation of the Galápagos Islands. In: *Plants and Islands*, ed. D. Bramwell. New York: Academic Press.

Van der Werff, H. 1983. Species number, area and habitat diversity in the Galápagos Islands. *Vegetatio* 54(3):167–75.

Wallace, A.R. 1892. *Island Life*, 2d ed. London: MacMillan.

Wiggins, I.L. and D.M. Porter. 1971. *Flora of the Galápagos Islands.* Stanford: Stanford University Press.

Williamson, M. 1981. *Island Populations.* Oxford: Oxford University Press.

Chapter 4: Plant Life

Arp, G.K. 1973. The Galápagos Opuntias: Another interpretation. *Noticias de Galápagos* 21:33–37.

Clark, D.A. and D.B. Clark. 1981. Effects of seed dispersal by animals on the regeneration of *Bursera graveolens* (Burseraceae) Santa Fé Island, Galápagos. Ecuador. *Oecologia* 49(1):73–75.

Colinvaux, P.A. and E.K. Schofield. 1976b. Historical ecology in the Galápagos Islands. II. *J. Ecology* 64:1013–28.

Connor, E.F. and D. Simberloff. 1978. Species number and compositional similarity of the Galápagos flora and avifauna. *Ecological Monographs* 48:219–48.

Dawson, E.Y. 1966. Cacti in the Galápagos Islands, with special reference to their relations with tortoises. In: Bowman 1966.

Eliasson, U. 1974. Studies in Galápagos plants. XIV. The genus Scalesia Arn. *Opera Botanica* 36:1–117.

Eliasson, U. 1984. Native climax forests. In: Perry 1984.

Grant, B.R. and P.R. Grant. 1981. Exploitation of *Opuntia* cactus by birds on the Galápagos, Pacific Ocean. *Oecologia* 49(2):179–87.

Hamann, O. 1979. On climatic conditions, vegetation types and leaf size in the Galápagos Islands. *Biotropica* 11:101–22.

Hamann, O. 1981. Plant communities of the Galápagos. *Dansk Botanisk Arkiv* 36(2):1–163.

Hamann, O. 1984. Changes and threats to the vegetation. In: Perry 1984.

Hamann, O. and S.W. Andersen. 1986. *Scalesia gordilloi,* a new Galápagos plant species. *Noticias de Galápagos* 44:13–14.

Hepper, F.N. 1979. Plants that live on Darwin's Islands. *Geographical Monographs* (London) 52:222–28.

Hooker, J.D. 1846. An enumeration of the plants of the Galápagos Archipelago, with descriptions of those which are new. *Trans. Linnaean Society of London* 20(2):163–233.

MacBryde, B. 1981. Some useful botanical literature and information for Galápagos guides. Unpublished manuscript. C.D.R.S., Galápagos.

Perry, R. 1974. Sunflower trees of the Galápagos. *Noticias de Galápagos* 22:11–13.

Porter, D.M. 1976. Geography and dispersal of Galápagos Islands vascular plants. *Nature* 264:745–46.

Porter, D.M. 1979. Endemism and evolution in Galápagos Islands vascular plants. In: *Plants and Islands,* ed. D. Bramwell. New York: Academic Press.

Porter, D.M. 1983. Vascular plants of the Galápagos: Origins and dispersal. In: Bowman et al. 1983.

Porter, D.M. 1984a. Relationships of the Galápagos flora. *Biological J. Linnaean Society* 21:243–51.

Porter, D.M. 1984b. Endemism and evolution in terrestrial plants. In: Perry 1984.

Schoenitzer, K. 1975. *Galápagos Plants.* Quito. Privately published.

Schofield, E.K. 1970. *Field Guide to Some Common Galápagos Plants.* Columbus: Ohio State University Research Foundation.

Schofield, E.K. 1973. Annotated bibliography of Galápagos botany, 1836–971. *Annals of the Missouri Botanical Garden* 60:461–77.

Schofield, E.K. 1980. Annotated bibliography of Galápagos, Ecuador botany: Suppl. I. *Brittonia* 32(4):537–47.

Schofield, E.K. 1984. *Plants of the Galápagos Islands.* New York: Universe.

Stebbins, G.L. 1966. Variation and adaption in Galápagos plants. In: Bowman 1966.

Svenson, H.K. 1946. Vegetation of the coast of Ecuador and its relation to the Galápagos Islands. I. Geographical relations of the flora. *American J. Botany* 33(5):394–426.

Van der Werff, H. 1978. The vegetation of the Galápagos Islands. Ph.D. thesis, Rijksuniversiteit, Utrecht.

Van der Werff, H. 1983. Species number, area and habitat diversity in the Galápagos Islands. *Vegetatio* 54(3):167–75.

Weber, W.A. 1966. Lichenology and bryology in the Galápagos Islands, with check lists of the lichens and broyphytes thus far reported. In: Bowman 1966.

Weber, W.A. and S.R. Gradstein. 1984. Lichens and bryophytes. In: Perry 1984.

Weber, W.A., S.R. Gradstein, J. Lavier, and H.J.M. Shipman. 1977. Bryophytes and lichens of the Galápagos Islands. *Noticias de Galápagos* 26:7–11.

Wiggins, I.L. and D.M. Porter. 1971. *Flora of the Galápagos Islands.* Stanford: Stanford University Press.

Chapter 5: Reptiles

Bartholomew, G.A. 1966a. Interaction of physiology and behaviour under natural conditions. In: Bowman 1966.

Bartholomew, G.A. 1966b. A field study of temperature relations in the Galápagos marine iguana. *Copeia* 2:241–50.

Bellairs, A. d'A. and J. Altridge. 1975. *Reptiles.* London: Hutchinson University Library.

Boersma, P.D. 1983. An ecological study of the Galápagos marine iguana. In: Bowman et al. 1983.

Burghardt, G.M. and A.S. Rand, eds. 1982. *Iguanas of the World.* New Jersey: Noyes.

Carpenter, C.C. 1966a. Comparative behaviour of the Galápagos lava lizards (*Tropidurus*). In: Bowman 1966.

Carpenter, C.C. 1966b. The marine iguana of the Galápagos Islands: Its behaviour and ecology. *Proc. California Academy of Sciences*, Ser. 4, 34:329–76.

Carpenter, C.C. 1969. Behavioural and ecological notes on Galápagos land iguanas. *Herpetologia* 25(3):155–64.

Cayot, L.J. 1981. Tortoise-plant interactions on Santa Cruz. Charles Darwin Research Station *Annual Report*, 94–95.

Christian, K.A. 1980. Cleaning-feeding symbiosis between birds and reptiles of the Galápagos Islands. *Auk* 97(4): 887–89.

Christian, K.A. and C.R. Tracy. 1980. The physical and biotic determinants of space and time utilisation by the Galápagos land iguana. *American Zoologist* 20(4):747.

Christian, K.A. and C.R. Tracy. 1981. Effect of the thermal environment on the ability of hatchling Galápagos land iguanas to avoid predation during dispersal. *Oecologia* 49(2):218–23.

Christian, K.A., C.R. Tracy, and W.P. Porter. 1983. Seasonal shifts in body temperature and use of micro habitats by Galápagos land iguanas. *Ecology* 64(3):463–68.

Darwin, C. 1845. *The Voyage of the Beagle.*

Dawson, W.R., G.A. Bartholomew, and A.F. Bennet. 1977. A reappraisal of the aquatic specialisations of the Galápagos marine iguana. *Evolution* 31:891–97.

de Vries, T.J. 1984. The giant tortoises: A natural history disturbed by man. In: Perry 1984.

Eibl-Eibesfeldt, I. 1966a. Marine iguanas. *Animals* 9(3):150–52.

Eibl-Eibesfeldt, I. 1984a. The large iguanas of the Galápagos Islands. In: Perry 1984.

Fitch, H.S. 1982. Reproductive cycles in tropical reptiles. *Occasional Papers of the Museum of Natural History, University of Kansas* 96:1–53.

Fritts, T.H. 1983. Morphometrics of Galápagos tortoises: Evolutionary implications. In: Bowman et al. 1983.

Fritts, T.H. 1984. Evolutionary divergence of giant tortoises in Galápagos. *Biological J. Linnaean Society* 21:165–76.

Green, D. 1984. Long distance movements of Galápagos, Ecuador, green turtles. *J. Herpetology* 18:121–30.

Greene, H.W and R.P. Reynolds. In press. Galápagos snakes: A simple model for the integration of systematics and natural history in conservation. In: *Conservation of Reptiles in the Galápagos Islands*, eds. H.L. Snell and T.H. Fritts. Albuquerque: University of New Mexico Press.

Hendrickson, J.D. 1966. The Galápagos tortoises, Geochelone Fitzinger 1835 (Testudo Linnaeus 1758 in part). In: Bowman 1966.

Herrero, S. 1990. Galápagos giant tortoises face major new threat. *Oryx* 24:168–69.

Higgins, P.J. 1978. The Galápagos iguanas: Models of reptilian differentiation. *Bioscience* 28(8):512–15.

Hoogmoed, J.M. 1989. Introduced geckos in Puerto Ayora, Santa Cruz, with remarks on other areas. *Noticias de Galápagos* 47:12–15.

Kushlan, J.A. 1981. Egg cache of a Galápagos gecko. *J. Herpetology* 15(1):121–22.

Laurie, A. 1983. Marine iguanas in the Galápagos. *Oryx* 17(1):18–25.

Laurie, A. 1990. Population biology of marine iguanas. I. Changes in fecundity related to a population crash. *J. Animal Ecology* 59:515–528.

MacFarland, C. and W.G. Reeder. 1974. Cleaning symbiosis involving Galápagos tortoises and two species of Darwin's finches. *Zeitschrift für Tierpsychologie* 34:464–83.

MacFarland, C.G., J. Villa, and B. Toro. 1974a. The Galápagos giant tortoises (*Geochelone elephantopus*). I: Status of the surviving populations. *Biological Conservation* 6:118–33.

MacKay, S. 1964. Galápagos tortoise and marine iguana deep body temperatures measured by radio telemetry. *Nature* 204:355–58.

Marlow, R.W. and J.L. Patton. 1981. Biochemical relationships of the Galápagos giant tortoises. *J. Zoology* (London) 195:413–22.

Meatyard, B.T., M.H. Jackson, and G.B. Estes. 1982. Cambridge Darwin Centenary Galápagos Expedition 1982. Unpublished report to sponsors.

Patton, J.L. 1984. Genetical processes in the Galápagos. *Biological J. Linnaean Society* 21:97–111.

Porter, D. 1815. *Journal of a Cruise Made to the Pacific Ocean*, 2 vols. Philadelphia: Bradford and Inskeep.

Pritchard, P.C.H. 1967. *Living Turtles of the World*. Jersey City, N.J.: TFH Publ.

Rauch, N. 1981. Reproductive behaviour of male and female marine iguanas. Charles Darwin Research Station *Annual Report*, 136–38.

Rauch, N. 1988. Competition of marine iguana females for egg-laying sites. *Behaviour* 107:91–106.

Reynolds, R.P. 1981. Land iguanas on North Seymour Island. *Noticias de Galápagos* 34:17–18.

Rodhouse, P. et al. 1975. Feeding and ranging behaviour of Galápagos giant tortoises. *J. Zoology* (London) 176:297–310.

Schafer, S.F. and C.O. Krekorian. 1983. Agonistic behaviour of the Galápagos tortoise. *Herpetologia* 39(4):448–56.

Schmidt-Nielsen, K. and R. Fange. 1958. Salt glands in marine reptiles. *Nature* 182:783–85.

Shoemaker, V.H. and K.A. Nagy. 1984. Osmo-regulation in the Galápagos marine iguana. *Physiol. Zoology* 57:291–300.

Snell, H.L. and T.H. Fritts. 1983. The significance of diurnal terrestrial emergence of green turtles in the Galápagos archipelago. *Biotropica* 15:285–91.

Snell, H.I., H.M. Snell, and C.R. Tracy. 1981a. Reproductive ecology of the Plaza Sur land iguana population. Charles Darwin Research Station *Annual Report*, 106–10.

Snell, H.I., H.M. Snell, and C.R. Tracy. 1981b. Variation among populations of Galápagos land iguanas (*Conolophus*): Contrasts of phylogeny and ecology. *Biological J. Linnaean Society* 21:185–207.

Snow, D.W. 1966. Giant tortoises. *Animals* 9(3):140–42.

Thornton, I. 1971. *Darwin's Islands*.

Trillmich, K.F. 1978. Feeding behaviour and social behaviour of the marine iguana. Charles Darwin Research Station *Annual Report*.

Trillmich, K.F. 1979. Feeding behaviour and social behaviour of the marine iguana. *Noticias de Galápagos* 29:17–20.

Werner, D.I. 1978. On the biology of *Tropidurus delanonis* (Iguanidae). *Zeitschrift für Tierpsychologie* 47(4):337–95.

Werner, D.I. 1983. Reproduction in the iguana *Conolophus subcristatus* on Fernandina Island. *American Naturalist* 121(6):757–75.

White, F.N. 1973. Temperature in the Galápagos marine iguana: Insights into reptilian thermoregulation. *Comparative Biochemistry and Physiology* 45(A):503–13.

Wright, J.W. 1983. The evolution and biogeography of the lizards of the Galápagos archipelago. In: Bowman et al. 1983.

Whyles, J.S. and V.M. Sarich. 1983. Are the Galápagos iguanas older than the Galápagos? In: Bowman et al. 1983.

Chapter 6: Sea Birds

Anderson, D.J. 1989. The role of hatching asynchrony in siblicidal brood reduction of two booby species. *Behavioural Ecology and Sociobiology* 25:363–68.

Boersma, P.D. 1974. The Galápagos penguin. Ph.D. thesis, Ohio State University.

Boersma, P.D. 1975. Adaptations of Galápagos penguins for life in two different environments. In: *The Biology of Penguins*, ed. B. Stonehouse. London: MacMillan.

Boersma, P.D. 1976. An ecological and behavioural study of the Galápagos penguin. *Living Bird* 15:43–93.

Cruz, J.B. and F. Cruz. 1990. Effect of El Niño Southern Oscillation on nestling growth rate in the dark-rumped petrel. *Condor* 92:160–65.

de Vries, T.J. and C. Hernandez. 1981. La historia natural de la fregata menor (Fregata minor) en la isla Genovesa. Charles Darwin Research Station *Annual Report*, 176–77.

Gould, S.J. 1983. *Hen's Teeth and Horses Toes*. New York: W.W. Norton.

Hailman, J.P. 1963. Why is the Galápagos lava gull the colour of lava? *Condor* 65:528.

Hailman, J.P. 1964. The Galápagos swallow-tailed gull is nocturnal. *Wilson Bulletin* 76:347–54.

Hailman, J.P. 1968. Behavioural studies of the swallow-tailed gull. *Noticias de Galápagos* 11:9–12.

Harris, M.P. 1969a. Biology of storm petrels in the Galápagos Islands. *Proc. California Academy of Sciences*, Ser. 4, 37(4):95–166.

Harris, M.P. 1969b. Breeding seasons of sea-birds in the Galápagos. *J. Zoology* (London) 159:145–56.

Harris, M.P. 1970. Biology of an endangered species, the dark-rumped petrel (*Pterodroma phaeopygia*) in the Galápagos Islands. *Condor* 72(1):76–84.

Harris, M.P. 1973. Biology of the waved albatross, *Diomedea irrorata*, of Hood Island, Galápagos. *Ibis* 115(4):483–510.

Harris, M.P. 1974. *A Field Guide to the Birds of the Galápagos*. London: Collins.

Harris, M.P. 1977. Comparative ecology of seabirds in the Galápagos archipelago. In: *Evolutionary Ecology*, ed. B. Stonehouse and C. Perrins, 67–76. Baltimore: University Park Press.

Harris, M.P. 1979. Survival and ages of first breeding of Galápagos seabirds. *Bird Banding* 50(1):56–61.

Harris, M.P. 1984. The seabirds. In: Perry 1984.

Imber, M.J. et al. 1992. Feeding ecology of the dark-rumped petrel in the Galápagos Islands. *Condor* 94:437–47.

Nelson, J.B. 1966. Fighting behaviour of Galápagos storm petrels. *Ibis* 108:430–32.

Nelson, J.B. 1968. *Galápagos: Islands of Birds*. London: Longmans.

Nelson, J.B. 1969. The breeding ecology of the red-footed booby in the Galápagos. *J. Animal Ecology* 38:181–98.

Nelson, J.B. 1977. Some relationships between food and breeding in the marine pelecaniformes. In: *Evolutionary Ecology*, ed. B. Stonehouse and C. Perrins, 78–87. Baltimore: University Park Press.

Nelson, J.B. 1978. *The Sulidae*. London: Oxford University Press.

Nelson, J.B. 1979. *Seabirds: Their Biology and Ecology*. Middlesex, England: Hamlyn.

Podolsky, R. and S.W. Kress. 1992. The attraction of the endangered dark-rumped petrel to recorded vocalizations in the Galápagos Islands. *Condor* 94:448–53.

Rechten, C. 1981. Study of the reproductive behaviour of the waved albatross on Española. Charles Darwin Research Station *Annual Report*, 179–80.

Schmidt-Nielsen, K. and W.J.L. Salden. 1957. Nasal salt secretion in the Humboldt penguin. *Nature* 181:1217–18.

Snow, B.K. 1966. Observations on the behaviour and ecology of the flightless cormorant. *Ibis* 108(2):265–80.

Snow, B.K. and D.W. Snow. 1968. The behaviour of the swallow-tailed gull of the Galápagos. *Condor* 70(3):252–64.

Snow, B.K. and D.W. Snow. 1969. Observations on the lava gull. *Ibis* 111:30–35.

Snow, D.W. 1965a. The breeding of Audubon's shearwater (*Puffinus l'herminieri*) in the Galápagos. *Auk* 82:591–97.

Snow, D.W. 1965b. The breeding cycle of the red-billed tropicbird in the Galápagos Islands. *Condor* 67:210–14.

Snow, D.W. and J.B. Nelson. 1984. Evolution and adaptations of Galápagos sea-birds. *Biological J. Linnaean Society* 21:137–55.

Snow, D.W. and B.K. Snow. 1966. The breeding season of the Madeiran storm petrel in the Galápagos. *Ibis* 108:283–84.

Snow, D.W. and B.K. Snow. 1967. The breeding cycle of the swallow-tailed gull, *Creagrus furcatus*. *Ibis* 109:14–24.

Tindle, R. 1984. The evolution of breeding strategies in the flightless cormorant (*Nannopterum harrisi*) of the Galápagos. *Biological J. Linnaean Society* 21:157–64.

Trillmich, F., K. Trillmich, A. Arnold, and D. Limberger. 1983. The breeding season of the flightless cormorant, at Cabo Hammond, Fernandina, Galápagos. *Ibis* 125(2)221–23.

Tuck, G. and H. Heinzel. 1978. *A Field Guide to the Seabirds of Britain and the World*. London: Collins.

Chapter 7: Coastal Birds and Migrants

Berrill, N.J. and M. Berrill. 1969. *The Life of Sea Islands*. New York: McGraw-Hill.

Harris, M.P. 1974. *A Field Guide to the Birds of the Galápagos*. London: Collins.

Kushlan, J.A. 1983. Pair formation behaviour of the Galápagos lava heron, *Butorides striatus/sundevalli*. *Wilson Bulletin* 95(1):118–21.

Peterson, R.T. 1961. *A Field Guide to Western Birds.* Boston: Houghton Mifflin.
Thornton, I. 1971. *Darwin's Islands.*
Tindle, R.W. and L.E. Tindle. 1978. Studies of the greater flamingo, *Phoenicopterus ruber ruber,* in the Galápagos Islands. Charles Darwin Research Station *Annual Report.*

Chapter 8: Land Birds

Abbott, I.J. and L.K. Abbott. 1978. Multi-variate study of morphological variation in Galápagos and Ecuadorean mockingbirds. *Condor* 80(3):302–08.
Abbott, I.J., L.K. Abbott, and P.R. Grant. 1977. Comparative ecology of Galápagos ground finches. *Ecological Monographs* 47:151–86.
Alatalo, R.V. 1982. Bird species distributions in the Galápagos and other archipelagoes: Competition or chance? *Ecology* 63:881–87.
Boag, P.T. 1983. Heritability of external morphology in Darwin's ground finches on Isla Daphne Major, Galápagos. *Evolution* 37(5):877–94.
Boag, P.T. and P.R. Grant. 1981. Intense natural selection in a population of Darwin's finches (Geospizinae) in the Galápagos. *Science* 214:82–85.
Bowman, R.I. 1961. Morphological differentiation and adaption in the Galápagos finches. *Univ. California Publ. in Zoology* 58:1–302.
Bowman, R.I. 1963. Evolutionary patterns in Darwin's finches. *Occasional Papers of the California Academy of Sciences* 44:107–40.
Bowman, R.I. 1979. Adaptive morphology of song dialects in Darwin's finches. *J. Ornithologie* 120(4):353–89.
Bowman, R.I. 1983. The evolution of song in Darwin's finches. In: Bowman et al. 1983.
Bowman, R.I. and S.L. Billeb. 1965. Blood-eating in a Galápagos finch. *Living Bird* 4:29–44.
Bowman, R.I. and A. Carter. 1971. Egg-pecking behaviour in Galápagos mockingbirds. *Living Bird* 10:243–70.
Carlquist, S.J. 1974. *Island Biology.* New York: Columbia University Press.
Christian, K.A. 1980. Cleaning-feeding symbiosis between birds and reptiles of the Galápagos Islands. *Auk* 97(4):887–89.
Curry, R.L. 1988. Group structure, within-group conflict and reproductive tactics in cooperatively breeding Galápagos mockingbirds. *Animal Behaviour* 36:1708–28.
Curry, R.L. and P.R. Grant. 1989. Demography of the cooperatively breeding Galápagos mockingbird in a climatically variable environment. *J. Animal Ecology* 58:441–464.
Darwin, C. 1845. *The Voyage of the Beagle.*
de Groot, R.S. 1981. Biology of the owls in the Galápagos. Charles Darwin Research Station *Annual Report,* 146–63.
de Groot, R.S. 1983a. Origin, status and ecology of the owls in the Galápagos. *Ardea* 71(2):167–82.
de Vries, T. 1975. The breeding biology of the Galápagos hawk. *Gerfaut* 65:29–54.
de Vries, T. 1976. Prey selection and hunting methods of the Galápagos hawk. *Gerfaut* 66:3–43.

Eibl-Eibesfeldt, I. 1966b. Darwin's finches. *Animals* 9(3):137–39.

Ervin, S. 1989. The nesting of the dark-billed cuckoo in the Galápagos. *Noticias de Galápagos* 48:8–10.

Faaborg, J. 1981. The evolution of polyandry in the Galápagos hawk. Charles Darwin Research Station *Annual Report,* 167–68.

Faaborg, J. 1986. Reproductive success and survivorship of the Galápagos hawk: Potential costs and benefits of cooperative polyandry. *Ibis* 128:337–47.

Faaborg, J., T. de Vries, C.B. Patterson, and C.R. Griffin. 1980. Preliminary observations on the occurence and evolution of polyandry in the Galápagos hawk. *Auk* 97(3):581–90.

Franklin, A.B., D.A. Clark, and D.B. Clark. 1979. Ecology and behaviour of the Galápagos rail. *Wilson Bulletin* 91(2):202–21.

Gould, J. 1841. *The Zoology of HMS Beagle,* Part III, *Birds,* ed. C. Darwin. London: Smith Elder.

Grant, B.R. and P.R. Grant. 1981. Exploitation of *Opuntia* cactus by birds on the Galápagos, Pacific Ocean. *Oecologia* 49(2):179–87.

Grant, B.R and P.R. Grant. 1989a. *Evolutionary Dynamics of a Natural Population, the Large Cactus Finch of the Galápagos.* Chicago: University of Chicago Press.

Grant, B.R. and P.R. Grant. 1989b. Natural selection in a population of Darwin's finches. *American Naturalist* 133:377–93.

Grant, P.R. 1981. Speciation and adaptive radiation of Darwin's finches. *American Scientist* 69:653–63.

Grant, P.R. 1983. The role of interspecific competition in the adaptive radiation of Darwin's finches. In: Bowman et al. 1983.

Grant, P.R. 1984a. Recent research on the evolution of land birds on the Galápagos. *Biological J. Linnaean Society* 21:113–36.

Grant, P.R. 1984b. The endemic land birds. In: Perry 1984.

Grant, P.R. 1986. *Ecology and Evolution of Darwin's Finches.* Princeton: Princeton University Press.

Grant, P.R. and B.R. Grant. 1992a. Demography and the genetically effective sizes of two populations of Darwin's finches. *Ecology* 73:766–84.

Grant, P.R. and B.R. Grant. 1992b. Hybridization of bird species. *Science* 256:193–97.

Grant, P.R. and K.T. Grant. 1979. Breeding and feeding ecology of the Galápagos dove. *Condor* 81(4):397–403.

Grant, P.R. and N. Grant. 1979. Breeding and feeding of Galápagos mockingbirds. *Auk* 96(4):723–36.

Harris, M.P. 1974. *A Field Guide to the Birds of the Galápagos.* London: Collins.

Lack, D. 1947. *Darwin's Finches.* London: Cambridge University Press.

Lack, D. 1953. Darwin's finches. *Scientific American* (April):3–7.

Lowe, P.R. 1936. The finches of the Galápagos in relation to Darwin's conception of species. *Ibis* 13(b):310–321.

MacFarland, C. and W. Reeder. 1974. Cleaning symbiosis involving Galápagos tortoises and two species of Darwin's finches. *Zeitschrift für Tierpsychologie* 34:464–83.

Millington, S.J. and P.R. Grant. 1983. Feeding ecology and territoriality of the cactus finch on Isla Daphne Major, Galápagos, Ecuador. *Oecologia* 58(1):76–83.
Peterson, R.T. 1967. The Galápagos: Eerie cradle of new species. *National Geographic* 131(4):540–85.
Rosenburg, D.K., M.H. Wilson, and F. Cruz. 1990. The distribution and abundance of the smooth-billed ani in the Galápagos Islands. *Biological Conservation* 1:113–24.
Schluter, D. 1982a. Distributions of Galápagos, Ecuador, ground finches along an altitudinal gradient: The importance of food supply. *Ecology* 63:1504–17.
Schluter, D. 1982b. Seed and patch selection by Galápagos ground finches: Relation to foraging efficiency and food supply. *Ecology* 63:1106–20.
Schluter, D. and P.R. Grant. 1982. The distribution of *Geospiza difficilis* in relation to *Geospiza fuliginosa* in the Galápagos. *Evolution* 36(6):1213–26.
Smith, J.N.M., P.R. Grant, B.R. Grant, I.J. Abbott, and L.K. Abbott. 1978. Seasonal variation in feeding habits of Darwin's ground finches. *Ecology* 59:1137–50.
Steadman, D.W. 1982. The origin of Darwin's finches. *Trans. San Diego Society for Natural History* 19:279–96.
Thornton, I. 1971. *Darwin's Islands.*
Yang, S.Y. and J.L. Patton. 1981. Genetic variability and differentiation in Galápagos finches. *Auk* 98:230–42.

Chapter 9: Mammals

Barlow, G.W. 1972. A paternal role for bulls of the Galápagos Islands' sea lion. *Evolution* 26:307–10.
Bonner, W.N. 1984. Seals of the Galápagos Islands. *Biological J. Linnaean Society* 21:177–84.
Clark, D.A. 1984. Native land mammals. In: Perry 1984.
Clark, D.B. 1980. Population ecology of an endemic neotropical island rodent *Oryzomys bauri* of Santa Fé Island, Galápagos. *J. Animal Ecology* 49:185–98.
Eibl-Eibesfeldt, I. 1984b. The Galápagos seals—Part 1. Natural history of the Galápagos sea lion. In: Perry 1984.
Leatherwood, S., W.E. Evans, and D.W. Rice. 1972. *The Whales, Dolphins, and Porpoises of the Eastern North Pacific: A Guide to their Identification in the Water.* San Diego: Naval Undersea Research and Development Center.
Maxwell, G. 1967. *Seals of the World.* London: Constable.
Miller, E.H. 1974. A paternal role in the Galápagos sea lions? *Evolution* 28:473–506.
Orr, R.T. 1966. Evolutionary aspects of the mammalian fauna of the Galápagos. In: Bowman 1966.
Orr, R.T. 1967. The Galápagos sea lion. *J. Mammalogy* 48(1):62–69.
Patton, J.L. and M.S. Haffer. 1983. Biosystematics of native rodents of the Galápagos archipelago, Ecuador. In: Bowman et al. 1983.
Peterson, R.S. and G.A. Bartholomew. 1967. The natural history and behaviour of the California sea lion. *American Society of Mammalogy Special Publication No. 1.*

Steadman, D.W. and C.E. Ray. 1982. The relationships of *Megaoryzomys curiori*, an extinct cricetine rodent from the Galápagos Islands. *Smithsonian Contrib. Paleobiology* 51:1–23.

Thornton, I. 1971. *Darwin's Islands.*

Trillmich, F. 1981. Mutual mother-pup recognition in Galápagos fur seals and sea lions. *Behaviour* 78:21–42.

Trillmich, F. 1984. The Galápagos seals—Part 2. Natural history of the Galápagos fur seal. In: Perry 1984.

Trillmich, F. and W. Mohren. 1981. Effects of the lunar cycle on the Galápagos fur seal. *Oecologia* 48(1):85–92.

Trillmich, F. and K.G.K. Trillmich. 1984. The mating systems of pinnipeds and marine iguanas: Convergent evolution of polygyny. *Biological J. Linnaean Society* 21:209–16.

Whitehead, H. 1987. Sperm whale behaviour on the Galápagos grounds. *Oceanus* 30:49–53.

Whitehead, H., S. Waters, and T. Lyrholm. 1992. Population structure of female and immature sperm whales off the Galápagos Islands. *Can. J. Fisheries and Ocean Sciences* 49:78–84.

Chapter 10: Terrestrial Invertebrates

Baert, L.L. 1990. Spiders of the Galápagos. Part V. Linphiidae. *Bull. British Arachnological Society* 8:129–38.

Clark, D.B., C. Guayasamin, O. Pazmino, C. Donoso, and Y.P. de Villacis. 1982. The tramp ant *Wasmannia auropunctata*: Autecology and effects on diversity and distribution on Santa Cruz Island, Galápagos, Ecuador. *Biotropica* 14(3):196–207.

Coppois, G. 1984. Distribution of bulimulid land snails on the northern slope of Santa Cruz Island, Galápagos. *Biological J. Linnaean Society* 21:217–27.

Coppois, G. and C. Glowacki. 1983. Bulimulid land snails from the Galápagos, Ecuador, 1: Factor analysis of Santa Cruz Island species. *Malacologia* 23(2):209–20.

Darwin, C. 1845. *The Voyage of the Beagle.*

Finet, Y. 1989. Recent molluscan fauna in the Galápagos: Taxonomic composition of the fauna. *Ann. Rept. Western Soc. Malacologists* 21:7.

Foster, W.A. and J.E. Treherne. 1980. Feeding, predation and aggregation behaviour in a marine insect (*Halobates robustus*, Hemiptera, Heteroptera, Gerridae) in the Galápagos Islands. *Proc. Royal Society of London, B., Biological Science* 209:539–54.

Foster, W.A. and J.E. Treherne. 1982. Reproductive behaviour of the ocean skater *Halobates robustus*, Hemiptera, Gerridae, in the Galápagos Islands, Ecuador. *Oecologia* 55(2):202–07.

Hayes, A.H. 1975. The larger moths of the Galápagos Islands. *Proc. California Academy of Sciences* 49(7):145–208.

Hickin, N. 1979. *Animal Life of the Galápagos.* Quito, Ecuador: Libri Mundi.

Linsley, E.G. 1966. Pollinating insects of the Galápagos Islands. In: Bowman 1966.

Linsley, E.G. 1977. Insects of the Galápagos (Suppl.). *Occasional Papers of the California Academy of Sciences* 125:1–50.

Linsley, E.G. and R.L. Usinger. 1966. Insects of the Galápagos. *Proc. California Academy of Sciences* 33(7):113–96.

Lubin, Y.D. 1982. Terrestrial invertebrates of the Galápagos Islands. Unpublished manuscript. C.D.R.S. Library, Galápagos.

Lubin, Y.D. 1984. Changes in the native fauna of the Galápagos Islands following invasion by the little red fire ant (*Wasmannia auropunctata*). *Biological J. Linnaean Society* 21:229–42.

Peck, S.B. 1990. Eyeless arthropods of the Galápagos Islands, Ecuador: Composition and origin of the cryptozoic fauna of a young, tropical oceanic archipelago. *Biotropica* 22:366–81.

Peck, S.B. 1991. The Galápagos archipelago, Ecuador: With an emphasis on terrestrial invertebrates, especially insects; and an outline for research. In: *The Unity of Evolutionary Biology; Proc. 4th Intl. Congress of Systematic and Evolutionary Biology*, ed. E.C. Dudley. Portland, Oregon: Dioscorides.

Peck, S.B. and J. Kukalová-Peck. 1990. Origin and biogeography of the beetles (Coleoptera) of the Galápagos Archipelago, Ecuador. *Can. J. Zoology* 68:1617–38.

Rick, C.M. 1966. Some plant-animal relations on the Galápagos Islands. In: Bowman 1966.

Silberglied, R.E. 1978. Inter-island transport of insects aboard ships in the Galápagos Islands. *Biological Conservation* 13:273–78.

Smith, A.G. 1966. Land snails of the Galápagos. In: Bowman 1966.

Treherne, J.E. and W.A. Foster. 1980. The effects of group size on predator avoidance in a marine insect. *Animal Behaviour* 28(4):1119–22.

Vagvolgyi, J. 1978. Speciation in the Galápagos land snail (*Naesiotus*). *American Zoologist* 18(3):648.

Chapter 11: Marine and Intertidal Life

Brusca, R.C. et al. 1980. *Common Intertidal Invertebrates of the Gulf of California*, 2d ed. Tucson: University of Arizona Press.

Cernohorsky, W.O. 1967. *Marine Shells of the Pacific*. Sydney, Australia: Pacific Publ.

Colgan, M.W. 1989. El Niño and Galápagos coral reef development: A study from the Urvina Bay Uplift, Isabela Island, Galápagos. *Ann. Rept. Western Soc. Malacologists* 21:6–7.

Constant, P. 1992. *Marine Life of the Galápagos*. Paris: Calao Life.

Cribb, J. 1986. *Subtidal Galápagos: Exploring the Waters of Darwin's Islands*. Camden East, Ontario: Camden House.

Glynn, P.W. and G.M. Wellington. 1983. *Corals and Coral Reefs of the Galápagos Islands*. Berkeley: University of California Press.

Grove, J.S. and R.S Lavenberg. 1990. *Galápagos Fishes: A Comprehensive Guide to their Identification*. Palo Alto, California: Stanford University Press.

Grove, J.S., S. Garcia, and S. Massey. 1984. Lista de los pesces de Galápagos. Guayaquil, Ecuador: *Boletin Cientifico y Technico, Instituto Nacional de Pesca*.

Hancock, A. 1945. Pacific marine algae of the Alan Hancock expeditions to the Galápagos Islands. *Pacific Expeditions*, 12.

Houvenhagel, G.T. and N. Houvenhagel. 1974. Aspects ecologiques de la zonation intertidale sur les côtes rocheuses des Iles Galápagos. *Marine Biology* 26:135–52.

Humann, P. 1982. *Marine Invertebrates*. Miami: Ocean Realm Publ.

Humann, P. 1983. *Corals of Florida, Bahamas, and the Caribbean*. Miami: Ocean Realm Publ.

Humann, P. 1993. *Reef Life Identification—Galápagos*. Jacksonville, Florida: New World Publ.

James, M.J., ed. 1991. *Galápagos Marine Invertebrates: Taxonomy, Biogeography and Evolution in Darwin's Islands*. New York: Plenum.

Keen, M.A. 1958. *Sea Shells of Tropical West America*. Berkeley: Stanford University Press.

McCosker, J.E. and R.H. Rosenblatt. 1984. The inshore fish fauna of the Galápagos Islands. In: Perry 1984.

Meatyard, B.T., M.H. Jackson, and G.B. Estes. 1982. Cambridge Darwin Centenary Galápagos Expedition 1982. Unpublished report to sponsors.

Merlen, G. 1988. *A Field Guide to the Fishes of the Galápagos*. Quito, Ecuador: Ediciones Libri Mundi.

Morris, P.A. 1974. *A Field Guide to Pacific Coast Shells (including shells of Hawaii and the Gulf of California)*. Peterson Field Guide Series #6. Boston: Houghton Mifflin.

Ricketts, E.F. and J. Calvin. 1962. *Between Pacific Tides*, 3d ed., revised by J.W. Hedgpeth. Berkeley: Stanford University Press.

Robinson, G.R. 1987. Negative impacts of the 1982–1983 El Niño on the Galápagos marine life. *Oceanus* 30:42–48.

Robinson, G.R. and E.M. del Pino, eds. 1985. *El Niño in the Galápagos Islands— The 1982–1983 Event*. Quito, Ecuador: Charles Darwin Foundation.

Scott, Sir Peter. 1974. Some Galápagos fishes. Unpublished notes and drawings. C.D.R.S. Library, Galápagos.

Thomson, D.A., L.T. Findley, and A.U. Korstich. 1979. *Reef Fishes of the Sea of Cortez*. New York: J. Wiley.

Tinker, S.W. 1958. *Pacific Sea Shells—A Handbook of Common Marine Molluscs of Hawaii and the South Seas*. Rutland, Vermont: C.E. Tuttle.

Wellington, G.M. 1975. The Galápagos coastal marine environment. Unpublished manuscript. C.D.R.S. Library, Galápagos.

Wellington, G.M. 1984. Marine environment and protection. In: Perry 1984.

Chapter 12: Conservation

Adsersen, H. 1989. The rare plants of the Galápagos Islands and their conservation. *Biological Conservation* 47:49–77.

Barnett, B.D. 1985. Chemical vasectomy of domestic dogs in the Galápagos Islands. *Theriogenology* 23:499–510.

Black, J. 1984. The path of conservation—Part 1. In: Perry 1984.

Bowman, R.I. 1984. Contributions to science from the Galápagos. In: Perry 1984.

Broadus, J.M. 1987. The Galápagos Marine Resources Reserve and tourism development. *Oceanus* 30:9–15.

Carrasco, A. 1992. El turismo a las islas Galápagos: Sus impactos en la economia, en la ecologia y en la sociedad. Presentation to the Fourth World Congress of National Parks and Protected Areas, February 1992.

Coblentz, B.E. and D.W. Baber. 1987. Biology and control of feral pigs on Isla Santiago, Galápagos, Ecuador. *J. Appl. Ecol.* 24:403–418.

Corley Smith, G.T. 1984. The path of conservation—Part 2. In: Perry 1984.

Cruz, F., J. Cruz, and J.E. Lawesson. 1986. *Lantana camara*, a threat to native plants and animals. *Noticias de Galápagos* 43:10–11.

Curry-Lindahl, K. 1981. Twenty years of conservation in the Galápagos. *Noticias de Galápagos* 35:8–9.

de Groot, R.S. 1983a. Origin, status and ecology of the owls in the Galápagos. *Ardea* 71(2):167–82.

de Groot, R.S. 1983b. Tourism and conservation in the Galápagos Islands. *Biological Conservation* 26:291–300.

de Neira, L.E.F. and J.H. Roe. 1984. Emergence success of tortoise nests and the effect of feral burros on nest success on Volcan Alcedo, Galápagos. *Copeia* 1984:702–07.

de Roy, T. 1987. When the aliens take over. *International Wildlife* Jan./Feb. 1987:34–37.

Evans, D. 1991. Ecuadorean whale sanctuary is created providing protection for the Galápagos Islands. *Ambio* 20:97.

Galápagos National Park Service. 1979. An outline of historical events related to the development and conservation of the Galápagos. Mimeographed sheets prepared for the Galápagos naturalist guides' course. C.D.R.S. Library, Galápagos.

Hamann, O. 1979. Regeneration of vegetation on Santa Fé and Pinta Islands, Galápagos, after the eradication of goats. *Biological Conservation* 15:215–36.

Hamann, O. 1984. Changes and threats to the vegetation. In: Perry 1984.

Hoeck, H.N. 1984. Introduced fauna. In: Perry 1984.

Jackson, M.H. 1984. Interpretation, natural history and management in the Galápagos Islands. M.E.Des. thesis, University of Calgary.

Jungius, H. and U. Hirsch. 1979. Changes in heart beat frequencies in Galápagos nesting birds due to human disturbance. *J. Ornithology* 120:299–310.

Kastdalen, A. 1982. Changes in the biology of Santa Cruz—1935 to 1965. *Noticias de Galápagos* 35:7–12.

Konecny, M.J. 1987. Food habits and energetics of feral house cats in the Galápagos Islands, Ecuador. *Oikos* 50:24–32.

Kramer, P. 1984. Man and other introduced organisms. *Biological J. Linnaean Society* 21:253–58.

Laurie, A. 1982. Marine iguanas—Where have all their babies gone? *Noticias de Galápagos* 35:17–19.

Lewin, R. 1978a. Galápagos: The endangered islands. *New Scientist* (20 July):168–72.

Lewin, R. 1978b. Galápagos: The rise of optimism. *New Scientist* (27 July):261–63.

Loope, L.L., O. Hamann, and C.P. Stone. 1988. Comparative conservation biology of oceanic archipelagoes: Hawaii and Galápagos. *Bioscience* 38:272–82.

Lubin, Y.D. 1984. Changes in the native fauna of the Galápagos Islands following invasion by the little red fire ant (*Wasmannia auropunctata*). *Biological J. Linnaean Society* 21:229–42.

MacFarland, C.G., J. Villa, and B. Toro. 1974a. The Galápagos giant tortoises (*Geochelone elephantopus*). I: Status of the surviving populations. *Biological Conservation* 6:118–33.

MacFarland, C.G., J. Villa, and B. Toro. 1974b. The Galápagos giant tortoises (*Geochelone elephantopus*). II: Conservation methods. *Biological Conservation* 6:198–212.

Reynolds, R. 1982. Some observations on the captive management of Galápagos tortoises and land iguanas at the Darwin Station and suggestions for the future. Herpetology report. Charles Darwin Research Station *Annual Report*, 115–19.

Ryan, P.R., ed. 1987. The Galápagos Marine Resources Reserve. *Oceanus* 30:1–104.

Schofield, E.K. 1973. Galápagos flora: The threat of introduced plants. *Biological Conservation* 5:48–51.

Schofield, E.K. 1989. Effects of introduced plants and animals on island vegetation: Examples from the Galápagos archipelago. *Conservation Biology* 3:227–38.

Steadman, D.W. 1986. Holocene vertebrate fossils from Isla Floreana, Galápagos. *Smithsonian Contrib. Zoology* 413:1–103.

Tindle, R.W. 1983. Galápagos conservation and tourism—11 years on. *Oryx* 17(3):126–29.

Thornton, I. 1971. *Darwin's Islands.*

Chapter 13: Visiting the Islands

Boyce, B. 1990. *A Traveller's Guide to the Galápagos Islands.* San José, California: Galápagos Travel.

Moore, A. and T. Moore. 1980. *Guide to the Visitor Sites of Parque Nacional Galápagos.* Galápagos, Ecuador: Servicio Parque Nacional.

Appendix 1:
Checklist of Plants and Animals

Coastal zone plants

Arid and Transition zone plants

Moist Zone plants

Reptiles

Seabirds

Coastal birds and migrants

Land birds

Darwin's finches

page

❏ Large ground finch   *Geospiza magnirostris*   188
❏ Medium ground finch   *Geospiza fortis*   188
❏ Small ground finch   *Geospiza fuliginosa*   188
❏ Sharp-billed ground finch   *Geospiza difficilis*   188
❏ Cactus ground finch   *Geospiza scandens*   188
❏ Large cactus ground finch   *Geospiza conirostris*   188
❏ Vegetarian finch   *Platyspiza crassirostris*   188
❏ Large tree finch   *Camarhynchus psittacula*   188
❏ Medium tree finch   *Camarhynchus pauper*   188
❏ Small tree finch   *Camarhynchus parvulus*   188
❏ Woodpecker finch   *Camarhynchus pallidus*   188
❏ Mangrove finch   *Camarhynchus heliobates*   188
❏ Warbler finch   *Certhidea olivacea*   188

Mammals

❏ Sea lion   *Zalophus californianus*   195
❏ Fur seal   *Arctocephalus galapagoensis*   200
❏ Rice rats   *Oryzomys and Nesoryzomys*   202
❏ Bats   *Lasiurus spp.*   203
❏ Humpback whale   *Megaptera novaeangliae*   204
❏ Common rorqual (finback)   *Balaenoptera physalus*   204
❏ Sei whale   *Balaenoptera borealis*   204
❏ Bryde's whale   *Balaenoptera edeni*   204
❏ Minke whale   *Balaenoptera acutorostrata*   204
❏ Sperm whale   *Physeter macrocephalus*   204
❏ Orca   *Orcinus orca*   204
❏ Short-finned pilot whale   *Globicephala macrorhyncha*   204
❏ Bottle-nosed dolphin   *Tursiops truncatus*   206
❏ Common (white-bellied) dolphin   *Delphinus delphis*   206

Terrestrial invertebrates

❏ Water boatman   *Trichocorixa reticulata*   169
❏ Land snail   *Bulimulus (Naesiotus) spp.*   212
❏ Longhorn beetle   *Stenodontes molarius*   214
❏ Ground beetle   *Calosoma spp.*   215
❏ Scarab beetle   *Trox suberosus*   215
❏ Cactus-eating weevil   *Gersteckeria galapagoensis*   215

Intertidal life

Marine life

Appendix 2:
Glossary of Terms

Abiotic: referring to the non-living parts of an ecosystem.

Aestivate: spend an unfavourable season or period of time in a state of dormancy; similar to hibernation; many Galápagos invertebrates aestivate during the dry season.

Andesites: extrusive volcanic rocks typical of volcanoes above a subduction zone; andesites are intermediate in composition between granites (typical of continental volcanism) and basalts (typical of oceanic volcanism); named after the Andes where they make up almost all of the major volcanoes; typically, they are light grey in colour and have numerous small white crystals scattered through a fine-grained homogeneous matrix.

Baleen: horny material that hangs in fringed sheets from the upper jaw of some whales (suborder Mysticeti), which is used to strain out the minute sea animals on which they feed (also called "whalebone").

Basalts: extrusive volcanic rocks typical of oceanic volcanoes and mid-ocean ridges; usually dark-coloured, this rock is formed from the melting of the earth's mantle zone; the Galápagos islands, the Hawaiian islands and Iceland are all almost entirely formed from basalts.

Bioluminescence: production of light by living organisms, including fireflies, numerous marine animals, many bacteria and fungi; the light is caused by an enzyme-catalyzed reaction which produces very little heat; frequently mis-called "phosphorescence," which refers to light given off as a result of previous illumination.

Biota: the plant and animal life of a region (same as flora and fauna).

Bolus: a small, round lump or mass of chewed food.

Boreal: of or pertaining to the northern zone of plant and animal life lying just south of the tundra; typically composed of coniferous forest.

Buccaneer: pirate, or sea robber, especially one who raided along the Spanish coasts of America during the seventeenth and eighteenth centuries; many were licensed by the king or queen of England, and formed an unofficial British navy.

Carrying capacity: the weight or amount of animals of a single or mixed population that can be permanently supported on a given area.

Chitin: chemical with long fibrous molecules which is the main component of the external skeleton of insects and crustaceans; it is a material of considerable strength and resistance to chemicals.

Cloaca: the opening or cavity into which both the intestinal and genitourinary tracts empty in birds, reptiles, amphibians and many fishes.

Crepuscular: species that are active during the twilight of dawn and dusk are said to be "crepuscular."

Ectothermic: species that regulate their body temperature by behavioural means are said to be "ectothermic" (as opposed to "endothermic," i.e., maintaining temperature by physiological means).

Endemic: native to and restricted to a particular area or region. In the Galápagos, some species may be endemic to individual islands, while others are endemic to the archipelago as a whole. Many others are "indigenous" (i.e., native but not endemic) or introduced by man.

Epiphyte: a plant that grows on another plant, but is not a parasite and produces its own food by photosynthesis; includes many orchids, mosses, lichens and other "air plants."

Feral: existing in a wild or untamed state, especially having reverted to such a state from domestication.

Garúa: fine misty rain or drizzle, typical of the dry or *garúa* season in the Galápagos; pronounced "gahrooah."

Genus: a classificatory unit of plants or animals with common distinguishing characteristics; it is the main subdivision of a family and is made up of a group of closely related species, or a single species; the genus name is capitalised and precedes the species name, which is not capitalised (e.g., *Geochelone elephantopus*, Galápagos giant tortoise).

Gular: on or of the throat region, especially of birds.

Habitat: the region or environment where a plant or animal naturally grows or lives.

Invertebrate: any animal without a backbone or spinal column; any animal other than a fish, amphibian, reptile, bird, or mammal.

Niche: the role or profession of an organism in the environment, including its activities and relationships in the community.

Olivine: a silicate mineral of magnesium and iron, existing usually as green crystals in many basaltic and other rocks; especially common on the brown sand beach at Punta Cormorant, Floreana.

Oxygen debt: incurred when an organism or part of an organism has been doing work with an inadequate oxygen supply; for example, after hard muscular work, the oxygen consumption of a person remains above normal until the oxygen debt has been repaid.

Pelagic: of or pertaining to the ocean or open sea; especially to distinguish from coastal waters.

Propagule: any part of a plant capable of growing into a new organism; e.g., spore, seedling, cutting.

Salina: a salt marsh, pond or lake.

Sea-floor spreading: the process by which new sea floor is created, pushing two tectonic plates further apart, usually associated with a mid-ocean ridge or rift valley.

Species: the fundamental biological classification, comprising a subdivision of a genus and consisting of a number of plants or animals all of which have a high degree of similarity. Members of a species can generally only interbreed among themselves, and show persistent differences from members of allied species.

Spermatophore: a case or capsule containing a number of spermatozoa (sperm), which is expelled by the male of some kinds of animals, such as scorpions.

Subduction: the process by which two tectonic plates collide, and one is forced to pass under the other, usually associated with mountains, volcanoes and earthquakes.

Taxon (pl. **Taxa**)**:** any taxonomic, or classificatory unit; e.g., subspecies, variety, species, genus, etc.

Tephra: collective term for all sizes of solid volcanic rock particles blown out of a volcanic vent.

Appendix 3:
Units and Conversions

Length

1 metre (m) = 10 decimetres (dm) = 100 centimetres (cm) = 1,000 millimetres (mm).

1 metre = 39.4 inches = 3.28 feet = 1.09 yards.

1 kilometre (km) = 1,000 metres = 3,281 feet = 1,094 yards = 0.62 miles.

Area

1 square metre (m^2) = 1.1196 square yards.

1 hectare (ha) = 0.01 square kilometres (km^2) = 1,000 m^2 = 11,960 square yards = 2.47 acres.

Volume and Liquids

1 litre (l) = 0.001 m^3 = 0.264 U.S. gallons = 0.22 imperial gallons = 61 cubic inches.

1 millilitre = 1 cm^3 = 0.001 litres

Weights

1 kilogram (kg) = 1,000 grams (g) = 35.3 ounces = 2.2 pounds.

1 gram = 0.035 ounces.

1 tonne = 1,000 kg = 2,204 pounds.

Temperature

Celsius or centigrade (°C): conversion to degrees Fahrenheit is F° = 9/5 °C + 32

(Water freezes at 0°C and boils at 100°C, normal human body temperature is about 37°C).

Appendix 4:
Information for Supporters of Galápagos Conservation

Maintaining the Galápagos Islands National Park in as near a natural state as possible requires a large expenditure of funds. An important function of the Charles Darwin Foundation for the Galápagos Islands is to raise money for conservation work in the Islands. While it is supported by several national and international institutions, the foundation remains largely dependent upon donations from people like you. Over a third of its annual income is derived from such personal donations. There are several means by which you may contribute financially to conservation in the Galápagos. In the United States, please send your tax deductible contributions to:

- **The Charles Darwin Foundation, Inc.**, Department 0553, Washington, DC 20073-0553, U.S.A.

No overhead is charged; all funds are used for scientific research, conservation, and education.

If you are a resident of the United Kingdom, please address your contribution to:

- **The Charles Darwin Foundation**, Barclays Bank, Acct. #31084534, 186 High Street, Ongar, Essex, U.K. CM5 9JL. Attention: Roger Perry.

In Canada, contributions, earmarked "for the Galápagos," may be sent to:

- **The World Wildlife Fund Canada**, Suite 504, 90 Eglinton Ave. East, Toronto, Ontario, Canada M4P 2Z7.

In Germany:

- **Zoologische Gesellschaft von 1858**, Alfred-Brehm Platz 16, D-6000, Frankfurt am Main 1, Germany.

In the Netherlands:

- **Vrienden van de Galápagos Eilanden**, ABN/AMRO Bank, Account #44.75.03.332, Driebergen, The Netherlands. Attention: Girard Ackers.

In other countries, please direct your contribution to your national World Wildlife Fund organisation or to:

- **The World Wide Fund for Nature** (formerly World Wildlife Fund-International), Avenue de Mont Blanc, CH-1196 Gland, Switzerland.

Since laws governing tax deductions vary from country to country, you may wish to seek specific tax information from the organisation receiving your contribution. If tax deductions are not sought, you may send your donation to:

- **The Charles Darwin Research Station**, Casilla 17-01-3891, Quito, Ecuador. Attention: Director.

Endowment Fund

Another option is to support the endowment fund of the Darwin Scientific Foundation, Inc.—a nonprofit organisation. The endowment fund was established to promote scientific research, education, and conservation of the natural resources in the Galápagos. Its annual income is directed to the most deserving activities and projects of the year. Donations and enquiries should be sent to:

- **Darwin Scientific Foundation, Inc.**, Department 0553, Washington, DC 20073-0553, U.S.A.

Index

MONICA J. JACKSON

About the Author

Michael Jackson was born in Kent, England, where he developed a keen interest in natural history. After obtaining his M.A. at Cambridge in Natural Sciences (Applied Biology), he left England to work in the Galápagos Islands as a naturalist guide. After spending a year in the Islands, he returned to England but was shortly back in the Galápagos as zoologist for the Cambridge Darwin Centenary Galápagos Expedition in 1982. The first edition of this book was written while living in Calgary where he studied at the University of Calgary for a Masters degree in Environmental Science.

Since 1986, Michael has been teaching sciences at St. Michael's University School in Victoria, British Columbia. Whenever possible he escapes to the outdoors to camp, fish, cross-country ski, kayak, hike, and scuba dive. He has been able to keep in touch with the Islands by leading several tours to Ecuador and the Galápagos for the University of Calgary, the University of British Columbia, and Wilderness Travel.